INDUCTION AND DEDUCTION

INDUCTION AND DEDUCTION

A STUDY IN WITTGENSTEIN

İLHAM DILMAN

OXFORD
BASIL BLACKWELL
1973

ISBN 0631 14640 7

Printed in Great Britain by
Western Printing Services Ltd, Bristol
and bound by the Kemp Hall Bindery, Oxford

PREFACE

It is a central contention of this book that the questions raised by philosophical scepticism are at the core of philosophy and that to come to terms with them is to further the kind of understanding that one seeks in philosophy.

The book is concerned with inductive and deductive reasoning: In what way do they differ from each other? How are we to characterize their distinctive features? These are not questions that I ask directly and neither does the book aim at arriving at a catalogue of differences. Such a task, I believe, would be misconceived. No. Rather the kind of difficulty which the philosophical sceptic raises highlights these differences by distorting them, or it recognizes them clearly enough but attaches a significance to them which turns them into something disturbing. It is in the course of a discussion of these difficulties that the differences in question become the subject-matter of the present study. For instance: How does the movement of one part of a mechanism determine the movement of another part and how does this differ from the way each step in a series of kinematic derivations is determined by the previous step? What is meant by establishing the validity of a deductive inference and how does it differ from establishing a causal connection between two events? In what sense does the justification of an inductive inference of the form 'Your headache will soon improve after you take this aspirin' take us outside what is mentioned in the statement? In contrast, how do we find a justification of a deductive inference within the statement of the premises and conclusion?

If in the former case we need the evidence of what happened at other times and other places when people with headaches took aspirin, how does this bear on our claim about what will happen now, in this case? What makes it into evidence for this claim? How does it lend support to my inference? Are we making an assumption about nature here? Are we relying on or employing a general principle which must be justified if our particular inference, on the basis of the evidence we have, is itself to be justified?

Although rightly, as Hume pointed out, we do not need this kind of evidence when we take a deductive step, do we not need some more general sanction or backing if we are to be justified in taking that step? If so, then presumably what gives this backing is some sort of principle which belongs to logic. But then, must not that principle itself be justified if the particular step that it sanctions is itself to be justified, that is if my inference is to be valid?

I face the first question in chapters 3 and 4 and the second in chapter 9: Can our belief in the uniformity of nature be justified? What makes it impossible for us to suppose that nature may not be uniform or that there may be uncaused events? (A discussion of these questions begins in chapter 1.) Are the laws of logic and the rules of grammar arbitrary? In what sense do they express necessary truths? (chapter 11). These two sets of questions mirror each other and my discussions of them, around which the whole book gravitates, complement each other. The questions obviously are directly connected with philosophical scepticism —the subject-matter of chapter 1.

Thus at the centre of each half of the book is what I say about the relation between those rules and principles which belong to the grammar of our reasonings and the actual inferences we make in particular cases, and what I say about whether these rules and principles are themselves justified and, if not, whether this means that they are arbitrary. My arguments here come from Wittgenstein and I believe that what he had to say on these questions is very central to his thinking. Therefore my discussions of induction and deduction and of philosophical scepticism in both connections are at the same time a study of Wittgenstein's contribution to these questions.

The first part of the book (chapters 2–7) takes the form of examining backwards each step in the line of reasoning which led Hume and Russell to scepticism with regard to inductive reasoning. The second part of the book (chapters 8–11) takes a different form. There I am concerned with some of the difficulties with which Wittgenstein was concerned in trying to understand the nature of a deductive step or connection, and what makes such a step binding on us, what makes a course of such steps impermeable to accidents. But the misunderstandings combated in both parts of the book parallel each other: 'When we reason from fact to fact either we are not reasoning at all or there are necessary connections in nature' (chapters 5 and 10). 'When we reason deductively from premise to conclusion our reasoning stands in need of an external sanction which is provided by principles of inference' (chapters 8 and 9). 'If these principles cannot be justified then our inferences are not valid' (chapters 9 and 11). 'If the principle of induction is not justified we have no reason for believing anything that we believe on inductive grounds' (chapters 4 and 7).

The book argues that what belongs to grammar or logic characterizes our ways of speaking, judging and reasoning. Such general characterizations or formulations give us grammatical propositions. These constitute a *very mixed class*. For instance, we have the propositions of mathematics which are not only the principles in accordance with which we reason when we apply mathematics in physics, engineering and accounting, but also the premises and conclusions of our arguments in pure mathematics. We have the law of contradiction, the principle of the uniformity of nature, the law of causality, such propositions as material things do not disappear when they are not perceived, there is no colour between red and green, water does not freeze when heated, and even there is no such thing as doubt in *this* case (*Cert.* §58), or *here* my eyes are shut (*Inv.* p. 224). Of course there are important differences between these, and obviously some of them can be arrived at by arguments in logic and pure mathematics and so can be doubted, proved and justified. Some are not normally formulated and do not belong to any calculus; they do not have such a dual role wherein they are both premises or conclusions and also the principles in accordance with which we move from premises to conclusions in other connections. They belong solely to the framework within which we think and reason. In their case too I can imagine a situation somewhat similar to one in which we ask for the justification of a complex logical or mathematical formula: What makes you think that there is no colour between red and green? Can you justify your claim that there is not? Only here the need for a justification does not arise from the kind of complexity that makes it difficult to recognize its internal consistency, its membership to a system. It arises from one's failure to recognize that it does really characterize our way of speaking and thinking. One is not given reasons for accepting what one understands but is reluctant to accept. One is shown that one does really accept it. This is shown in the way one speaks and reasons.

But is one justified in accepting it, in speaking and judging that way? Does one have reasons for doing so? I argue that we have no reason for believing in the uniformity of nature, for instance, and that there can be no justification for such a belief. I ask what this belief comes to, how it is manifested in what we do in various connections in the course of our life and, more particularly, in scientific investigation. I try to bring out the importance of this belief for much that we do and to show that rejecting it is not an open option for us. This is, of course, very closely connected with the question I raise later (in chapter 11) whether 'rules of grammar' are arbitrary. It is also connected with the question whether mathematics needs the kind of foundations in logic on which Russell and Whitehead tried to base it (chapter 12).

To put in a nutshell what I regard to be at the core of my discussions of both inductive and deductive reasoning: Rules of grammar and principles of reasoning do not justify a way of reasoning, a practice of judgment and investigation. They define it. They are not anything independent of or over and above the way we actually proceed in our reasonings and investigations. It is what we actually do in particular cases that gives them content. There are a great many cases, of course, where what we actually do in a particular case—e.g. an inference that we draw—can be justified. If the justification that we give takes the form of appealing to a rule or principle of reasoning, what the rule does is to enable us to see what we find uncertain or questionable in relation to what we do not find so. If there were not numerous cases where what we say, think and infer is unquestionable to us—and this involves what Wittgenstein called 'agreement in judgment'—then there could be no justification anywhere. It is these cases that form the bedrock of our practices, our forms of reasoning. They are what Wittgenstein had in mind when he quoted Goethe's words:

> . . . and write with confidence
> In the beginning was the deed (*Faust* I).

I would like to acknowledge a very great debt to John Wisdom and to Rush Rhees for what I say in the following pages. Wisdom has not actually seen the contents of this book. But he has given me the foundations for writing it by his example and encouragement ever since I came into contact with him as a student, and also by his contributions to the subject, both published and unpublished. Rhees has seen what I have written and has given me both criticism and generous encouragement. But what I have learned from him goes back to the time I had the good fortune to be his colleague. Thirdly, I would like to thank Professor Peter Winch for his very helpful suggestions and criticisms.

I am grateful to the editor of *Analysis* for allowing me to use here 'Wittgenstein, Philosophy and Logic', which appeared in the December 1970 issue of *Analysis*. Chapter 12 is a revised version of that article.

December 1972   İLHAM DILMAN

TABLE OF CONTENTS

CHAPTER 1

INTRODUCTORY: PHILOSOPHY
AND SCEPTICISM

I

Can anyone know anything outside himself, anything beyond
what is accessible to him in sense experience, anything that is not
confined to the here and now? Can one know, for instance, that
one's senses are not deceiving one, that material things exist?
Can any amount of recollection, however much corroborated by
records, give one reason for believing in the reality of the past?
How can present or past experience give one grounds for expecting anything, or believing that there is a future? Is it possible
to prove that one is not alone, that one is not the only sentient,
intelligent being in existence?

It seems that for all we know life may be one long dream. All
our memories may be completely delusive. As Russell put it:
The world may have come into existence five minutes ago with a
population complete with memories of an unreal past. Again it
seems that for all we know none of our expectations may be
fulfilled as from now—the sun may not rise though the earth
is not hit by a star, the bread we eat may poison us though it
contains no arsenic. For all I know when my friend says 'red'
he may not mean what I mean by 'red' although he uses the word
in connection with traffic signals that say 'stop', pillar boxes
and blood.[1] For all I know Smith may pour boiling water on
his foot, scream and groan, and yet feel a tickling sensation
which he calls 'pain'. Or he may feel nothing at all. For all I
know no one may feel anything though they react just like I do
when I am hurt, pleased or angered. Perhaps what I see around
me are hats and coats that cover automata.

The philosophical sceptic has no positive grounds for thinking
any of this. What worries him is that he cannot deny it with
justification, or so it seems to him, that he cannot prove anything

[1] See Appendix below.

to the contrary. As Kant put it: 'It is a scandal to philosophy that the existence of things outside of us must be accepted merely on faith' (*Critique of Pure Reason*, p. 34). It seems to him a genuine possibility that the whole of life may be a dream or that the past may be a figment of our imagination, one that he cannot rule out. Equally it seems to him on the cards that the whole of human reason is sick at the core or a mere illusion, since for all we know the principles of human reason may be inconsistent. So he asks whether there can be any guarantee or general proof that the inferences we can draw from these will at no point lead to a contradiction.[2] If not, then surely there is no line between valid and invalid inferences, no line between sanity and madness.[3] So it seems. He is worried that he cannot show this to be otherwise, that he cannot use logic to prove that the logical distinctions in terms of which we evaluate arguments are founded on reality and not merely determined by human conventions.

These worries may be confined to specific features of human life—to mathematics, scientific methods, moral values, religious practices. Is there any real distinction between science and pseudo-science, morality and convention, religion and superstition? How can it be shown that these distinctions are not ultimately dictated by our whims and interests. If the line between what is acceptable and what is not, what is right and what is not, what is genuine and what is false, what is real and what is illusory, in these regions of human life cannot be founded on some independent reality, if the norms that guide us in our actions, decisions, assessments and evaluations cannot themselves be justified, it seems that there cannot be any real, binding reason why one should say or do this rather than that in the context of these activities. For all we know the steps we take in our reasonings and deliberations may be nothing more than moves in a game we happen to play. Thus, as Russell puts it: If the inductive principle cannot be proved or justified 'we have *no reason* to expect the sun to rise tomorrow, to expect bread to be more nourishing than a stone, or to expect that if we throw

---

[2] See chapter 12, sec. III below.
[3] The second part of this book is largely a study of how the line between valid and invalid inferences, sense and nonsense, is determined.

ourselves off the roof we shall fall' (*Problems*, p. 69). Glaucon's request in the *Republic* that Socrates should show him why moral considerations matter, that he should justify his conviction that they are of supreme importance, is very similar to Russell's search for a justification of why we should be guided by experience. Just as Russell thought that unless the inductive principle can be justified it would be irrational to put one's trust in past experience, Glaucon seems to have thought that unless a moral life can be justified it would be irrational not to steal, rape and murder if one can get away with doing so. Just as it may be a delusion that life is not a dream or that the world did not come into existence five minutes ago, it may equally be a prejudice and a delusion that some things are not permitted. In short, in the absence of what the philosophical sceptic seeks it seems that moral behaviour as well as scientific caution and good sense are irrational—as irrational as our belief in the existence of other people or the reality of the past. In all these cases the rationality of some deep going feature of human life seems to be at stake.

This concern to prove or justify the reality of human knowledge, to provide a general guarantee of the rationality of human life, to demonstrate that outside our thoughts there is a reality independent of us, that the norms and standards which regulate our thought and behaviour are independent of our desires and decisions, goes deep in philosophy. It runs into all its big questions.[4] Yet what is it that the philosophical sceptic is concerned with? And why is it 'the whole business of philosophy' to meet such scepticism? Do knowledge and action in human life wait on the refutation of scepticism? It does not seem that the kind of proof, guarantee or justification which the philosophical sceptic seeks is something that we really need. It does not seem that we compromise our rationality in continuing to live as we do without it. Are we wrong to think so?

It has been pointed out by Berkeley that if there were not 'external bodies we might have the very same reasons to think there were that we have now' (*Principles* §20). Hence if one denies their existence 'there is no damage done to the rest of

[4] See Rush Rhees, 'Wittgenstein's Builders', *Arist. Soc. Proc.*, 1959–60, p. 174.

mankind, who, I dare say, will never miss it' (§35). Even Mc-
Taggart pointed out that 'we sacrifice neither the experience of
everyday life nor the results of science by denying the existence
of matter'[5] (*Some Dogmas of Religion*, pp. 95–6). In other words,
the existence of material things, which the sceptic claims we
cannot know, is an idle hypothesis. If Descartes' demon, who is
supposed to deceive me, never lets me down, how could he still
be said to deceive me? If this is what the demon does, there is
nothing irrational in the way I trust my senses. One could say:
As long as the demon never lets me down, I don't care if he
'deceives' me.

Is it not otherwise, however, with the sceptic who worries
whether we can trust our past experience—'that great guide of
human life'? Perhaps the hypothesis of a material world is an
idle one; not so the hypothesis that nature is uniform. But if it
is not idle we should expect scientists to be prepared to give it
up in the face of conflicting evidence, namely specific non-
uniformities. This is not so however. For while scientists are
certainly prepared to revise or abandon the causal hypotheses,
scientific laws and theories with which they have been working,
they allow nothing to count against the principle of the uniformity of nature. In fact, specific non-uniformities, which may
trouble scientists, stand to the uniformity of nature somewhat
in the same way that specific sensory illusions, delusions and
hallucinations stand to the existence of a material world. Just as
our 'belief' in the existence of a material world tells us nothing
about when a sensory perception is veridical and when it is not,
so is our 'belief' in the uniformity of nature silent about when a

---

[5] Berkeley would agree with McTaggart that 'we only sacrifice a theory
of metaphysics' and that this is what he was combating. Nevertheless he
was divided over the question whether what he opposed was the creation
of philosophers. He wrote: 'Yet the prejudice [that matter is something
that can only be known indirectly] is riveted so deeply in *our* thoughts,
that we can scarce tell how to part with it' (§74). He said that the mind of
man retains a great fondness for the notion of matter which, he argued,
involves a contradiction (*ibid.*). So he oscillated between attributing this
contradiction to the 'vulgar opinion' (§4) and attributing it to 'the
philosophical notion' (§9). The truth is that what gives rise to 'the meta-
physical theory of matter' which Berkeley was concerned to combat are
temptations to which we are *all* susceptible and which are as old as
human language and thinking.

specific uniformity is to be expected and when not. We would not even distinguish between what is and what is not a uniformity if we did not 'believe' in the uniformity of nature. Unless we all 'believed' in the uniformity of nature, and that means trusting, for instance, that the floor boards on which I stand will not suddenly give way under my feet or crumble into dust, we could not even contemplate a specific non-uniformity.[6] We can no more understand what it means for nature as such to be non-uniform than we can make sense of the suggestion that the material world may be unreal and all our sense perceptions illusory.

If the scientist believes that the floor boards cannot collapse unaccountably, that there must be a cause for every event, this is not anything that may turn out to be unfounded. It is not something that is itself based on investigation. A particular causal hypothesis may be mistaken, it may turn out to be unfounded, and one who understands it knows what it is meant to exclude. But what is the law of causality meant to exclude? What would constitute an exception to it? That a particular material disintegrates or turns into dust without a cause? Such a claim is not open to investigation. The disintegration, rotting, rusting, wearing of any material raises causal questions for a scientist and an investigation of these questions is an investigation into the causes of these phenomena; not an investigation of whether or not they have a cause. That these phenomena may have no cause is, in this sense, unthinkable[7] or, as Wittgenstein puts it in the *Tractatus*, 'what the law of causality is meant to exclude cannot even be described' (6.362). Unlike a causal hypothesis or law, the law of causality is not itself a general law or hypothesis, but 'the form of a law' (6.32).

It is the grammar of causal investigation that excludes the *possibility* of an uncaused event, and more generally the scientist's whole *way* of investigating nature that excludes the possibility of inexplicable events. So to look for an explanation when the floor boards suddenly give way is to embark on a scientific investigation. To trust that an explanation will be found is to trust the

[6] See chapter 3 below.

[7] As for indeterminacy in quantum physics, it could be said that certain facts in a particular area of scientific investigation may make it pointless for scientists to stick to the methods that have served them well elsewhere.

B

methods of investigation employed. This trust is, of course, based on their past success, but it is on all fours with our trusting the floor boards on which we tread. Normally we do not suppose that they are riddled with wood worm or dry rot. We do so only in exceptional circumstances—e.g. when the house is old and damp and has been badly neglected. Such trust, the matter-of-course actions and reactions in which it is manifested, is a fundamental feature of human life, one without which it would be hard to imagine not only scientific investigation and inductive justification, but any form of reasoning, thought and speech.

The principle of the uniformity of nature, then, is not a very general hypothesis; to think so is to misunderstand its logic.[8] When a scientist meets a specific non-uniformity he does not conclude that here is a respect in which nature is not uniform. He looks for an explanation of what he takes to be an anomaly— the kind of explanation he has used or will use in other situations. In other words he never accepts a specific non-uniformity as final and irreducible. He tries to represent it as part of a wider uniformity—thus: Floor boards do not generally give way under our feet (uniformity). When they do (non-uniformity) this may be because e.g. they are riddled with wood worm or dry rot. Under such conditions floor boards do give way under our weight (uniformity). This is a feature of scientific procedure. Within the grammar of scientific investigation no non-uniformities are final. The scientist's faith in the uniformity of nature is, therefore, part of the attitude he must adopt if he is to go on with scientific research and investigation.

We see that *as an hypothesis* the claim that nature is uniform is as empty as the claim that there is a material world, or that material things continue to exist even when no one perceives them. The sceptic says: 'For all we know nature may not be uniform and the scientist's belief to the contrary may come from the devil.' But how would a Cartesian demon deceive us here? By making us never accept a non-uniformity as final, when it is, by convincing us that there is an explanation whenever we are faced with a non-uniformity, when there is not, and by putting into our minds fictitious explanations which work. This, however, needs questioning: When is a non-uniformity final and

[8] For a more detailed argument see chapters 3 and 4 below.

when is it not? Does this not depend on how far scientists go in their inquiries, how far they succeed in unifying their ways of explaining different phenomena? Whether or not there is an explanation—does this not depend on whether scientists eventually succeed in explaining the phenomena in question? Can an explanation be fictitious when it does really work? One could shrug one's shoulders: as long as the explanations which the demon puts into our minds work I don't care. It doesn't matter whether or not we are 'deceived' in this sense, since such deception is no deception, and our scientific methods are as reliable as they ever will be—they are as good as those that might have come from a benevolent God.

We are not wrong, then, in our feeling that we can get on perfectly well without the proof or guarantee which the philosophical sceptic seeks and that we are not less rational for managing our lives without it. It is not for this that coming to terms with scepticism figures prominently in philosophical inquiry.

II

Russell rightly contrasted the philosopher who says 'For all we know the sun may not rise tomorrow' with the astronomer who says 'The sun may not rise tomorrow' because he has spotted a star moving towards the earth. The latter's reasons for doubting that the sun will not rise are quite different from those of the philosopher. His doubts spring from what he has observed; it has a specific, inductive basis. To find out whether he is justified in his fears involves checking his observations, making new observations, going over his calculations. His claim that contrary to our expectations the sun *may* not rise tomorrow means that there is *some* probability that it will not rise—however small. Whether there is any such probability depends on the facts.

In contrast the line of reasoning which leads to philosophical doubt does not rely on anything that could be otherwise. The philosophical sceptic does not contrast the inference which he finds doubtful with others about which he feels confident. It is not anything that he finds wanting here as opposed to there which makes him uncertain. His doubt, as in Hume's case, is based on the fact that inductive inferences are supposed to proceed upon a supposition for which it is impossible to give either *a priori* or *a posteriori* reasons. If this is true, it is certainly true come what may. The question of whether our belief that the sun will rise tomorrow is justified or not, as the philosopher asks this, is therefore a purely *a priori* question. When he says that the sun *may* not rise tomorrow he simply means that there is no logical absurdity in supposing that it will not rise.

The astronomer questioned a widely held belief because he knew something which others did not know. The philosopher's doubt, on the other hand, is 'as to whether the laws of motion will remain in operation until tomorrow' (*Problems*, p. 61). If the astronomer doubted *this* he could not question our belief that the sun will rise tomorrow, his observations could not give him any reason for thinking that we may be mistaken. Certainly the philosophical sceptic, like the astronomer, has made a discovery, namely that what is presupposed by all inductive inferences can be justified neither *a priori* nor *a posteriori*. Only this is a discovery about our reasonings, not about the world. But does it show that our inductive procedures are untrustworthy? Does this even make sense?

Take another example—the philosophical sceptic who says that no one can know the thoughts and feelings of another person. He may put this by saying that our notion of the knowledge we are supposed to have of other people's minds involves a contradiction. Surely he does not wish to imply that this man who says he knows that Mary is fond of her mother does not stand to other men making similar claims about friends and acquaintances as his words suggest—any more than the sceptic about induction wishes to deny that there is a difference between an inductive inference that is justified and one that is not, a difference which it pays us to note in our life and actions. He is trying to say that the kind of knowledge this man claims to have of Mary's feelings does not stand to other kinds of knowledge as his words suggest. In other words, he does not wish to deny that this man may have very good reasons for what he claims *relative* to other people making similar claims. He does not mean to doubt what this or any other man claims about Mary's feelings, any more than the sceptic about induction means to doubt that the sun will rise tomorrow. So there is no discrepancy between the way he acts and what he says. He is interested to understand what it *means* to make a claim about another person's feelings.

When we say of a man that he knows something, or when the man says this of himself, these words are meant to indicate how he is placed relative to other men talking and thinking about the same kind of thing. Whether or not the use of the word 'know' is justified in a particular case depends on whether he is in fact so placed. If he is not, then he should not say that he knows, but perhaps only that he believes. The sceptical philosopher who says that we should not speak of knowledge in any of these parallel cases does not wish to deny that we constantly need to know of men talking and thinking of other people how they stand relative to each other. He does not wish to deny that the word 'know' used here adequately meets the need to say something about this relation—the relation between cases of men concerned with other people's feelings. He would gladly agree with Berkeley that 'we ought to speak with the vulgar' (*Principles* §51).

Yet he would also agree that 'we ought to think with the learned'. Why? What would be lost if the philosopher *thought* with the vulgar? Not an appreciation of how the particular case of any man concerned with other people's thoughts and feelings stands in the manifold of similar cases, but an appreciation of how the whole manifold stands in relation to other such manifolds—cases of people who claim knowledge of other things. The former is a question of fact, the latter one of grammar. The philosopher who finds a contradiction in our conception of the knowledge we have of other people's thoughts and feelings is concerned with the grammar of this knowledge. He is concerned to reject a particular model of it: 'We cannot know the minds of other people *in the way* we know our own.' But it *seems* to him that if we cannot know what other people think and feel in this way then we cannot know it at all—just as it seems to the sceptic about induction that if the grounds of an inductive conclusion do not entail it the inference to this conclusion is not justified. This is the kind of difficulty which the sceptic struggles with and finds insurmountable.

Take yet a different case—that of the sceptic with regard to our knowledge of material things. What are the difficulties which he finds insurmountable? What consequences do these difficulties force him to embrace? There are several difficulties, but of these two particularly have loomed large in the history of 'scepticism with regard to the senses'. It is not too difficult to see that each of these is connected with a feature of the grammar of a physical reality. Material things cannot be equated with our sense impressions, they exist independently of anyone's sense impressions. This *seems* to make it impossible for our senses to give us reasons for the claims we make about material things: How can we know the reality of something that transcends our sense experience? If it is possible for one to have such impressions as would lead anyone to believe there is a dagger before him when this is not true, if the presence of these impressions is compatible with the non-existence of the dagger, how can any sense impression give one reason to think that a dagger is before one? The second difficulty stems from the fact that propositions about physical objects make claims about the future: a physical reality is one that lasts—unlike an hallucination or after-image. But then, how can we know any proposition about a physical thing when we can always be made to correct ourselves later? It *seems* that anything that anyone may say about a physical object can turn out to be false and that, therefore, no such proposition can be beyond the reach of doubt.

'We cannot prove the existence of material things since all we have to go by are our sense impressions and the existence of material things is logically independent of them.' The picture is that of prisoners who only know what goes on outside their cell by looking at mirrors or television screens. Yet nothing of what they see on these screens may be real. This is a perfectly genuine possibility. That what *they* see is real is an hypothesis which may or may not be true and which they may or may not have reason to believe. Similarly, the sceptic thinks, the existence of the material world is an hypothesis (*Problems*, pp. 22–3). But if so, how can it be proved? This whole trend of thinking is fraught with contradictions: Can we all be deceived all the time? Is it possible for all propositions about physical objects to be false? Is it possible that we have never asserted one such true proposition and yet understand what it means to talk about physical objects? Can it be said, without contradiction, that if our sense impressions give us reasons for what we say about physical objects, they do so at best in the way that images in one's driving mirror give one reason for thinking that the car behind is getting ready to pull out? Berkeley rightly thought not. He recognized that the notion of matter, as something that can only be known indirectly, involves a contradiction.

'We cannot prove the existence of material things since even in the best of circumstances we cannot be sure that we shall not have to revise our opinion.' But is this true? Are there no circumstances in which a mistake is not even conceivable? Moore was addressing himself to this question when after having declared positively and confidently that he was in a lecture room, as his audience could see, and not in the open air, standing up and not either sitting or lying down, dressed and not absolutely naked, holding some sheets of paper with writing on them, he said that there was nothing dogmatic in his confidence. He thought that it would be absurd to think that he was being dogmatic. 'I should have been guilty of absurdity [he wrote] if, under the circumstances, I had *not* spoken positively about these things, if I spoke of them at all' ('Certainty', *Phil. Papers*, p. 225). As far as I know, Moore never explained why he thought it would be absurd for him to doubt that he is holding some sheets of paper in his hand or to doubt that he has a hand. It was Wittgenstein who explained that here Moore had put his finger on something extremely important and of first-rate relevance to all scepticism.

Physical-object statements like 'This is a tree' (Malcolm reports him to have said—see *Ludwig Wittgenstein, A Memoir*, pp. 87–92) in some circumstances play a role similar to that of mathematical propositions. If I put five beads in a box and then another five and then on counting the beads I find nine I would say that one must have disappeared. Similarly, if I am sitting under a tree in the garden, a tree that I can see clearly and recognize well, then normally nothing would convince me that there is not a tree there. I could walk up to it in dense fog, try to touch it, in order to make sure. But on a clear day, in broad daylight, when I am standing only three yards away from it, and it is clearly visible to my friends, I would not need to go up to it and touch it. Touching it, under those circumstances, cannot make it more certain that there is a tree before me. It would be an idle ceremony. Moore says 'I know that that is a tree and this a finger' in circumstances where it does not have any sense to make sure. This is precisely what he may have wished to bring to our attention. Malcolm reports him to have once said that he agreed with Wisdom that in circumstances such as these one knows these things in the strict sense that one will not have to correct oneself later.

In these circumstances we are not prepared to allow anything as counting against the truth of the proposition that this is a tree. We do not take seriously the possibility of being mistaken. We do not admit such a possibility here. To the sceptic this is yet further evidence of our 'carelessness and inattention', of our being creatures of instinct and habit. Wittgenstein anticipates this reaction: 'But if you are *certain*, isn't it that you are shutting your eyes in the face of doubt?' His answer is: 'They are shut' (*Inv.* p. 224).

That we react in this way in the kind of situation which Moore focused on, that we take this sort of attitude to a great many propositions about trees and stones, chairs and tables, is an *important fact* about us. It underlies the possibility of our being able to talk and reason in the way we do. Wittgenstein said that 'a language-game is only possible if one trusts some-thing' (*Cert.* §509). He meant, if one trusts something naturally, instinctively, as a matter of course. 'Language [he said] did not emerge from some kind of ratiocination' (§475). The trust he was thinking of is pre-logical. To try to base it on reason is like trying to lift yourself by your bootstraps.

Thus such propositions as 'The earth has existed for hundreds of years', 'There is a table there even when I turn round, and even when no one is there to see it', 'Water will boil when heated, and not freeze', belong with propositions of logic.

One cannot make experiments if there are not some things that one does not doubt. . . . The *questions* that we raise and our *doubts* depend on the fact that some propositions are exempt from doubt, are as it were like hinges on which those turn. That is to say, it belongs to the logic of our scientific investigations that certain things are *in deed* not doubted. But it isn't that the situation is like this: We just *can't* in-vestigate everything, and for that reason we are forced to rest content with assumption. If we want the door to turn, the hinges must stay put (*Cert.* §§337, 341-3).

Thus if it is to be possible for us to doubt or wonder whether what seems like palms and water in the distance is an oasis or a mirage, if there is to be a finding out that it is the one or the other, then when we are drinking the water and bathing our hands in it we must regard it as senseless to continue to doubt. At that point nothing that could be countenanced must be counted by us as evidence that we are having an hallucination. In other words, unless we take this attitude on such occasions as when we are drinking the water, we cannot doubt, wonder, or even tentatively believe and try to make sure about anything on other occasions. As Wittgenstein put it: 'If there is a making sure *here* [e.g. when we are actually drinking the water] then there is no making sure at all' (Malcolm's *Memoir*).

What is in question has wider application than this. When I say 'This is a tree', under such circumstances as it would be absurd for me to express this with any hesitation or reservation, then although what I say is *based* on sense experience it is not arrived at by any form of inference. I do not have any evidence for what I say, and I could not now think of any evidence against it. Similarly, the belief that fire will burn me is based on past experience, and yet it is an unreasoned belief—though not unreasonable. It is instilled in me much in the way that similar beliefs and expectations are instilled in animals. The very possibility of inductive reasoning, sophisticated instances of which we meet in the sciences, is founded on instances where we take inductive steps habitually and without having reasons. It is the cumulative effect of past experience that brings us to take such steps almost automatically. It is an *important fact* about us that we learn from experience in this way, that we develop such reactions as a result of past experience. If, in fact, we did not learn those simple inductive lessons that children and animals learn, even if we survived, inductive reasoning could not get going at all.[9]

Compare with the teaching of arithmetic. Given a certain training, we react to the order 'add 2' in a certain way. This

[9] This topic is discussed in greater detail in chapter 3.

need not have been the case. Wittgenstein considers the case of a pupil whose reactions to the teaching differs from our normal reactions—and compares him with a person who naturally reacts to the gesture of pointing with the hand by looking in the direction of the line from the finger-tip to the wrist (*Inv.* §185). If his natural reactions to our instructions and examples are different from ours the teaching will soon stop. He will not be able to acquire the ability to reason mathematically. More important still, if the majority of people did not share the natural reactions which Wittgenstein's pupil lacks, the techniques of elementary arithmetic, as we now know them, could not have developed among us. Those techniques are founded on the important fact that we do react in such-and-such ways as a matter of course.

My working out the answer to a problem in pure or applied mathematics is a piece of mathematical reasoning. I can justify my answer by showing you how I have reached it, by going over it with you step by step. I can explain why I took this step here, performed that operation there; and you may be able to show me that I have made a mistake at this point, taken the wrong turning at that one. You may even be able to show me that my whole way of reasoning about the problem is wrong. You will convince me by reasoning with me. You and I have reasons here because we have mastered the techniques of elementary arithmetic; these reasons that we have and recognize are reasons in mathematics. But how were we brought to the mastery of these techniques? Wittgenstein describes that teaching as *training*. Training is here being contrasted with the giving of reasons and explanations. The latter presupposes that certain techniques have already been learned.

How do I know, though, how to take the training? How am I to be guided by my teacher's examples and instructions? Wittgenstein writes: 'If that means "Have I reasons?" the answer is: my reasons will soon give out. And then I shall act, without reasons' (*Inv.* §211). Supposing that the child is being taught how to continue the series '+ 2' and after 1000 he writes down 1002 —the correct number. What was his reason for writing down just this number? (Do I have reasons for thinking that this colour before me is red? *Inv.* §381.) If you say that the way he understands '+ 2' is his reason for writing down 1002 after 1000, this would be pretty empty. For what he actually writes down is the criterion of how he understands what he has been asked to do. And the instructions that enable him now to write down 1002, whatever form they take, do not *in themselves* determine what he is to write down at each point. There is always an interpretation of the orders, rules and examples given him on which whatever he writes down is just what he ought to have written down. So Wittgenstein says that interpretations by themselves do not determine the meaning of any expression, sign or gesture. He asks: 'What has the expression of a rule—say a signpost—got to do with my actions? What sort of connection is there here?' He answers: 'Perhaps this one: I have been trained to react to this sign in a particular way, and now I do so react to it' (*Inv.* §198). This cannot itself be a connection of logic, and it is here that we reach bedrock—the point at which Wittgenstein says: 'This is simply what I do' (§217).

Given a certain training, then, we all react to certain orders and examples in these ways as a matter of course, without thinking. These actions and reactions, the trust and convictions which they exhibit, provide part of the 'stage-setting' in which mathematical reasoning goes on. My having reasons here, where I have worked out the solution to a mathematical problem, depends on my taking certain steps without reason, blindly, naturally. The reasons that I give in connection with the problem will give out in the end. If I needed still further reasons, then I could have no reasons at all. (Compare with: If there is a making sure *here*, then there is no making sure at all.)

It is the same with my 'knowledge' or 'belief' that I am not the only conscious being in existence, that there are other human beings like me. (Compare with our 'belief' in the uniformity of nature.) What we have here is not so much a belief as a conception within the framework of which I may hold different beliefs—for instance, that my friend is in pain:

'I believe that he is suffering.' Do I also *believe* that he isn't an automaton? (*Inv.* p. 178).

Compare with:

I have a telephone conversation with New York. My friend will tell me
that his young trees have buds of such and such a kind. I am now
convinced that his tree is. . . . Am I also convinced that the earth
exists? (*Cert.* §208).

Wittgenstein would say that the latter proposition belongs to
my frame of reference: What could stand up right if that were
to fall? Could I, for instance, have a telephone conversation with
a friend in New York?

Similarly, if I believe that he is suffering then I am necessarily
taking a certain conception of what is before me. We do not have
a second belief here that is open to doubt or question. Of course,
during a visit to Madame Tussaud's I may doubt, for a moment,
whether what seems to be an attendant is really an attendant
and not one of the wax figures to be found there. (And my friend
may whisper: 'I believe he is one of the attendants.') My doubt,
short-lived as it is, has a specific basis: Is he a live human being
or only a wax imitation? Suppose it moves and begins to talk.
This will clear my doubt. I see that he is one of the attendants,
a live human being. This discovery changes my whole attitude
and orientation to what is before me. If a moment ago I had
thought of it as a wax figure I could not have intelligibly supposed
that it might be hungry or bored. There would have been no
logical room for me to hold this belief.

It could, of course, be said that at first I *believed* one thing,
namely that what is before me is a wax figure, and that soon after
I came to *believe* something else, namely that all the time I was
looking at one of the attendants. But this is different from the
case where I first *believe* that he is in pain and then come to see
that he was pretending. In the former case Wittgenstein speaks
of 'attitude':

Our attitude to what is alive and to what is dead, is not the same (*Inv.*
§284).
My attitude towards him is an attitude towards a soul. I am not of the
opinion that he has a soul (p. 178).

Having this attitude means reacting to people in certain ways—

for instance, resenting what they say, being insulted, hurt, angered or irritated by their words and deeds, being grateful for what they do, pitying them, feeling embarrassed in their presence, and so on. This attitude, these reactions are a pretty basic feature of the life we live. Without them it is hard to think what human life would be like and whether we would be human at all. They form part of the framework in which we attribute emotions, intentions and plans to human beings, hold them responsible for what they do, praise, blame, criticize, punish and forgive them. These various 'language-games', as Wittgenstein would call them—thanking, cursing, praising, judging, passing sentence—are based on these matter-of-course reactions which constitute our 'attitude towards a soul'.

Wittgenstein speaks of these as a 'special chapter of human behaviour' (Z. §542). He says that they are the prototype of a way of thinking (Z. §541) and that the language-games in question may be regarded as extensions of this mode of response (Z. §545). My relation to what I react in these ways is part of my concept of a human being (Z. §543). Thus to think, for instance, that 'we tend someone else because by analogy with our own case we believe that he is experiencing pain too' is 'putting the cart before the horse' (Z. §542). The horse is our natural reaction to someone who has hurt himself and is crying. The mistake of putting the cart before the horse lies in the sceptic's idea that unless such a reaction, e.g. tending someone who has hurt himself, is based on reason and can be justified it is irrational. If that stands in need of justification then none of our beliefs and conjectures about our friends and acquaintances can be justified. (If there is a justification *here*, then there is no justification at all.)

We are indeed creatures of instinct and habit when it comes to the way we resist putting our hands into a flame, avoid bumping into a lamp-post, perform elementary operations in arithmetic, cry out when we are in pain, tend someone else who does so, react with horror in certain situations. Examples can be multiplied endlessly. But the sceptic is wrong to see here evidence of the limitation of our reason, or worse, to think that our rationality rests on quicksand. (Hume: All inferences from experience are effects of custom, not of reasoning.) What he has to be shown is that where there is no instinct and habit there is no reason either. This is a purely conceptual point; but it is an important one. It is the sceptic's perseverance, his refusal to take refuge in 'carelessness and inattention', that has enabled us to appreciate it. If we were not ourselves susceptible to the tendencies to which he gives in without fear, if we were unwilling to travel with him, we would never have seen this.

III

I began by saying that coming to terms with or meeting scepticism is of fundamental importance in philosophy. But this does not mean that it is 'fundamental to anything else'. It isn't as if we have to rescue fundamental assumptions from the attack of the sceptic before we can get on with our other business. The idea that philosophy should refute scepticism, for instance, so that the scientist can build on more secure foundations is, as I have tried to show, a misconception. The reason why it is so important for philosophy to meet scepticism can only be appreciated when we are clear about the object of the sceptic's concern.

The sceptic himself is not clear about this. He thinks that he is concerned with very general assumptions for which we ought to be able to give reasons. We have seen that he is wrong about this. What he is concerned with are features of the framework within which we make assumptions, embark upon investigations, engage in various forms of reasoning, sort out what is true from what is false, distinguish appearance and illusion from reality. Wittgenstein talked of this as *grammar*. What is at issue then is whether the grammars within which we talk and reason, raise and settle doubts, are themselves responsible to any reality, whether the grammatical frameworks within which we distinguish between what is real and what is not are arbitrary. Are our ways of thinking, reasoning, inferring, calculating in any way grounded in nature or are they bounded for us by arbitrary definitions?

I have already hinted at the way they may be grounded in nature, though this does not mean that our ways of reasoning are sanctioned by nature, that our norms are supported by facts. What distinguishes them from anything that may be called arbitrary is the way they enter our lives, how we take them for granted in so much of what we say and do. It is the activities that revolve around them that 'determine their immobility' (*Cert.* §152).

It is not so much our particular actions and activities, what we do, say and infer on particular occasions that get support from them as they from our particular actions. Our particular actions get support from each other.[10] As for what we say and do on particular occasions in agreement with each other, they depend for their very sense on much *else* that we do in *other* connections. In other words, while what gives content to the norms that can be extracted from our practices are what we do in carrying out those practices in particular cases, what holds them fast for us is the way in which the sense and point of what we do in each particular case depends on the wider surroundings of our life: 'One might almost say that these foundation-walls are carried by the whole house' (*Cert.* §248).

The norms in question, the rules of grammar, characterize ways of reasoning and judging, and some of them characterize fundamental features of human life. They are *groundless* in the sense that they are themselves expressions of what we count as grounds in various situations for the judgments we make and the inferences we draw. But they are *not arbitrary* in the sense that so much in our life hangs together with them: 'Thinking and inferring is of course bounded for us by natural limits corresponding to the body of what can be called the role of thinking and inferring in our life' (*Remarks* I, §116).

This question of whether what belongs to grammar and cannot be proved or justified is arbitrary is, I think, the most fundamental question raised by philosophical scepticism.[11]

Rhees once quoted Socrates' statement in the *Phaedo*: 'Let us beware of admitting into our souls the thought that probably no arguments are sound' (90E). He said that what this statement emphasizes especially 'is the rather extraordinary fact that people ever do have the idea that some arguments are sound. That they

[10] See chapter 9 below.
[11] We shall examine it in some detail in our study of both inductive and deductive reasoning—in particular in connection with the uniformity of nature and logical necessity.

have so to speak got to be guided by arguments, or got to accept certain conclusions.' It is just *this* that the philosophical sceptic wonders at, just *this* that he wants to come to grips with. Behind his arguments and conclusions lies a concern to understand man's relation to reality and how his diverse activities are governed by this relation: How does an arrangement of signs which says something differ from, say, an arrangement of bricks? How does drawing a conclusion or calculating differ from the sequence of steps in a dance? How do the movements of a builder on a building site differ from those of an ape imitating him? In short: What is a proposition? What is an inference? What is a thought?

His desire to see clearly how we can know the many things we claim to know, how we can reason to and support these claims, stems from this concern—concern with the conditions of intelligibility and rationality, criteria of knowledge and understanding. It is not so much that he wishes to understand these things as that his questions are rooted in difficulties about them. These difficulties are at once the motive power that drives him on and also a stumbling block to his efforts—in so far as they are directed to a better understanding of man's relation to reality. Therefore to meet or oppose scepticism means to resolve these difficulties, to remove the implicit contradictions to which they commit the sceptic, and so to move towards a better understanding. In so far as the understanding in question is what the philosopher seeks one could say, with Rhees, that 'the refutation of scepticism is the whole business of philosophy'. What needs to be added is that the search for better understanding in philosophy *is* a struggle with difficulties. Our gain lies in what we come to understand *en route*. In St. Augustine's words, quoted by Wittgenstein: 'The search says more than the discovery' (*Z.* §457). One could say that the discovery is in the search, in the struggle with difficulties. It has no independent life and cannot be expressed directly—in the form of a thesis.

It is, of course, not for nothing that the sceptic takes the line which he does take, and his statements often obscurely hint at something important. We have already seen that when he complains that it is impossible to prove the existence of a material world or to justify inductive reasoning what he says is perfectly true, though not anything that needs to disturb us. To see this, however, one needs to do a great deal of philosophical spade work. Again, he complains that it is impossible for anyone to know somebody else's thoughts and feelings. Here too there is truth in what he says, namely that one cannot know someone else's feelings, answer questions about another person's mind, in the same way that one knows one's own feelings, answers questions about one's own mind. But this does not mean that one cannot know what another person feels, that one cannot have proper grounds for answering questions about his mind. Still, if the sceptic is right in thinking that a person's way of answering questions about his own mind differs from anyone else's way of answering those *same* questions, he is wrong in his idea of how they differ. For he thinks that they differ as a man's way of answering questions about what goes on in his own house differs from someone else's way of answering those same questions, someone who has never entered that house. 'If *this* is the way we know what other people think and feel then we don't know it at all—we can't know it at all.' (Compare with: If we know the existence of material things at best in the way that prisoners in a cave know what is outside their cave from shadows they see on the walls of their cave, then we do not know that there are material things; we cannot even have a conception of matter. Berkeley: The idea of matter involves a contradiction.)

To meet the sceptic here means coming to appreciate how it is that we can answer questions about other people's minds, and have proper grounds for doing so, *without denying* that our way of answering such questions does differ from our way of answering similar questions about ourselves. This would involve coming to see what this difference amounts to and how it characterizes our concept of mind. It would also involve appreciating the sense in which we base our answers to these questions about other people on their behaviour and on what they tell us about themselves; the sense in which although what they feel is not identical with the behaviour in which it finds expression, it is nevertheless not something alongside or behind that behaviour. For instance, the joy which someone feels is not a *further* occurrence to his joyous exclamations, movements and smiles. If there is anything behind these it is the particular

C

circumstances in which they add up to real joy as opposed to a pretence or parody of it. So when these expressions lead us to believe that he feels joy we are not inferring to something behind them, although when *he* says that he feels joy he does not base what he says on these expressions. If he were to deny it we would conclude that we had been mistaken, provided we had no reason for doubting his sincerity, no grounds for suspecting that he might be deceiving himself. Sometimes, of course, we have such grounds—in which case to know what he really feels and thinks we have to talk with him, try to gain and deserve his confidence, and to reflect on his words and circumstances. But if we have grounds for doubting his testimony in this particular case, there are many cases where we have no such grounds.

The possibility of reflecting about another person's situation, words and behaviour with a view to forming a judgment about his feelings, hopes, intentions, aspirations and character pre-supposes that there are circumstances where we are prepared to take other people's testimony at face value—just as if we can, in special circumstances, wonder if our senses are deceiving us there must be a great many occasions where we would regard such a supposition as unintelligible. As we have seen, my sense perceptions can turn out to be deceptive in one situation because I regard them as reliable in other situations. Similarly, if an-other person's testimony about his feelings can be deceptive in one situation, or even in a whole series of situations, this is because there are circumstances in which we regard them as reliable and beyond question.

'Joy is not joyful behaviour' (*Z.* §487). But the difference between real and simulated joy is not to be found in what goes on in a man's consciousness. It is to be found in his outer circumstances. Similarly the difference between a man who feels no joy and one who conceals the joy he feels is not to be found in what goes on in the latter's consciousness. All sorts of things may go on there. But these stand to the joy he feels much in the same kind of relation as his smiles and joyous exclamations. ' "Joy" ', as Wittgenstein put it, 'designates noth-ing at all. Neither any inward nor any outward thing' (*Z.* §487). But it is *manifest* joy that enables us to understand what hidden joy means. Hidden joy is not, so to speak, the real thing divorced from its external strappings, and its identity lies in its connection with manifest joy.

I have not attempted to meet scepticism about our knowledge of other people's thoughts and feelings. It would take a long and many-sided discussion to do so. I have merely tried to call attention to *some* of the questions one would have to discuss in coming to terms with such scepticism. My point is that coming to terms with philosophical scepticism here involves getting clear about all these questions and others. It is not too difficult to see, therefore, that in meeting scepticism we not only clear up confusions but also further understanding.

Often in what the sceptic says truth and falsehood are intermingled. In clearing up the confusions that mislead him not only are we able to move from what he says (e.g. that the whole of life may be a dream, that the world may have come into existence five minutes ago) but also get to what he is trying to say. His insight becomes accessible, though it no longer disturbs us:

A. 'You *cannot* say this—not in the way you want us to understand it.' This involves bringing out the internal incoherence in some of the things he says or suggests. It will help him to reformulate his questions, to express himself differently. For instance: 'Empirical truths are never certain.' 'I mean they are not certain in the way that mathematical truths are certain.' 'I see that this does not mean that empirical truths are less certain than mathematical truths.'

B. 'You *needn't* say this—that empirical truths are never certain and, therefore, never to be counted on—if you do not make such-and-such assumptions—for instance, that because they make claims about the future they stand open to correction so that it is for ever on the cards that they may be false.'

It is not enough to show the sceptic that something he says is incoherent. The implicit assumptions that make the line of thought which culminates in what is incoherent the only one open to him must be brought into daylight. When they are seen for what they are they will lose their attraction and leave the sceptic free to move in a different direction. Wittgenstein described this as showing the fly out of the fly bottle. Merely arguing against what the sceptic says will only increase the pressure against which he is speaking without providing him with either relief or insight. If we are merely concerned to show that he is wrong we shall be unable to penetrate beneath the surface of his worries. As I said, if we are to learn anything from the sceptic we must be prepared to enter into his worries and face his difficulties.

The problems with which the sceptic is concerned are deep in the sense that struggling with them brings one to something deep. If the form of words in which they find expression embodies confusion, this does not mean that his problems are not perfectly genuine, that they are merely 'symptoms of confusion'. Answering his questions may well involve transforming them, but this is not to say that one is not answering his questions, meeting his difficulties. Wittgenstein characterized them as 'deep disquietudes' and said that 'their roots are as deep in us as the forms of our language and their significance is as great as the importance of our language' (*Inv.* §111).

To see the importance of language means to see that man's moral, intellectual and spiritual life is not conceivable in the absence of those ways of living which could not have developed apart from language. Wonder at the existence of language, at the existence of an independent reality which we take into consideration whenever we say or do something. I have tried to show that this is central to philosophical scepticism. If one leaves this out one will have left out what gives philosophical inquiry the kind of depth it can have. As Rhees puts it:

Philosophical difficulties are rooted not so much in 'linguistic confusions' as in confusions about language. . . . We cannot understand the problems of philosophy until we have reflected on language. Not just on how words are used, but on what using words is. . . .

Such reflection may help us to understand how it is that language— thinking and speaking and the understanding that there is in life among men—has led men to wonder what things are. A start from ideas of 'linguistic confusions' may issue in philistinism; and generally has (*Without Answers*, p. 134).

Summary. I have argued that the philosophical sceptic is concerned with the grammar or formal features of our modes of knowledge, reasoning and life—some of them features without which we would not be the kind of beings we are. He asks what reality corresponds to these features, whether we have any reason why we live and think the way we do. It seems to him that if the norms of reasoning we observe in different connections in our life cannot be justified then our rationality is an illusion.

I have argued that we are not wrong in our feeling that we can get on perfectly well without the kind of proof, guarantee or justification which the philosophical sceptic seeks and that we are not less rational for managing our lives without it. More strongly, the idea of a proof or justification of our norms of reasoning, of the formal features of our life is a confused one. A justification of what the sceptic wants to see justified would be like trying to lift oneself by one's bootstraps. On the other hand, this does not mean that it makes no difference how we go on, what we say, that our norms of reasoning are arbitrary, that there is no reality to these norms, that the practice and procedures in which these norms are observed are games we happen to play.

I have argued that to bring this out is to meet philosophical scepticism and to answer the sceptic's worries. To do so is to further the kind of understanding we seek in philosophy. The sceptic's questions may embody conceptual confusion; but that is not to say that they are symptoms of confusion *tout court* or pseudo-questions. For in them he is seeking the kind of understanding we are able to obtain if we take his questions seriously and try to come to terms with his difficulties. I have argued that the questions he asks, the issues he raises are important—in fact they are central to philosophy.

Part I

INDUCTIVE REASONING

CHAPTER 2

INDUCTION AND SCEPTICISM

Induction is where we reason from a piece of information, however complex or elaborate this may be, to a conclusion which is
logically independent of it. It is in the light of something that
goes beyond the information itself that we infer the conclusion.
In this induction differs sharply from deduction. There the
relation between premise and conclusion, by virtue of which I
am justified in inferring the latter from the former, is internal
and can be gathered from the premise and conclusion alone (see
chapter 8). Hence in deduction what the conclusion states is
already contained in the premise or premises. What verifies or
establishes the truth of the premises also verifies or establishes
the truth of the conclusion. There is no need to check the latter
once the truth of the premises has been established. Doing so
would not be doing anything new or different. Whereas in induction collecting the information or evidence from which the
conclusion is inferred and verifying the conclusion are not
equivalent. For instance, the doctor may know from the patient's
symptoms and from the X-ray picture he takes that the patient
has an enlarged liver. But when he finally operates on the
patient he comes to know this in a different way. There is a
difference between establishing the truth of the conclusion
directly and collecting the best evidence which justifies it inductively. In deduction there is no room for such a contrast
since the best possible evidence for the premise or premises is
necessarily also the best possible evidence for the conclusion.

Hence in induction our reasoning takes us beyond what we
already know, it widens our knowledge. We can thus move from
what we see to what we do not at the time see. From watching
the hands of the clock I can infer that the parts of the mechanism
behind its face are moving—and even perhaps that they are
moving in a certain way. This is a new piece of knowledge in the
sense that at the time I make the inference I do not see the

mechanism, nor how its parts are moving. The new piece of knowledge I thus reach, whether certain or probable, may be expressed in the form of a particular proposition in the present tense—e.g. the mechanism is moving in such and such a way. Or it can be expressed in the future tense—e.g. you will soon hear a chime, it will strike five. In the first case we argue from something in the present to something else in the present; from one state of affairs in the present we infer the existence of another distinct state of affairs also in the present. In the second case, from a present one we infer a future state of affairs, one not yet in existence. We make a prediction. In a way it could be said that we are predicting in the first case too: we are predicting what we shall see or find out if we look inside the clock. We can, in this way, also infer a past event, that is predict that we shall find further and better evidence of its having taken place. In all these cases we move from particular evidence to particular conclusions in the past, present or future tense. We can also move from particular evidence to general conclusions, that is generalize.

This movement of thought, this kind of inference is very common. We constantly draw such inferences or act on them. This kind of inference permeates all our empirical knowledge, all our actions, decisions and intentions. In our everyday thinking and behaviour we constantly take inductive steps, act on inductive beliefs, anticipate, generalize. Hence scepticism about induction, like scepticism about our knowledge of the physical world, cuts very deep.

Some philosophers have doubted whether inductive inference is a form of reasoning at all. They thought that ultimately it rests on an item of faith, that all inductive inference presupposes what cannot be justified by reason at all. Hence it seemed to them that the distinction between what we normally regard as a well-founded inductive conclusion and an unsupported conjecture is a spurious one. It seemed to them that we have as little reason to believe or put our trust in the former as we have for doing so in the case of mere conjectures. The faith and confidence we place in well-supported inductive conclusions seemed as blind as the unshakeable beliefs of a superstitious man, as blind as mere habit itself. Hence philosophical sceptics in turn questioned the reality of this distinction, the foundations of inductive inference, our right to trust any conclusion arrived at by induction; they came to doubt whether inductive reasons are really reasons, and whether we can really extend our knowledge by inductive inference at all.

Locke who never gave free reign to scepticism was by no means untroubled by it. It seemed to him that no inductive science can be free from blemish:

We can go no further [he wrote] than particular experience informs us of matter of fact, and by analogy to guess what effects the like bodies are, upon other trials, likely to produce. But as to a *perfect science* of natural bodies, we are, I think, so far from being capable of any such thing, that I conclude it lost labour to seek after it (*An Essay Concerning Human Understanding*, p. 271).

Here is the expression of a truth, the inevitability of which Locke comes near grasping, namely that physics, chemistry and astronomy must remain different from mathematics and geometry, though the latter may be used in physical, chemical and astronomical reasoning. Yet, Locke regards this as a shortcoming. He thinks that physics lacks the perfection which mathematics has. But the line between finding inductive knowledge imperfect, finding it inadequate, and finding it undeserving of the title of knowledge is a thin one, and the doubts which Locke held in check, at the expense of greater philosophical depth, know no bounds.

Hume did not have Locke's equanimity and gave way to these sceptical doubts. He then tried to pacify and reassure us. He even denied that he was a sceptic:

My practice, you say, refutes my doubts [he wrote]. But you mistake the purport of my question. As an agent, I am quite satisfied in the point; but as a philosopher who has some share of curiosity, I will not say scepticism, I want to learn the foundation of this inference (*Inquiry*, Sec. IV, Pt. II).

Certainly there is an important difference between ordinary doubt and the kind of doubt which both Hume and Russell raise. In so far as Hume tries to point this out he is right. Nevertheless he was not clear about what distinguishes philosophical doubt from its everyday counterpart. He often thought that the only distinctive feature of the doubts he raised in his philosophical inquiries was their absolute generality. Both he and Russell often spoke as if there was no other difference. Russell said:

If the inductive principle is unsound, we have no reason to expect the sun to rise tomorrow, to expect bread to be more nourishing than a stone, or to expect that if we throw ourselves off the roof we shall fall (*The Problems of Philosophy*, pp. 68–9).

Thus they both thought that grounds for philosophical scepticism are grounds for doubting what in our daily life we accept without doubt and take for granted in our everyday reasonings. They were thus sometimes surprised that their philosophical arguments did not undermine their everyday convictions. Hume's explanation was that 'nature will always maintain her rights and prevail in the end over any abstract reasoning whatsoever' (*Inquiry*, Sec. V, Pt. I).

It is happy [he wrote] that nature breaks the force of all sceptical arguments in time and keeps them from having any considerable influence on the understanding. Were we to trust entirely to their self-destruction, that can never take place, until they have first subverted all conviction, and have totally destroyed human reason.

Sometimes the fact that their everyday convictions had remained intact led them to think that they were not really sceptics. Sometimes they flatly denied that it was their intention to question our everyday convictions:

None but a fool or a madman will ever pretend to dispute the authority of experience or to reject that great guide of human life (*Inquiry*, Sec. IV, Pt. II).

Sometimes they tried to pacify their audience and to reassure themselves:

Though in all reasonings from experience there is a step taken by the mind which is not supported by any argument or process of the understanding, there is no danger that these reasonings, on which almost all knowledge depends, will ever be affected by such a discovery (*Inquiry*, Sec. V, Pt. I).

Both Hume and Russell saw this as evidence that this step taken by the mind is causally determined or the result of blind habit. Russell said that 'our instincts cause us to believe that the sun will rise tomorrow' (*Problems*, p. 63), and Hume said that 'all inferences from experience are effects of custom' (*Inquiry*, Sec. V, Pt. I).

There are, of course, cases where what we believe and the confidence with which we believe it are not based on argument and are impervious to ratiocination. It is, for instance, usually of little avail to argue with someone who suffers from 'feelings of persecution'. Such a man's beliefs are not easily amenable to reason. Again, a great many of our everyday beliefs and expectations will not be easily shaken by reasoning (see chapter 3). On the other hand, there are cases where one can alter a man's expectations, undermine the certainty of his convictions, by reasoning with him. If one succeeds in showing him that the reasons he has for what he believes are not good, that the grounds on which his expectations are based are inadequate, one will undermine his confidence.

Hume and Russell send a fear into our hearts because in what they say they often imitate one who says to another that what he believes is unreasonable, that he has no grounds, or very inadequate ones, for what he expects: If the principle of induction cannot be justified 'it becomes plain that we have no ground whatever for expecting the sun to rise tomorrow, or for expecting the bread we shall eat at our next meal not to poison us' (*Problems*, p. 62). 'We may be in no better position than the chicken which unexpectedly has its neck wrung' (p. 63). It would be wrong, therefore, to say that it was not their intention to undermine our confidence in conclusions arrived at by induction. This was not their end certainly; but they were prepared to follow their argument to the bitter end whatever it may be, not to take refuge in 'carelessness and inattention'.

The truth is that, like many philosophical sceptics, Hume and Russell were divided in their reactions to how they meant what they said.[1] In so far as they did mean to frighten us, in so far as they thought that our convictions have no firm foundations, their pacification was inadequate. For if you tell someone that there is no good reason to count on something that matters to him you will give him little comfort by adding that although he has no good reason he will continue to rely on it just the same. No, comfort, if it is needed, is to be found in a different direction. If sceptical reasoning makes little difference to our confidence, that is not because we are impervious to reasoning in these matters, but because of the kind of reasoning with which the sceptic faces us (see chapter 1).

However until we see this and realize that there is no ground for alarm we ought to be frightened. Otherwise it means that we are either too frightened to take the sceptic's arguments seriously or that we are too practically orientated for philosophy to mean a great deal to us.

[1] Compare with the way Russell tries to soften his claim that memory cannot give us knowledge of the past: 'There can be no doubt that memory forms an indispensable part of our knowledge of the past' (*The Analysis of Mind*, pp. 159, 165). He makes it quite plain, however, that he thinks it a perfectly real possibility that the world had come into existence five minutes ago 'complete with records and memories' and then adds that he is not suggesting that we cannot be sure that this is not the case. When he then adds that he is 'not suggesting that the non-existence of the past should not be entertained as a *serious hypothesis*' (p. 160) this does not cut much ice.

CHAPTER 3

UNREASONED BELIEFS

In *An Inquiry Concerning Human Understanding* Hume wrote:

When a child has felt the sensation of pain from touching the flame of a candle, he will be careful not to put his hand near any candle but will expect a similar effect from a cause which is similar in its sensible qualities and appearance. If you assent, therefore, that the understanding of the child is led into this conclusion by any process of argument or ratiocination, I may justly require you to produce that argument (Sec. IV, Pt. II).

He did not think that such an argument can be produced. His reason for thinking so was that any such argument or process of reasoning would necessarily involve some general principle which the child could not have learnt prior to learning such inductive lessons in particular cases as that a candle flame burns the hand.

There is nothing sceptical about this point as such and it should not be confused with Hume's qualms about whether *any* inductive claim or conclusion can be justified. Two questions, I think, need to be distinguished in connection with Hume's concern 'to learn the foundation of inductive inference': (i) Must everything that may be called an inductive belief be based on reasons if it is to be a rational belief? Can it be always based on reasons? (ii) Can an inductive conclusion be *ever* based on reasons or justified? Are inductive reasons really reasons? Hume confused these questions and he thought that since inductive justification in the end brings us to cases where our convictions and expectations rest on habit it follows that 'all inferences from experience are effects of custom, not of reasoning' (*Inquiry*, Sec. V, Pt. I).

In this conclusion Hume was wrong. But he was right in thinking that there is something important about the fact that as children we learn such inductive lessons as that a candle flame burns the hand and is painful to touch and that reasoning plays no part in our learning these lessons. The truth is that beliefs such as these are logically more primitive than any inductive law or principle from which they may be derived. If they needed justification then no inductive step or conclusion could be justified.[1]

In *Philosophical Investigations* Wittgenstein wrote:

The character of the belief in the uniformity of nature can perhaps be seen most clearly in the case in which we fear what we expect. Nothing could induce me to put my hand in the flame—although after all it is *only in the* past that I have burnt myself (§472).
The belief that fire will burn me is of the same kind as the fear that it will burn me (§473).

The point is that if we speak of the belief in the uniformity of nature we are referring to a pretty fundamental feature of human life. Without it it is hard to imagine not only scientific investigation and reasoning, but any kind of thought and speech. But what is this 'belief'? To see what it amounts to look at the way I fear that fire will burn me. The belief shows itself in a multitude of reactions and expectations of this kind. Believing in the uniformity of nature is not anything over and above acting and reacting in these ways in a multitude of situations. Having the belief *is* acting and reacting in these ways.

Therefore it would be wrong to say that we act in these ways, for instance that nothing would induce us to put our hands in the flame, because we believe in the uniformity of nature: 'Have we in some way learnt a universal law of induction, and do we trust it here too?—But why should we have learnt one universal law first, and not the special one straight away?' (*Cert.* §133). Our acting in these ways habitually, blindly, as a matter of course, forms part of the framework on which the workings of language and thinking in general, and the possibility of inductive reasoning in particular, are based.

'When I write a letter and post it [says Wittgenstein] I take it for granted that it will arrive—I expect this' (*Cert.* §337). This does not mean that a letter which I post may not reach its

---

[1] See chapter 1, sec. II above.

destination—any more than I may put my hand in the fire and not feel pain. But what kind of reason or explanation do we give in such cases? We say that *normally* letters get to their destination, a man who puts his hand in a flame feels pain. In *this* case the letter did not arrive, I felt no pain, because the postman was careless, my hand was anaesthetized. Apart from the norm there would be nothing to explain in these cases, nothing to give reasons for, nor could we intelligibly speak of the postman as having been careless or my hand as anaesthetized. If fire did not normally burn and cause pain when touched there would be nothing to explain in this particular case.

But can we not give a reason for expecting to be burnt by fire? It may seem at first that we can, even though we do not in fact *need* to do so. But the possibility of giving reasons and the need to do so cannot be separated altogether. For unless we can imagine circumstances in which people may need reasons for such a belief we shall not know what role a reason can have in connection with it. But if what we are looking for does not play the kind of role that reasons normally have in connection with beliefs that people have, if it is not something that makes a difference to what they say and do, it will be no more than an idle wheel, a false support. This is part of what Wittgenstein has in mind when he writes:

'Why do you believe that you will burn yourself on the hot-plate?'—
Have you reasons for this belief; and do you need reasons?
When I ask this, a hundred reasons present themselves, each drowning the voice of the others (*Inv.* §§477–8).

In connection with such beliefs it is not clear what will count as a reason, nor what role a reason is supposed to have.

Wittengenstein points out that the question 'On what grounds do you believe this? might mean 'From what are you now deducing it or have you just deduced it?' It might also mean: 'What grounds can you produce for this assumption on thinking it over?' (*Inv.* §479). Thus we could give a physical explanation of why fire burns the flesh and a physiological one of why this produces pain in a living being. These are not, of course, reasons why people expect to be burnt by fire and to feel pain. In fact,

D

these explanations take such expectations or beliefs for granted. They cannot add support to our convictions, they cannot increase our certainty. If we were not already convinced about a great many facts such as these, if we did not regard them as unquestionable, we could not so much as begin to explain anything.

The belief that fire will burn me if I touch it, as the fear that it will burn me, is *not reasoned*. It has not been arrived at by reasoning, it is not based on reasons. But it is not unreasonable in the way that the neurotic girl's fear of every man she meets is unreasonable. The reasons she gives will usually be bad reasons in the sense that they do not justify her fears. Or they may be rationalizations in the sense that they do not explain why she fears that the men she meets will try to seduce her. But the belief that fire will burn me if I touch it far from being unreasonable is, in fact, a paradigm of a reasonable belief. It would be unreasonable to doubt or question it (*Cert.* §220). In fact, in this belief we have an example of something about which we could not even be mistaken. A mistake here would topple all judgment with it (§558). One might say: 'If that is false, then I am crazy.'

Such beliefs, then, as that fire will burn me if I touch it, that the pencil in my hand will fall to the ground when I let go of it, that water boils when heated and not freeze, are not only not based on reasons, they are (to use a simile from Wittgenstein) the hinges around which our reasonings revolve. If we did not have and share such beliefs, if we did not regard them as unassailable, if we did not acquire them by experience, as animals do, we could not think and reason in the way we do. That is the possibility of our carrying out empirical and scientific investigations, of our framing explanatory hypotheses and checking them, of our formulating scientific laws and empirical generalizations and justifying them, depends on there being a large number of beliefs, like those mentioned, which we all take for granted, are not prepared to question, and for which we do not need justification. Thus the fact that we acquire such beliefs as a result of experience underlies the possibility of thinking and concept-formation in general, and of inductive reasoning in particular.

When, for instance, we perform an experiment to establish or verify a law of nature, such as Hooke's law, which states that as the force applied on a metal bar increases the bar stretches proportionately, the stretch in question varying with the metal, there are a great many regularities on which we rely and which go unmentioned in the experiment. I do not doubt, for instance, that the weights I place in the pan attached to the metal bar will remain constant during the experiment, or that the screws or clamps holding the bar in place will not turn into jelly. If I did I could not even set up the experiment. Thus the possibility of supporting Hooke's law inductively, of performing the above experiment, depends on beliefs of this sort being exempt from doubts. It depends on our not needing to make sure that they are true, on our not counting anything as grounds for or against believing them. It is in this sense that these convictions are like hinges on which our experimental investigations and inductive justifications turn.

But what holds these hinges in place? Partly the attitude that we have learnt to take towards them. Repeated experience instils these beliefs in us as in animals. In what we are taught we come to take them for granted and refuse to question them:

When a child learns language [writes Wittgenstein] it learns at the same time what is to be investigated and what not . . .
Just as in writing we learn a particular basic form of letters and then vary it later, so we learn first the stability of things as the norm, which is then subject to alterations (*Cert.* §§472–3).

This is part of learning to speak, judge and reason. What we thus accept without question enables us to make judgments, to support and criticize them. These truths form an important part of the common understanding that makes it possible for us to communicate with each other, to argue, reason, agree and disagree. Given the way we judge, act and reason, it is impossible for us to give them up without giving up that whole way of judging.

These truths which are beyond question for us in this way form a system, experience does not teach them to us in isolation, and in the system they give one another mutual support (*Cert.* §142). Each is held fast by what lies around it (§144). Testing, confirmation, doubts and mistakes take place in the system; our arguments, criticisms and judgments have their life within it. The truths thus held in place are the fixed stars around which these activities revolve; the movement around them determines their immobility (§152). Each is so anchored in all my questions and answers that I cannot touch it (§103).

Thus we do not refuse to question them because they have been established very firmly. They are not 'truths' in this sense. They belong to our frame of reference (§83), they form part of 'the scaffolding of our thoughts' (§211), they constitute 'the matter-of-course foundation' for the researches we carry out (§167). Their groundlessness is a matter of their role in our ways of speaking and judging. They are not propositions which in our credulity we have accepted without grounds; they are not presuppositions for which we are unable to find any justification. They do not, as Hume thought, bear witness to the weakness and limitation of human reason. On the contrary, reflection on language and on what is involved in different forms of reasoning shows that in any area of speech and thought there are widely shared matter-of-course reactions and beliefs which belong to the framework of our judgments and reasonings and as such are beyond dispute and justification. Such a framework is necessary if there is to be any argument and justification.

We see that Hume was right in thinking that such a belief as that contact with fire is painful is not based on reasons. It is logically more primitive than any general law from which it may be derived or which may be used to justify it. But he did not see clearly that it does not *need* justifying. I have argued that to think that its lack of justification opens the door to scepticism is to misunderstand what is involved in justifying a belief in *actual* cases—in situations where giving a justification makes a difference to what we actually say and do. For a mode of speech and reasoning is possible only if there are certain things that people trust without reason and justification. Beliefs such as the one in question are precisely those regularities that we trust as a matter of course. They are what we accept without justification and regard as being beyond dispute. If Hume thought that they need justifying that is because he recognized that they have a special position in connection with the justifications we actually give but was unclear about what this position amounts to.

I have tried to connect the fact that we learn from experience in the way Hume suggested, as a fact which conditions the possibility of speech and thought in general, and inductive reasoning in particular, with the special place we give in our language and investigations to what we thus learn: (i) Given past experience we come to expect contact with fire to be painful. This is an important fact about us. We do not reach this expectation by ratiocination. It is an unreasoned expectation—one of the points where we begin and where our substantiations end. (ii) What we thus come to expect is given a special place in our speech and thought. In Wittgenstein's words, it is given the stamp of incontestability, shunted on to an unused siding which lies apart from the route travelled by inquiry.

We had seen in chapter 1, section II, that if, like the philosophical sceptic, we allowed *every* proposition about physical objects to stand open to correction, if we did not draw the line somewhere and say that under these circumstances these propositions are immune to the challenge of the future, we should have made it impossible for any physical object proposition to be falsified. This is what the sceptic does by his refusal to admit that there is an end to doubt. In doing so he deprives his own words of any sense and intelligibility—such words as: 'perhaps we are mistaken in our belief that there are physical objects', 'perhaps, unknown to us, a malicious demon is deceiving us'. We have seen that we can know on purely *a priori* grounds that a malicious demon cannot deceive us in the way that Descartes urged us to imagine it. For if it is possible for us to be mistaken in a particular situation about the existence or the properties of a physical object, there must be some physical object propositions which in certain circumstances cannot turn out to be false, or about which we cannot be mistaken. We can see this by reflecting on what it *means* for a belief about a physical object to turn out to be false.

Similarly for inductive beliefs: If my expectation that this pencil in my hand will fall to the ground if I let go of it and will not stay suspended in mid-air needed justifying, then no inductive belief or expectation could have a justification: 'We expect *this*, and are surprised at *that*. But the chain of reasons has an end' (*Inv.* §326).

CHAPTER 4

INDUCTION AND THE UNIFORMITY
OF NATURE

Hume asked: 'What is the nature of that evidence which assures us of any real existence and matter of fact beyond the present testimony of our senses or the records of our memory?' His answer was that this type of inference 'arises entirely from experience' (*Inq*. Sec. IV, Pt. I). When we are confronted with an 'entirely new' situation, when we lack previous experience or information based on other people's experience, we cannot know what inference to make. Reason alone, unassisted by experience, will be unable to guide us here, as it does in cases of formal inference. In all inductive reasoning there is a step taken by the mind which cannot be justified *a priori*.

Hume asks whether it can be justified *a posteriori*: 'What is the foundation of all conclusions from experience?' This question seems to him to be on all fours with the first question and he lets it pass as intelligible. He answers: 'Even after we have experience our conclusions from experience are *not* founded on reasoning or any process of the understanding.' Past experience *alone* can give us no reason for this kind of conclusion. For when, on the basis of past experience, we make an inference we assume that the future will be like the past: 'All our experimental conclusions proceed upon the supposition that the future will be conformable to the past.' So unless we have reason for accepting this supposition our inference will not be justified.

But what reason have we for accepting it? How can we justify the belief that nature is uniform? How can we know that the future will conform to the past? Here Hume reaches deadlock. It cannot be known or justified *a priori* since, as Hume thinks, whether or not nature is uniform is a contingent matter. It cannot be known or justified *a posteriori* either, since all knowledge or justification *a posteriori* would have to presuppose it: 'The proof of this last supposition by probable arguments, or arguments regarding existence [writes Hume] must be evidently going in a circle and taking that for granted which is the very point in question.'

Russell expressed this as follows:

It has been argued that we have reason to know that the future will resemble the past, because what was the future has constantly become the past, and has always been found to resemble the past, so that we really have experience of the future, namely of times which were formerly future, which we may call past futures. But such an argument really begs the very question at issue. We have experience of past futures, but not of future futures, and the question is: Will future futures resemble past futures? This question is not to be answered by an argument which starts from past futures alone. We have therefore still to seek for some principle which enables us to know that the future will follow the same laws as the past (*The Problems of Philosophy*, pp. 64-5).

Hume did not think that any such principle can be found. He said: 'At this point it would be very allowable for us to stop our philosophical researches.' In the *Abstract* he said: 'This conformity (betwixt the future and the past) is a *matter of fact*, and if it must be proved, will admit of no proof but from experience. But our experience in the past can be a proof of nothing for the future, but upon a supposition that there is a resemblance betwixt them. This therefore is a point which can admit of no proof at all, and which we take for granted without any proof.'

We see that Hume thought that this conformity betwixt the future and the past is a factual assumption. He insisted in more than one place that 'the course of nature may change'. However he found it impossible to give any reason for thinking that it will not change. Russell who followed Hume closely in his early writings continued the search. 'The problem we have to discuss [he wrote] is whether there is any reason for believing in what is called "the uniformity of nature" ... On our answer to this question must depend the validity of the whole of our expectations as to the future, the whole of the results obtained by induction, and in fact practically all the beliefs upon which our daily life is based' (pp. 63-5).

Why is it that the supposition that the future will be like the

past 'can admit of no proof at all'? What would have to continue
to be the case for it to be true? In what sense is nature supposed
to have been uniform up to the present? In what sense has the
future turned out to be conformable to the past? Certainly not
in the sense that all our predictions have come true. Obviously
it must be possible for us to be mistaken in what we predict.
Again, the truth of the supposition in question was never
thought to be incompatible with changes in specific sequences
of events which have been regular and repetitive. Russell said:
'The belief in the uniformity of nature is the belief that everything that has happened or will happen is an instance of some
general law to which there are no exceptions' (p. 63). That is,
nature has at least so far been uniform, what was to take place
in the future has conformed to what took place in the past, in
the sense that all events classed together on specifiable criteria
have been in accordance with certain simple laws. In short, for
Russell the uniformity of nature, the conformity between the
future and the past, is a matter of the same laws holding all along
and throughout spheres of phenomena demarcated by certain
criteria. For Hume it is a matter of like causes having like
effects.

Let us consider these two criteria of uniformity. To begin with
Hume's criterion. Let us suppose that B is an event which has
always followed A so as to justify the causal hypothesis that A
is the cause of B, and that in a given instance A is not followed
by B. This may or may not be taken as falsifying the causal
hypothesis in question, but in neither case would it be taken to
clash with Hume's dictum 'like cause like effect'. For where we
take it to falsify the causal hypothesis, we would deny that A
had ever been the cause of B. We would *not* say that what had
caused B in the past, or on other occasions, was no longer doing
so, or not doing so in this instance. We would say that what we
thought was the cause of B is not, and never has been, its cause.
In some cases we may have to revise our conception of the
causes of the kind of event or phenomenon of which B-like
events are an instance. This would mean modifying the scientific
theories in question. Where, on the other hand, the causal
hypothesis is not taken as falsified, an explanation is advanced
of why in this instance, or these instances, B does not occur even

though A does. We may account for this failure in terms of some feature of these instances which distinguishes them from others, or in terms of some difference in their circumstances or surroundings. It is, of course, not an arbitrary matter which course we take.

We see that our ways of inquiring into and explaining natural phenomena are such as to allow only two alternative courses in the kind of eventuality we have considered. In neither case, however, do we have an instance in which Hume's criterion of uniformity fails to be satisfied. Is it any wonder that what was in the future has always turned out to be conformable to what had taken place in the past in the sense relevant to Hume's discussion! This is made plain in the following passage by Russell:

If we are challenged as to why we believe that the sun will continue to rise heretofore, we may appeal to the laws of motion: the earth, we shall say, is a freely rotating body, and such bodies do not cease to rotate unless something interferes from outside, and there is nothing outside to interfere with the earth between now and tomorrow. Of course it might be doubted whether we are quite certain that there is nothing outside to interfere, but this is not the interesting doubt. The interesting doubt is as to whether the laws of motion will remain in operation until tomorrow (p. 61).

It is true that there may be circumstances in which we may wonder whether, doubt if, the sun will rise tomorrow. These are circumstances which would give us some *inductive* reason for thinking, expecting, fearing that it will not rise. If we were right and the sun exploded or was hit by another star, this would be uninteresting to Russell. For it would *not* show that nature is not uniform, in the sense relevant to his discussion. It would not show that Hume's supposition had been falsified.

Indeed, in the absence of special circumstances one wouldn't have any reason for fear or doubt. Russell acknowledges this when he says: 'We are all convinced that the sun will rise to-morrow. This is a matter about which none of us, in fact, feel the slightest doubt.' We feel no doubt for, as things are, we have no reason for doubting this. The proviso 'as things are' is, of course, perfectly proper. We all know that a minor planet or asteroid may one day collide with the earth. Astronomers have no reason now for expecting this to happen. They may even have good reasons for ruling out that it will happen within the next ten or twenty years.[1] Hence they may say that there is not the slightest possibility that the sun will not rise for the next decade or twenty years. Their reasons are, of course, specific inductive reasons, and no one who knows what is in question would dream of suggesting that the astronomers have no right to make such a claim since it is logically possible for the sun not to rise tomorrow. Logical possibility, i.e. the coherence of the description of an event, gives us no reason at all for thinking that there is some possibility that an event of that description will occur.

Russell thinks that a person who entertains his *uninteresting* doubt is imagining or anticipating a possibility which, were it to become actual, would not show that the course of nature had changed. That is why he finds what is being imagined uninteresting. It is uninteresting because, were it to come about, it would be accountable in terms of our laws of motion and gravitation. He writes:

The belief that the sun will rise tomorrow might be falsified if the earth came suddenly into contact with a large body which destroyed its rotation; but the laws of motion and the law of gravitation would not be infringed by such an event. The business of science is to find uniformities, such as the laws of motion and the law of gravitation, to which, so far as our experience extends, there are no exceptions. In this search science has been remarkably successful, and it may be conceded that such uniformities have held hitherto. This brings us back to the question: have we any reason, assuming that they have always held in the past, to suppose that they will hold in the future? (p. 64).

I asked: What would have to continue to be the case, what would have to remain unchanging among the various things that change from day to day, from generation to generation, from place to place, if Hume and Russell are to be satisfied that their

---

[1] They *could* not have reason for ruling it out indefinitely and altogether, i.e. for thinking that it will *never* happen. There are interesting questions here about the grammar of 'never', about time and logic, closely relevant to our discussion which I cannot go into now.

supposition is true, that nature is uniform? We have just seen Russell's answer to this question. Let us probe deeper into it. Let us suppose that in the development of a particular branch of science certain recurrent events come to the notice of scientists. These do not accord with the laws scientists expect them to come under, and their deviation from the course which accords with those laws cannot be explained by means of any of the relevant laws. I am imagining that what has been discovered, although of a recognizable kind, proves intractable to any simple orthodox explanation. Here, in the absence of any good reason for treating these events in a completely separate way, scientists may find themselves forced to modify and perhaps even to abandon some laws which have so far served them well. Does this constitute an 'interesting' situation for Russell? Does it count as a non-uniformity of nature?

Let us suppose that some laws are abandoned. What does this amount to? It amounts to the formulation of new laws intended to apply *both* to the phenomena which defied the old laws and to the phenomena to which the abandoned laws applied. No new law will be considered satisfactory which does not apply to *both*. If, on the other hand, scientists do not succeed in formulating such new laws, the relevant criteria of classification will have to be re-examined and perhaps modified. I am speaking as if the laws and the criteria were quite separate from one another, and of course this is not so. What I am trying to emphasize, however, is that in the kind of eventuality we are imagining scientists will be forced to modify the relevant theory or explanatory system in one way or another. Sometimes the modification will have to go very deep, radically affecting their, and eventually our, conception of the phenomena in question. But in no such case will scientists speak of a non-uniformity of nature.

Yet from one point of view we do have a non-uniformity here, since an existing law has been broken. For instance, bodies which have so far always been observed to behave in accordance with certain laws are now observed to behave sometimes in accordance with these laws and sometimes not, although no difference in their circumstances can be discovered to account for this. That is, we have the same bodies, in the same circumstances, not always behaving in the same ways. But 'same' and 'similar' are relative terms. The bodies and their circumstances are the same or similar on certain specifiable criteria which rule out various differences as irrelevant. These criteria, built into the scientist's explanatory system or theory, are open to examination and revision. What one has so far regarded as an irrelevant difference may come to be considered relevant. Thus when one is speaking of uniformity in specific cases of this sort one is using special systems of classification. The uniformity in question is not independent of one's system of classification, it is necessarily relative to such a system.

Consider, for instance, the uniformity to be found in the chemical reactions and physical properties of substances identified by professional chemists, as opposed to substances classified for everyday purposes by their tastes, colours, visible textures, and so on. For instance, if we try to determine the melting point of butter by simply taking a large number of samples, slowly heating them up until they begin to melt, recording their temperatures at this point, we shall be more likely to be struck by the variety in our findings than by their uniformity. If we spread out these tests over a long period of time and carry them out in different places the variety in our findings will be even greater. Notice that even here we have started at a certain level of sophistication, in that we are using a graded thermometer and the samples in question are artificial products which have to some extent at least been made to measure.

What would be the chemist's reaction to our experiments? He would say, to begin with, that our samples, strictly speaking, were not samples of the same substance, that the term 'butter', although good enough for commercial purposes, covers substances which vary considerably in their ingredients and so in their properties. He would say that our experiments were carried out under conditions of different barometric pressure. He would add that in so far as we could regulate the barometric pressure and use accurate instruments of measurement, then if we analysed a given sample of butter whose melting point has been accurately determined, and synthesized a new sample which matched the relevant specifications of the first accurately, then allowing for experimental error, we would find the second sample to have the same melting point as the first. What sort of statement is this?

And why is it made with an assurance that precedes any checking or confirmation?

Notice that the proposition asserted is a conditional one. It states, roughly, that *if* the barometric pressures are the same, and *if* the samples match each other in all relevant respects, *then* the temperatures at which they start to melt will be the same. In so far as the scientist moves in the direction of making the truth of the consequent clause into a criterion of the fulfilment of the antecedent conditions, the truth of the statement in question will begin to assume a necessary character. He will then become more and more reluctant to allow the antecedent conditions specified to be fully satisfied when the consequent one does not obtain. Is it any wonder that the proposition in question cannot be falsified and that he can be certain of it *a priori*! But then the connection that he refers to will thereby cease to be a connection in nature; the proposition he asserts will no longer state a connection between sets of natural phenomena.[2] It will have been transformed into a statement of how certain complicated sets of conditions for identifying phenomena of certain kinds are to be connected. The way such a proposition is used in scientific investigation may be compared to the way geometry and trigonometry are used in finding out actual heights and distances.

You will notice that our samples have to meet a greater number and variety of stringent requirements before they can satisfy our criteria of uniformity of performance. But the greater and more stringent these requirements are the less will conditions which meet them be likely to recur. Perhaps one will be able to reproduce them artificially, though even then one will at best only approximate uniformity in one's results. That is the uniformity in question is only an ideal which in practice we can at best approximate artificially, in laboratory conditions. As Simone Weil puts it:

On the scale of our senses there is no appearance of determinism except in the laboratory. Ask a meteorologist or a peasant if they see much determinism in storms or rain: look at the sea, and say if the shapes

---

[2] See chapter 10 below.

of the waves appear to reveal a very rigorous necessity! The truth is that nineteenth-century physicists believed there were no more things in heaven and earth than in their laboratory—and indeed in their laboratory only at the moment when an experiment succeeded. Their excuse was their professional obsession, but those who shared their belief without their excuse were fools (*S.N.L.G.*, p. 68).

She is right. We are, indeed, most impressed by the so-called uniformity of nature when we contemplate natural phenomena from the safe distance of the mathematical physicist's study. What is in question, however, is an ideal that has an important role to play in scientific investigation.

Thus a chemist may write down an equation for a chemical reaction, specifying certain conditions. There will be no doubt in his mind that whenever those conditions are satisfied, correctly identified samples of the chemicals in question will always react in accordance with the equation. Whenever the actual result diverges from the one he has worked out on paper, he will say that the conditions have not been properly satisfied, the samples not correctly identified, or perhaps that they contain impurities. This procedure is, of course, not arbitrary. He has ways of checking for possible defects, he has theories by means of which he can connect each defect in the particular experiment with the divergence from the expected result. That is he has ways of accounting for each failure—ways which have proved their worth in many other instances.

The connections which enable him to predict actual results and explain failures of prediction are theoretical. They are stated in what are called 'laws of nature'. These laws are statements of uniform association, that is statements of how changes in one magnitude or condition are correlated or vary with changes in another. But the properties and conditions in question are identified, the magnitudes measured, by methods which presuppose other such laws. Take the notion of equality in weight for instance. One who has no idea how it is judged will have no understanding of what is meant by 'weight'. But our ways of determining equality in weight, our methods of measurement, presuppose certain laws of nature—such as the laws of statics. That is, what method, what operation we choose in defining equality in weight in part depends on facts of nature, on certain regularities in the course of events, which call for investigation. For instance, our criterion of equality in weight which states that two bodies A and B are of equal weight if they balance each other in the opposite pans of scales constructed in accordance with certain specifications (e.g. have arms of equal length) presupposes the law of the lever. If the law of the lever did not hold our method or criterion for measuring weights would have had to be different. Hence the law of the lever may be said to enter or be presupposed by other laws stating various functional dependences between the weight of objects and other magnitudes.

The way our various scientific laws are woven together, the way they presuppose our various concepts and also enter into their determination, contributes to our impression of the uniformity of nature. Hence to understand what this uniformity consists in we have to consider both the nature of scientific theorizing and the basis of concept formation. When we have done so we shall see that the uniformity in question is not a matter of fact, as Hume and Russell thought, though it does depend on certain very general facts in a way which we shall consider presently.

I suggested that the scientist who is impressed by the so-called uniformity of nature is impressed by the uniformity which is portrayed by laws of nature which involve one another and between them define or determine the concepts which they relate. Only 'portray' is the wrong word here, or at least one which there is some danger of misunderstanding. Einstein wrote: 'The simpler our picture of the external world and the more facts it embraces, the more strongly it reflects in our minds the harmony of the universe' (Einstein and Infeld, *The Evolution of Physics*, p. 225). Yes. But on a common-sense level, in our every-day dealings with reality in practical situations, what happens to the harmony and order of the universe? Are we still impressed by the uniformity of nature? The harmony which Einstein, more than others, had a glimpse of is one that belongs to his 'picture', which is an extremely abstract one. Just as the rigid and un-changing order which we find when doing geometry is one that belongs to our geometry and which nature has sometimes been said, misleadingly, only to approximate. The harmony which

Einstein was impressed with has its source in the theories and equations which he was developing. The relation between the picture, the theories, and the actual facts and phenomena of nature is very different from the relation between a portrait and the sitter, between ordinary descriptions, statements of fact and generalizations and the facts which they state, describe or generalize.

It is difficult to say anything adequate about this relation in a brief space. Both Wittgenstein (*Tractatus*, 6.341) and Toulmin have compared scientific theories with co-ordinate systems. This is an analogy that goes deep. However, it may obscure the sense in which scientific theories are empirically founded. So both Wittgenstein and Toulmin safeguarded against this danger by emphasizing how much the theories which scientists develop to describe and explain natural phenomena ultimately depend on what facts their investigations bring to light. Thus having compared mechanics with a system of co-ordinates for describing mechanical phenomena and having said that all the properties of such a system 'can be given *a priori*' (6.35), Wittgenstein emphasized that 'the laws of physics, with all their logical apparatus, still speak, however indirectly, about objects in the world' (6.3431). He said: 'The possibility of describing the world by means of Newtonian mechanics tells us nothing about the world: but what does tell us something about it is the precise *way* in which it is possible to describe it by these means. We are also told something about the world by the fact that it can be described more simply with one system of mechanics than with another' (6.342). That is (i) the laws of mechanics belong with our systems of measurement and representation. One should not confuse them with the results stated in accordance with them. It is those results which our empirical investigations and measurements confirm or disconfirm. Still (ii) given the purpose for which the system of co-ordinates is designed and how it is to be used, what geometrical features it is to have depends on how things are.

This dependence, however, is *indirect* in the sense that no actual fact *in itself* can force us to abandon or modify the system we adopted. The system has to establish its worth 'over a longer term'. So, in the long run, it may turn out that a given system of co-ordinates does not provide the best way of representing the range of facts we are interested in. Therefore, we could still say that 'the possibility of explaining particular phenomena in a particular way is something which *has to be found out*' (*The Philosophy of Science*, p. 94).

The part played by one who develops a new theory is, in Toulmin's words, 'no more than that played by anyone who introduces a language, symbolism, method of representation or system of signs' (*ibid.* p. 128). The theory is prompted by reflection on certain classes of facts, by the perception of analogies between phenomena so far treated as dissimilar. It helps us to connect them in new ways, suggests the possibility of treating them in ways we had not thought of before, transforms our apprehension of them, and encourages us to anticipate new facts. Thinking of Newton and Freud, Professor Wisdom said, 'Each introduced a word and from it bred a notation which encourages us towards new experience and also enables us to co-ordinate old experience' (*Philosophy and Psycho-Analysis* p. 253). Writing of the account which the chemist gives of a particular experiment in accordance with his theories, he said that it connects 'the incident before us with thousands of others with which we should never have connected it but for his myth of the molecule' (*ibid.* p. 186).

In *The Evolution of Physics* Einstein and Infeld illustrate this with many examples. In a section entitled 'The Field as Representation' they write: 'We have tried to translate familiar facts from the language of fluids, constructed according to the old mechanical view, into the new language of fields. We shall see later how clear, instructive, and far reaching our new language is' (p. 142). They then go on to show how this way of representing phenomena brought out further resemblances— between electric, magnetic and now optical phenomena: 'This great result is due to the field theory. Two apparently unrelated branches of science are covered by the same theory. The same Maxwell's equations describe both electric induction and optical refraction' (p. 157). Later on in the book Einstein speculates about the analogy between the relation of an electrical charge to its field and the relation of a physical body to its gravitational field. In a passage worth quoting he says:

E

We cannot build physics on the basis of the matter-concept alone. But the division into matter and field is, after the recognition of the equivalence of mass and energy [E = mc²], something artificial and not clearly defined. Could we not reject the concept of matter and build a pure field physics? What impresses our senses as matter is really a great concentration of energy into a comparatively small space. We could regard matter as the regions in space where the field is extremely strong. In this way a new philosophical background could be created. *Its final aim would be the explanation of all events in nature by structure laws valid always and everywhere.* A thrown stone is, from this point of view, a changing field, where the states of greatest field intensity travel through space with the velocity of the stone. There would be no place, in our new physics, for both field and matter, field being the only reality. This new view is suggested by the great achievements in field physics, by our successes in expressing the laws of electricity, magnetism, gravitation in the form of structure laws [*viz.* of the kind Maxwell formulated], and finally by the equivalence of mass and energy. Our ultimate problem would be to modify our field laws in such a way that they would not break down for regions in which the energy is enormously concentrated (pp. 257–8, *i.m.*).

The possibility of treating widely different types of phenomenon in the same way, of representing them by means of the same system of co-ordinates, of bringing them under the same few simple laws, the same form of description—it was this prospect that excited Einstein and made him speak of 'the harmony of the universe'. No one, perhaps, came nearer than he did to realizing this possibility. His general theory of relativity is the most conspicuous landmark in this direction. Its aim (in his words) is 'to build a physics valid for all-co-ordinate systems' (pp. 225–6), i.e. not only for inertial ones as Newton had done. What this comes to is still (in Wittgenstein's words) to 'impose a unified form on the description of the world' (6.341). That is, the uniformity we are speaking about belongs to our ways of speaking about, representing and explaining natural phenomena. As Toulmin puts it: 'The fact that an astrophysicist uses the same law, when explaining the motion of the parts of a double-star, as has already been used to account for the motion of falling apples, the moon and the satellites of Jupiter, represents a uniformity in his techniques for dealing with the four systems. This uniformity in technique reflects the presumption that the four phenomena can be regarded as similar in type, viz. gravitational . . . So it is not Nature that is Uniform, but scientific procedure; and it is uniform only in this, that it is methodical and self-correcting' (pp. 147–8).

Let us review the course of our discussion so far. I asked: 'What is the nature of the supposition which Hume and Russell are distressed at being unable to prove? Why does it admit of no proof?' To see why it does not, I asked: 'What would constitute its disproof?' Hume's answer was: An instance where a familiar cause does not produce its familiar effect. Russell's answer was: An instance where a law which expresses a specific uniformity ceased to hold. We examined instances which appeared to satisfy these descriptions. It turned out that none of them were to be described in ways that would bring them into conflict with Hume's supposition or make them 'interesting' for Russell.

The descriptions in question are not internally inconsistent or self-contradictory. So Hume is right in thinking that the contradictory of his supposition cannot be ruled out *a priori*. Yet though the words 'like cause unlike effect', for instance, are not self-contradictory, nevertheless nothing is allowed to wear such a description. Why not?

We have seen that there is a sense in which nature is full of non-uniformities and that the future constantly lets us down in what it brings. Yet mostly this does not worry the scientist, and when it does it still does not discourage him. His faith in the uniformity of nature seems unshakeable. Where, in an extreme case, he has to give up a law which has so far served him well he still has to keep an eye on the past, on instances to which the old law applied, when formulating a new law to take up the place of the old one. It would not be a law if he did not do so.

Our dilemma then is this: Hume's supposition, the uniformity of nature, cannot be proved, and yet the scientist's faith in it seems unshakeable—he will not admit any instance to be so described as to constitute an 'interesting' exception to the uniformity of nature. But this is not a piece of dogmatism. It has to do with the kind of approach to natural phenomena that is at the heart of scientific investigation; it is bound up with the kind of account which he seeks of physical events and processes.

He *cannot* admit the possibility of a familiar cause not producing its familiar effect *and* go on investigating nature *in the same way as before*. The kind of attitude and procedure which constitutes scientific investigation as we know it excludes admitting such a possibility. His methods preclude certain ways of describing situations that may face him. In short the so-called principle of the uniformity of nature is a proposition that belongs to the framework of scientific investigation.

Hume's dictum that like causes always produce like effects does not state an hypothesis or assumption, it involves no claims about the future. It sets no limits to what the future may bring and it is in no danger of being falsified by the course of events. In that sense it is true come what may, though its denial is not self-contradictory. It fixes or indicates limits to what we shall *say* in certain eventualities. These limits have to do with the logic of scientific discourse and inductive reasoning in general. As an empirical hypothesis Hume's supposition about the conformity betwixt the future and the past, about the uniformity of nature, is either constantly falsified or it is empty in the sense that its truth is compatible with any and every possible states of affairs. It may even be argued that it is devoid of sense since one cannot sensibly speak about nature as a whole, of its following one course rather than another, or of its changing its course. When Hume says that 'the course of nature may change' he is not speaking sense if he means that 'everything may change'. He is not speaking sense unless he is thinking of specific changes in contrast with others, or over and against an unchanging background. These considerations apply equally to his claim about the conformity betwixt the future and the past.

The supposition, then, which Hume claimed is involved in all inductive reasoning is no ordinary supposition at all. If anything it is a statement of grammar. If one wishes to speak of its basis, one has to look not simply at nature, but at the complex of human activities which constitute scientific investigation—forecasting, explaining natural phenomena, justification of predictions and explanations.

II

Still is there not some truth in the conviction that it is a *fact* that there is at least some order or uniformity in natural phenomena without which it would not be possible to investigate them, suggest explanations, and make predictions at all? I think there is. I shall now try to explain this.

I have argued that language is the source of the system that we find in nature, and that the uniformity or haphazardness we find in physical occurrences is relative to the language we use. As Toulmin puts it: 'The kinds of regularity we encounter in everyday life, which form the starting-points of the physical sciences, are hardly ever *invariable*; and correspondingly the degree of system in everyday language is limited. Only rarely can one infer from an everyday description of the circumstances of a phenomenon what form it will take' (p. 47). Although science takes its start from everyday language and the reality of certain questions asked in it, that language is gradually modified in the development of science. So the language of science, especially of the more sophisticated sciences, differs from the everyday language in which we talk about physical things, processes and events, in more than one respect. One respect in which it differs from everyday language is in the classifications it uses. Toulmin asks: 'What is the point of the physicist's reclassification? To see this [he goes on] recall that it is his aim to find ways of inferring the characteristics of phenomena from a knowledge of their circumstances. This aim is one which ordinary language, being largely devoid of system, does not serve very well' (p. 52). After giving an example Toulmin continues: 'How different is the situation in the physical sciences. There the specification of a system carries rigorous implications about its behaviour . . . Indeed, the classification system scientists employ changes as time goes on, and the way in which it does so shows what their ideal is: that, from a complete specification of the nature of any system they have under investigation, it should be possible to infer how it will behave, in as many respects and to as high a degree of accuracy as possible' (p. 53).

When we think about this question of the uniformity of nature most of us are inclined to say that it is *because* there is uniformity in nature that the scientist is able to give a coherent picture and account of natural phenomena. When challenged we are inclined to imagine situations which defeat all attempts to give such a

coherent account, to predict what would come next, to give
reasons for what happens. But what is this degree of haphazardness other than the scientist's failure to present a coherent
picture of what happens, to explain it in terms of the existing
theories? I wish to suggest that it is not because of extreme
haphazardness here that his theories fail, but rather that we *call*
the situation in which such a failure occurs 'haphazard'. What
we mean is that no explanation is forthcoming. One cannot
explain such a failure in terms of the haphazardness of what
takes place because that failure is our criterion of haphazardness, it is not its result. To say that there is no explanation
because the events are haphazard is to go round in a circle. For
if the haphazardness of the events imagined is to be able to
explain the scientist's failure it must be possible to identify
the haphazardness apart from the failure.

It is not because we believe that the future will be like the past
that when faced with the kind of situation imagined we believe
that we shall be able to give an account of what happens in it.
But rather, if we want to talk of a belief that the future will be
like the past, that belief *is* our belief that we shall be able to give a
coherent picture or account in such extraordinary situations. One
is inclined to think that if only we could find reasons for Hume's
'supposition' this would guarantee success in the face of such
eventualities. The desire is for such success to be guaranteed *a
priori*, that is in advance, all at once and once and for all. What is
desired here is self-contradictory. Nothing can guarantee that
scientists will solve their problems. They have to try until they
hit upon a solution. In some cases it has taken centuries for a
viewpoint to be developed from which solutions emerged to
long-standing problems. There is nothing sceptical in my suggestion.

I am not saying that a situation may not be reached wherein
scientists give up. They may give up. But if they did, it would
not do to say that the reason for it is that nature is no longer
orderly and amenable to scientific study. This *cannot* be an
explanation of the scientists' defeat. Here one can envisage two
very different kinds of genuine explanation: either (i) a sociologi-
cal one, or (ii) one that would *necessarily* constitute a progress
in science and so go some way towards placing the defeat behind

one's back. For defeat here means a failure to give a coherent account of certain phenomena in terms of the existing scientific theories. An explanation of why the existing theories fail here may take one of two possible forms: either (a) that of indicating weaknesses in these theories, or (b) that of indicating positive complications in the phenomena in question. To do either is to carry on with scientific investigation and speculation, to take it forward.

On the one hand it seems nonsensical to say that a form of investigation or reasoning is made possible by the way things are, by some very general facts about nature. On the other hand, it seems obvious that if things behaved differently, in certain specifiable respects, then we might not have sought for the kind of explanation we now seek, we might not have evolved the techniques of investigation that we now use. The idea we are examining is that our methods of investigating and reasoning about nature depend in the end on certain very general facts about nature—facts which lead us to speak of order and uniformity in natural phenomena. Let us consider this in comparison with our familiar methods of measurement. We may not have been able to measure lengths in the ways we now do, by using measuring rods, if the results we obtained fluctuated, if different measurements of the same object at different times and by different people did not agree. If they did fluctuate we might still have been able to measure lengths, though not in the way we now do, provided we were able to discern some regularity in these fluctuations—that is, provided we could correlate these fluctuations with changes in the circumstances in which the measurements are taken. Leaving aside this complication, it is obvious that the possibility of our conveniently using our present methods of measuring length depends on the constancy of our results. This obviously is a *fact* and so could have been otherwise. On the other hand one could not describe what is in question as a constancy in the lengths of the measuring rods. One cannot say, for instance, that if our measuring rods changed their lengths haphazardly we could not measure lengths and distances. For any claim about measuring rods having different lengths at different times presupposes the existence of established methods of measurement.

Results of measurements are, of course, facts, but they could not, without circularity, be said to underlie the possibility of the methods by means of which they are obtained. The very identity of these facts presupposes the existence of methods of measurement by means of which they are assessed. The concepts in terms of which they are stated depend on what constitutes the application of these methods. I am not saying that the length of an object depends on how we measure it, that what we measure is dependent on our methods of measurement. What I am saying is that our *notion* of what we measure, namely length, is dependent upon our methods of measuring the lengths of objects and the criteria that are internal to these methods. That notion has its identity in and cannot exist apart from that complex institution of measuring.

The possibility of speaking about or referring to the *lengths* of objects requires certain complex activities that we carry on in certain contexts—e.g. superimposing objects followed by cutting them in certain ways. Such activities lie in the background when we refer or point to the length of an object or indicate the distance between two points. Our notion of length belongs with these activities and appears in the role it plays there. Such words as 'length' and 'weight' have their fixed place or position in the complex institution of measuring, in the peculiar comparisons we carry out and the inferences we draw from them. These give the notions in question their peculiar grammar and identity. They fix the body of implications that can be drawn from ascriptions of length to objects, they determine what it makes sense to say here and what not. In short they determine what we mean by 'length'. That is why Wittgenstein says that this meaning is learnt by learning to measure (*Inv.* p. 225).

Such institutions develop gradually and over a long period of time in the process of men wrestling with practical problems which face them in the kind of life they live. One example of the kind of practical problem I mean would be that of chopping trees to block the entrance to a cave. One can imagine that the methods of comparison and measurement in which the concept of length makes its appearance would have developed in and out of situations of this sort. Men must have come to talk of the *length* of objects as a result of having to meet this sort of problem.

The methods of comparison they thus came to develop, our techniques of measurement which are the more sophisticated counterparts of these, provide the post at which our ascriptions of length are stationed. The sense of what we say when we make such ascriptions, the reality of this way of talking, presupposes these techniques, these modes of comparison, and the kind of life, the sort of activities, in which they are used. The concept of length thus corresponds to our particular way of dealing with situations that arise in our ways of living (*Remarks* V, §46). For instance, we want to buy linoleum to cover our floor and wish to bring home a sufficient amount of it without having to bring the whole roll. So we ask for the length and width of the floor. In the process of meeting this problem we formulate various questions in which the concept of length is employed. The concept leads us to make investigations, it is the expression of our interests and directs them (*Inv.* §570).

What I am trying to point out is that if the practices in which such concepts as length have their identity are made possible by such general facts of nature as the constancy of our results, if without them we might not have found these particular techniques convenient and useful and so might not have developed them, then we must remember that had our ways of living been different what we find convenient and useful would have equally been different. In that case too we would probably have developed different techniques and different concepts. If, therefore, we say that such facts determine our concepts, we must remember that this determination is via our interests which are not even conceivable apart from our particular ways of living. We must also remember that this dependence between our ways of speaking, the concepts we use, and our ways of living, the interests that guide our activities, is a two-way one. The facts alone and in themselves cannot account for our techniques, norms and concepts.

Besides the general facts of nature that are in question cannot be described in terms of the concepts used in stating the results we arrive at by means of the methods which they make possible or give point to. As we have seen, what our methods of measurement may be said to be founded on is not anything that can be stated apart from the activities we engage in. Wittgenstein refers to it as 'a certain constancy in results of measurement' (§242). The constancy belongs to or characterizes our results. Wittgenstein compares it with what he calls 'agreement in judgments' of which he speaks as 'part of the framework on which the working of our language is based' (§240). Just as 'what we call "measuring" is partly determined by a certain constancy in the results of measurement', so also what we call 'calculating' is partly determined by the important fact that mathematicians in general agree about the results of their calculation. If there were no such agreement 'then neither would human beings be learning the techniques which we learn' (*Inv.* p. 226). You cannot separate the techniques which constitute mathematics from these 'important facts'. These facts partly determine the identity of our techniques. They also give point to them.

Agreement in human judgments, constancy in results of measurement: both are contingent facts. Yet, within certain limits and in one form or another, both are essential to the possibility of distinguishing between correct and incorrect uses of words and measuring techniques. The idea of a correct way of using a word or measuring something in contrast with incorrect ways, of a regular use of words or a method of measurement, is in turn essential to the idea of what is said or the result obtained being true or false. So the idea of truth and falsity, the idea of an independent reality which one can investigate, measure, and speak about, and with which one's results and statements can accord or conflict, presupposes norms that one can maintain, rules that one can observe, methods that one can follow. I have argued that the kind of regularity implied by the idea of a method, the kind of regularity we have in procedures that are governed by criteria, is fundamental to the kind of regularity which scientists discern in natural phenomena—the kind of regularity which makes them and us speak of 'the uniformity of nature'.

Any specific regularity in nature may cease to obtain and so is a matter of contingent fact. But this need not shake the scientist's faith in the uniformity of nature. For the possibility that he will succeed in discerning a new regularity that never ceased to obtain cannot be ruled out by facts alone: 'Why would it be *unthinkable* that I should stay in the saddle however much the facts bucked?' (*Cert.* §616). However, certain facts in a particular area of scientific investigation may make it pointless for scientists to use methods that have served them well elsewhere—for instance, indeterminacy in quantum physics. As Wittgenstein puts it: 'Certain events would put me into a position in which I could not go on with the old language-game any further' (§617). But even here methods which have been useful so far or elsewhere are not ruled out of court: 'Even if an irregularity in natural events did suddenly occur, that wouldn't *have* to throw me out of the saddle' (§619). Still, if the circumstances are sufficiently different from the ordinary circumstances in which familiar scientific methods have proved to pay, who is to say that we are proceeding with the *same* methods in the new circumstances?

I have not argued that there are no uniformities in nature, but that what uniformities we perceive, detect and make use of in our predictions and explanations are relative to our language and systems of classification. The possibility of finding uniformities in nature is bound up with the kind of regularity that exists in human affairs—among them scientific techniques of investigation and theoretical speculation. This is not to say that the uniformities we find in nature are man made.

But to say that there are uniformities in nature is not to say that nature is uniform. For if there are uniformities there are also non-uniformities. What I have opposed is the idea that the so-called principle of the uniformity of nature is a very general statement of fact, that it states a very abstract truth about 'the constitution of the universe'.

Someone may say: 'If induction leads to true results it must be because the universe has such-and-such a constitution.' For instance, Keynes' 'limitation of independent variety'. In Strawson's words: 'The universe is such that induction will continue to be successful.' One answer to this is that induction does not always lead to true results. Another answer is that it doesn't make sense to seek an explanation of why induction generally leads to true results as it makes sense to seek an explanation of why such-and-such a method of psychotherapy is generally a success in the treatment of hysteria.

A third answer is that the claim that we can reason inductively because the universe is constituted in such-and-such a way is an explanation only in name. For our view of the universe is not something that we have arrived at by means of investigation; it is not something that can be identified apart from our ways of living. How we look on the world is a matter of what questions we ask, how we investigate them, how we reason about and support the things we say, what we accept as an explanation of the things that interest us. Therefore how we investigate and reason about natural phenomena cannot be explained in terms of features of the world as we picture it without circularity. As Wittgenstein puts it: 'I did not get my picture of the world by satisfying myself of its correctness; nor do I have it because I am satisfied of its correctness. No: it is the inherited background against which I distinguish between true and false' (*Cert.* §94). 'It is the substratum of all my inquiring and asserting' (§162).

We do reason inductively, we are concerned to know the causes of events. Scientific methods are immensely influential in a society like ours. We look on the world in certain ways, we picture it in such-and-such a way. But the picture is not itself the result of the assessments we have made; it is rather a means of assessment: 'It helps us in the judgments of various situations' (*Cert.* §146).

I have argued that the so-called principle of the uniformity of nature is a feature of our picture of the world, that it belongs to the framework of our scientific investigations. This is not to deny that this principle rests on certain very general facts of nature, that what makes our methods of scientific investigation and reasoning possible, given our interests and what we find useful and convenient, are in part certain very general facts of nature. But these facts do not justify these methods and principles. The relation between them and the principles is neither deductive, nor inductive, nor any other kind of logical relation.

INDUCTION, UNREASONED BELIEFS
AND THE UNIFORMITY OF NATURE

General law of induction
or principle of the
uniformity of nature

Inductive conclusions
based on various kinds
of evidence (great
variety).

Such beliefs[3] as—e.g.
that the pencil will fall
down if I let go of it, or
that fire will burn me if
I touch it. (Unreasoned
beliefs and expectations
—but not unreasonable.
Far from it, it would be
unreasonable to doubt or
question them.)

I *General Facts
about Nature*
Particular regulari-
ties we trust as a
matter of course.

II *General Facts about Us*
(i) Given past experience
we come to expect
fire to burn us—this
is an important *fact
about us.*
(ii) What we thus come
to expect is given a
special place in our
speech and thought.
Wittgenstein: It is
given the stamp of
incontestability,
shunted on to an
unused siding which
lies apart from the
route travelled by
inquiry.

Facts ⇄ Ideals   Beliefs ⇄ Rules

Chapter 3. Our idea of the uniformity of nature and its place in our
various everyday reasonings.

Chapter 4. The scientist's conception of this uniformity and the role
this plays in his experimental investigations and theoretical
reflections. (The role of *ideals* in scientific research and
speculation.)

---

[3] In any area of speech and thought there are widely shared matter-of-
course reactions and beliefs which belong to the framework of our
judgments and reasonings and as such are beyond dispute and justification.
Such a framework is necessary if there is to be any argument and justification. A mode of speech and reasoning is possible only if there are certain
things that people trust without reason and justification—in deed.

CHAPTER 5

DEDUCTION AS THE SCEPTIC'S MODEL OF COMPARISON

Hume asked: 'What is the nature of that evidence which assures us of any real existence and matter of fact *beyond* the present testimony of our senses or the records of our memory?' He answered that this kind of inference 'arises entirely from experience'. He then asked: 'What is the foundation of all conclusions from experience?' He answered: 'The supposition that the future will be conformable to the past.' But why did Hume ask this second question? Why was he not satisfied that what we know from past experience is good enough as ground for an inductive conclusion? At least part of his reason was that the grounds of an inductive argument do not entail the conclusion. This is, of course, perfectly true. But why should anyone want it to be otherwise? Why should the lack of entailment be a source of dissatisfaction?

In *The Problems of Philosophy* Russell writes:

It must be conceded that the fact that two things have been found often together and never apart does not, by itself, suffice to *prove* demonstratively that they will be found together in the next case we examine. The most we can hope is that the oftener things are found together, the more probable it becomes that they will be found together another time, and that, if they have been found together often enough, the probability will amount *almost* to certainty. It can never quite reach certainty, because we know that in spite of frequent repetitions there sometimes is a failure at the last, as in the case of the chicken whose neck is wrung. Thus probability is all we ought to seek (pp. 65–6).

Here Russell notes a feature of all inductive arguments without which they would not be what they are, namely inductive arguments. From this he concludes that we have no right to be certain of the conclusion of an inductive argument on the basis of the argument alone. We must have something additional to the grounds we have if the argument is to give us a right to trust its conclusion. What we need is a general principle which we can trust independently of any such argument and which will ensure that the grounds in question entail the conclusion.

If this principle is conceived as an additional premise and is, therefore, a contingent truth it cannot turn the inductive argument into a deductive one unless it incorporates the conclusion in question. But in that case it will also incorporate the doubts it is meant to remove. We have already seen that if the principle is so conceived it will itself be subject to the doubts it is meant to cure. If, on the other hand, it is a general principle in accordance with which we draw inductive conclusions it will be logically less primitive than the specific inductive inferences we have learned to make in particular cases. It cannot, therefore, add to the sanction we already have for making them. Neither can it change its character and turn the inductive steps in these arguments to deductive ones.

Some philosophers who saw this clearly enough thought that weakening the conclusion from 'it is certain that p' to 'it is likely that p' might achieve the desired result. Hume saw that this move could not change the original situation. He held that there are not even 'probable arguments' for putting our trust in past experience and making it the standard of our future judgment (*Inq.* Sec. IV, Pt. II).

Given that no principle can be found which will both turn an inductive inference to a deductive one and be immune from the doubts it is meant to remove, the question that we need to ask is this: Why should we need it at all? Why are we inclined to think that unless the grounds of an inference entail the conclusion those grounds alone cannot give us a right to accept it? The answer to this question is not simple. We want to see inductive inferences turned into deductive ones before we feel they can be trusted because of our idea that all forms of reasoning must have a common essence best exemplified in deductive reasoning. This idea prompts people to compare induction with deduction and it makes the differences which the comparison brings out into a source of dissatisfaction.

But given the idea that all forms of reasoning must have a common essence, why do we think that it is best exemplified in

instances of deductive reasoning? Partly at least because there
what conclusions are warranted in particular instances, and
what conclusions are not, is determined in a general manner
and within very definite limits. Valid and invalid inferences are
separated in a clear-cut way and there are no degrees of validity.
It is not too difficult for us to satisfy ourselves in a given case
that the necessary and sufficient conditions for a valid inference
are fulfilled. Once we have satisfied ourselves on this point no
grounds are left for doubt or hesitancy. Once we have done so
we can be certain that if our premises are true our conclusion
must be true. There is nothing that can go wrong. We know
this in advance of the situation in which the inference is made.

In the case of inductive inferences we are unable to find such
criteria. Whether or not our evidence is considered conclusive
depends on the circumstances, on what we already know, and on
how our knowledge is organized. The conclusiveness of our
grounds varies from one situation to another, from one field of
investigation to another. This seems to make their trustworthi-
ness something arbitrary. We fail to find general and definite
standards with which to measure our individual judgments in
particular cases and so we think that there is no measure to which
our judgments are responsible. Behind this conclusion lies our
idea that a difference in degree cannot add up to a difference in
kind, that an indefinite measure is no measure at all. Since the
difference between what is generally considered a well-supported
inductive conclusion and what is considered a poorly supported
one is one of degree we think that it cannot amount to a real
difference. This makes it seem that a well-supported inductive
conclusion is no better than one which is only poorly supported
or not supported at all. As Russell has argued, when we believe
that the sun will rise tomorrow 'we may be in no better a position than the chicken which unexpectedly has its neck wrung'
(*Problems*, p. 63).

Here Russell has given way to the inclination, so persistent in
philosophy, to count as fatal in any degree what in a high degree
we already count as fatal (Wisdom, *O.M.* p. 185). There is a
close connection, I believe, between this craving for consistency,
encouraged by abstract thinking, and the desire to have things
mapped out tidily and once and for all—the desire to cope with

every conceivable situation in advance and not to have to deal with difficulties as they come up. These cravings, I believe, are in part responsible for the kind of fascination which formal disciplines like deductive logic and mathematics have exercised on so many philosophers.

Part of Russell's argument is that there is no real difference between the scientist who makes sophisticated predictions and the chicken which expects to be fed when the man who has fed it regularly in the past appears on the scene. Why does Russell think that there is no real difference between the two cases?

Take the case of a scientist who puts forward a causal hypothesis and compare it with the landlady who tells her lodger that if he drinks the cup of coffee she has made for him he will be able to keep awake. When questioned why she thinks this she replies that a cup of black coffee had this effect on her previous lodger. Is this a well-supported inductive belief? Is it reasonable for her to be as confident as she is? The answer is No on both counts. One has only to bring to mind how a scientist investigating the effect of coffee on sleep would proceed to see how the landlady's evidence for her belief is inadequate. Yet what is the difference but the *number* of positive observed instances and the *width* in the variety of conditions in which the instances are found? And, of course, the difference between the support of 5, 10, 50, and 100 instances is one of degree.

Looked at in this way it is quite natural for one to wonder how a difference in the number of positive instances should make all the difference between certainty and doubtfulness. But the fact is it does. Although it is true that there is no sharp line between strong and weak inductive arguments, well-founded beliefs and unfounded dogmas, and hence an area in which we don't know whether or not certainty is warrantable, the difference between the two outskirts of this borderline area is sufficiently important for us to be marked with different pairs of words.

In her paper 'The Problem of Justifying Inductive Inference' Miss Ambrose points out that 'some inductive arguments closely parallel deductive ones' (*Essays*, p. 199). She writes that if a person were to say 'I have known thousands of cases, and no exceptions, of people being burnt upon touching a hot stove, but it is not probable that I shall be burnt the next time I touch

F

one', then we would be inclined to say, 'You do not know what "probably" means.' What this person says, she points out, comes near to being a self-contradiction (p. 198). She examines the analogy between inductive and deductive arguments and compares,

       (a) 'Some number of cases make p probable'

and   (b) 'Some number multiplied by 2 equals 14' (see pp. 192–3).

In the latter case there is a number which makes the proposition necessary, or necessarily true. There is one and only one number, namely 7, for which this is true, and what number this is is quite definite, i.e. precisely delimited. So we can frame and do have strict rules for assessing or finding that number, for checking whether a suggested number is the right one. Here there is no room for doubt, uncertainty or hesitation. In the former case, however, there is no one number such that that number of cases makes p probable—necessarily probable, if one can say so. But though there is no one such number there is a whole range of them. However, while in the first case the range, confined as it is to one and only one number, is definite, in the second case it is not. There is no sharply delineated range of number of positive instances which will give probability to or make certain the inductive conclusion. There are nevertheless cases, as Miss Ambrose points out, where it would be a misuse of language to say 'Still p is not probable.' 'But even here [she goes on] we are not as sure there is an entailment relation between the observational premise and the conclusion "p is probable" as we are in the case of deductions which are valid in virtue of their form' (p. 199).

     There are two reasons why this is not so: (i) The indefiniteness of the range in the number of positive instances needed and hence the lack of strict rules governing the use of the words 'probable', 'certain', 'hence', etc. (ii) The way this range varies from one subject of investigation to another. It may take more to make evidence sufficient or conclusive in one field than in another. As I said earlier this depends on what we already know and on the way what we know is organized. For instance, in physics far fewer observations than one would expect on general grounds is usually considered adequate to establish a law or hypothesis (Toulmin, *P.S.* p. 110). In fact, on purely general grounds the force of an inductive reason would altogether disappear. As Professor Black writes: 'What reason is there to suppose that if a number of observed As are all Bs, all As are therefore B? The answer, so far as I can see, is that *in general* there is no reason. It all depends upon the As, the Bs, and what we already know about them' (*Problems of Analysis*, p. 188).

We see that here we have no strict or general rules governing the use of such expressions as 'certainly' and 'probably'. There are no simple, all-embracing criteria for the conclusiveness of evidence. As Wisdom once put it:

One may with regard to the question 'When is deductive argument good?' make some very considerable attempt to give an answer in terms of definite rules, rules which amount to a definition of the good deductive argument and the bad deductive argument. But it is notorious that with regard to inductive, scientific reasoning the attempt is by no means such a success; the attempt to give an account in general terms of when scientific reasoning, inductive reasoning, is good or bad has been a failure not only compared with the attempt to give such an account of deductive reasoning but also as compared with what we may achieve when asked about reasoning concerning probabilities ('Proof and Explanation', *V.L.*).

Wisdom was, of course, thinking of *a priori* reasoning concerning probabilities, which has in fact been cast into the form of a calculus. It is easy to confuse probable conclusions derived deductively with probable predictions and think that by weakening the conclusion of an inductive argument we can convert it into a deductive one. Some of the so-called attempts at justifying induction have taken just this form. But this is not the point under consideration now. What concerns us at present is the fact that there are no strict and general rules, no calculus, of inductive reasoning. This leads to scepticism because of our inclination to identify thinking and reasoning with calculating. We do so because we think that unless one is reasoning in accordance with strict rules, definite criteria, one is not really reasoning at all, because we think that if the application of a concept is not governed by strict criteria then it must be arbitrary, because we think that where there are no strict rules we can draw any conclusion we like. Hence upon failing to discover strict and general rules here we think either that there are such rules though we are ignorant of them (Locke), or that there are none and that one inductive conclusion is as good as another (Hume and Russell).

Locke saw clearly that the way we actually reason about natural phenomena is not geometrical in form, that we have no way of calculating the course of events or the properties of substances as we have for calculating 'the properties of a square or a triangle' (*Essay*, p. 269). He said that there is no hope of our discovering 'general, instructive, unquestionable truths' about nature, and that 'certainty and demonstration are things we must not, in these matters pretend to' (p. 270). The reason for this, he thought, is our ignorance of 'the real essences' of things, 'our want of ideas that are suitable to such a way of proceeding' (p. 312). The real essence of a thing, according to Locke, is 'that foundation from which all its properties flow and to which they are all inseparably annexed' (p. 213). Where we have a concept of the real essence of a thing, as we do in geometry, then the application of that concept is governed by precise rules. 'If things were distinguished into species [Locke wrote] according to their real essences, it would be as impossible to find different properties in any two individual substances of the same species, as it is to find different properties in two circles, or two equilateral triangles' (p. 226). He believed that if only we knew the real essence of substances, if only our concepts 'were exactly copied from precise boundaries set by nature, whereby it distinguished all substances into certain species' (p. 232) then we would not have to rely on inductive methods of reasoning about nature as we do. That is although Locke saw that the way we reason about nature differs radically from geometrical reasoning, he thought of this as an accident. He did not understand properly why reasoning about actual things and phenomena cannot take the form of a calculus and why reasoning that does take that form ceases to be about the actual, reasoning about an 'ideal gas' for instance, though it still does and, indeed, must have a role to play in such reasonings.

To repeat, where we reason inductively we are not guided by strict rules, and what counts as good, sufficient and conclusive grounds for an inductive conclusion varies with the subject of investigation and how much has been achieved in it. There are cases where we will not be sure whether the evidence we have is conclusive or not, and here even experts may disagree—as they do not in mathematics. But then there are many cases where we feel no such hesitation and there is overwhelming agreement. Where there is no general agreement we have, to some extent at least, to be 'guided by our noses', by good judgment rather than by logical acumen. A good nose is something that can be trained, it is acquired by experience in the relevant field of inquiry. To use one's nose is not to proceed arbitrarily, and those who have a good nose will often assess the evidence similarly, agree in their evaluations of it. The less there are strict and general rules, the more we have to judge each case on its own merits, the more we have to rely on 'our nose', though this does not mean that cases do not bear on each other.

I have tried to point out that the continuity between well-founded and unfounded beliefs is a direct consequence of the lack of strict rules in inductive reasoning and to show how implicit assumptions about language and reasoning turn it into a ground for scepticism. A philosopher who, because of this continuity, complains that inductive reasoning is not really reasoning has drawn an unwarrantable conclusion and suffers from a limitation in his ideas of the nature of reasoning. Yet an argument, like Russell's, which leads to such a paradoxical result can be an eye-opener. Not only may it wake us up to the differences between inductive and deductive reasoning, but it may also lead to a better understanding of the connections between language and reasoning, between the rules in accordance with which we reason and the criteria that govern the use of our concepts,[1] and the relation between geometry and physics.

Wisdom has pointed out on more than one occasion that an argument like Russell's does not come wholly from confusion. It is true, he says, that 'it seems to be going too far to put Rutherford with the chicken', to deny that there is any real difference between inductive inferences which we regard as justified and those we regard as poorly supported. Certainly

---

[1] See chapter 9.

Russell's argument does not show that 'we have been deluded for centuries respecting these scientists'. But it is not true that it achieves nothing: 'What it accomplishes is to revive before the mind the difference between the "therefore" in inductive argument and in demonstrative argument'—between a necessary connection and a causal one[2] (*V.L.*).

In 'Philosophical Perplexity' he pointed out similarly that such a sceptical, paradoxical conclusion as 'inductive arguments do not really give any probability to their conclusions' is certainly misleading in that it makes us think that our confidence in scientific research has been misplaced, but that there are two important perceptions behind this paradox (*P.P.A.*, pp. 48–9). One of these is that there is a difference in logic between such seemingly similar pairs of statements:

(a) The results obtained by investigation into the causes of lung cancer have very much increased the probability that smoking is a cause of lung cancer.
(b) My having drawn 90 balls from a bag which we know to contain 100 balls, each either white or black, has very much increased the probability of the proposition that all the balls in that bag are white.

(a) It was 5–1 against the dog from trap 1; but I hear a rumour that each of the others has been provided with a cup of tea, and I think we may now take 4–1 against him.
(b) There were six runners, there are now only five, we still know nothing of any of them, so it is now 4–1 against the dog from trap 1.

The first of these statements is justified *a posteriori*, the second *a priori*. There are many similarities in these ways of talking. For instance, in both cases there are occasions where we express the probability in numerical ratios. Hence it is easy to fail to notice the difference between them, difficult to understand in what way they are different. The paradox draws attention to this difference and can be reformulated as saying that an inductive argument *cannot* ever make its conclusion probable *in the way* that a deductive argument employing a calculus of probability

---

[2] In chapter 10 below we shall consider what this difference amounts to and what prevents us from recognizing it.

does. New evidence that comes to light may, of course, increase the probability of an empirical hypothesis. But it cannot do so in the way that the draws in Wisdom's example increase the probability of all the balls in the bag being white.

The other perception behind the paradoxical words is 'the shocking continuity between the scientist's arguments by the method of difference and the savage's *post hoc ergo propter hoc*, between the method of agreement and the reflexes of rats' (*P.P.A.*, p. 49). I have already commented on this.

Russell highlights this continuity. He also brings into prominence a similarity between certain human beliefs and the chicken's expectations at the sight of the man who has fed it in the past. He speaks of both as 'a blind outcome of past experience'. We have seen the sense in which both are *unreasoned* and we have considered the position which such beliefs have in a whole way of thinking and reasoning in the case of human beings.

We have also seen that an unreasoned belief is not necessarily unreasonable. But while my belief that I shall burn myself if I touch a flame is perfectly reasonable, we cannot say this of the chicken's belief that the farmer who is approaching it will again give it food. It is not that the chicken's belief is unreasonable, but that the surroundings are missing for the category of reasonableness to be applicable to it. We have seen that with human beings this kind of belief has a special position in a complicated mode of life, a whole network of activities. These include collecting evidence, setting up and performing experiments, drawing inferences, evaluating them, distinguishing between well-grounded beliefs and unsound ones. These activities and distinctions, in turn, play a role in our lives; they make a difference to a great deal of what we say and do. It is their position in this network of activities that we are thinking of when we call such beliefs reasonable. What makes them reasonable, as we have seen, is not that they are based on good grounds, but that it would be a piece of unreason to doubt them (*Cert.* §325). To doubt them would mean doubting all judgment and reason. For they are like the hinges around which revolve all these activities in which judgment and reason operate. Where these activities are absent what would it mean to call them reasonable?

Yet they are conspicuously absent in an animal's life. This is an important difference which Russell ignores when he compares the scientist with the chicken. Animals, of course, learn from past experience, as human beings do. But there is nothing in their life that could be called criticism of their beliefs and expectations. There is no place there for standards of soundness and reliability where such beliefs and expectations are concerned. After having compared the belief that fire will burn me with the fear that it will do so, Wittgenstein points out that on being asked for the grounds of such a belief 'one *bethinks* oneself of them' (*Inv.* §475). But what would it be for the chicken to do so?

No doubt the chicken responds to features of its environment with the regularity with which a barometer responds to changes of atmospheric pressure. On the basis of what the barometer reads we can anticipate changes in the weather—rain and storms and sunshine. But it is we who do the anticipating, not the barometer. We cannot attribute expectations to the barometer as we can to the chicken. This has to do with what else we can attribute to the chicken—for instance, sensory capacities. What enables us to do so are the circumstances that surround the chicken's behaviour. But although the chicken can and the barometer cannot have expectations, certainly neither can make inferences. Their behaviour may exhibit much regularity, but to neither can we intelligibly attribute the kind of knowledge that a human being expresses when he says 'now I can go on' (*Inv.* §151).

So we are once more confronted with the need to distinguish between the kind of regularity we find in causal sequences and the kind of regularity we find in human affairs—the kind of regularity exemplified in the case of a person who observes a rule. Without the latter there can be no inferring or predicting. In many animals we find the rudiments of what we need if there is to be any reasoning at all. For instance they learn from experience. But while they stop at that point, human beings quickly develop beyond it. Bit by bit the life of the human infant becomes such that there is a place for reasoning in it. In assimilating the case of the scientist to that of the chicken Russell obscures this.

CHAPTER 6

EXPLANATION AND JUSTIFICATION BY EXPERIENCE HAS AN END

Hume said that as a philosopher he wants to learn 'the foundation' of inductive inference (*Inq*. Sec. IV, Pt. II). He asked rhetorically: 'Who will assert that he can give the *ultimate reason* why milk or bread is proper nourishment for a man, not for a lion or tiger?' (*ibid*. Sec. IV, Pt. I, *i.m.*). He wrote:

It is confessed that the utmost effort of human reason is to reduce the principles productive of natural phenomena to a greater simplicity, and to resolve the many particular effects into a few general causes, by means of reasoning from analogy, experience, and observation. But as to the causes of these general causes, we should in vain attempt their discovery, nor shall we ever be able to satisfy ourselves by any particular explication of them. These ultimate springs and principles are totally shut up from human curiosity and inquiry. Elasticity, gravity, cohesion of parts, communication of motion by impulse—these are probably the ultimate causes and principles which we shall ever discover in nature; and we may esteem ourselves sufficiently happy if, by accurate inquiry and reasoning, we can trace up the particular phenomena to, or near to, these general principles. The most perfect philosophy of the natural kind only staves off our ignorance a little longer (*ibid*. Sec. IV, Pt. I).

One ought to distinguish here between different kinds of question. To begin with there are ordinary causal questions and requests for explanation. For instance one may be inquiring into the cause of an accident. It may be found that the car had faulty brakes or that the driver was drunk. One could then ask why the brakes were faulty or the driver drunk—why he took so many drinks when he had to drive back home, or why having taken the drinks he insisted on driving the car himself. Usually, as we push our questions further back, our understanding of what happened increases. The cloak of anonymity that surrounds it gradually lifts and we begin to see how it differs from the many other accidents we have heard or read about. The fact that we do really increase our understanding in this way may make us think that our understanding will not be complete or adequate until there is no room for any further question of the sort we have been asking. When we recognize that we can continue pushing our questions further back endlessly we may come to think that we can never have complete understanding of any event.

Obviously people do sometimes think they have an adequate understanding of something when they do not, and sometimes they take an explanation given to them as 'the last word'. For them to come to see not only that every explanation can be questioned, but that one can always push a request for explanation further back may be very salutary. Here what is inevitable and absolutely necessary will strike them as something new and refreshing. If they express this by saying that there cannot be a final, ultimate explanation of anything, thinking of actions, events, regularities in phenomena, then they will be saying what is necessarily true—as necessarily true as saying that there is no last number in the series of natural numbers, or that there is no segment in a geometrical line that cannot be further divided. But if this makes them think that there cannot be a complete or adequate understanding of these things then they will have been misled.

What one needs to be clear about here is that while there is no logical limit to how far back we can push our request for explanation, nevertheless within the context of our inquiry there are limits of relevance. What counts as complete and adequate understanding is determined by the nature and purpose of our inquiry. Given the purpose for which we embark on it, and the kind of inquiry that is in question, our requests for further explanation will become pointless beyond a certain point, and the information they call for will cease to contribute to the understanding we are seeking. One can say that there are limits, not sharp ones, to what is relevant to the questions we investigate when we ask such questions as 'What was the cause of the accident?', 'Why did that wall fall in the storm when the others did not?' Such questions are specific and the inquiries they call for have a terminus—though where that terminus lies is relative to our purposes, and to the knowledge and assumptions we bring into the inquiry.

People are apt to feel the same difficulty in connection with explanations of the meaning of a word. If such an explanation is given in words then one could ask for a similar explanation of the meanings of the words used in the explanation. If it consists in pointing or giving examples then again one can ask for an explanation of how the pointing is to be taken, what the examples are meant to illustrate. For any definition, rule, sign or example can be taken in more than one way and so can be misunderstood. There is no way of making it impossible for a man to whom we are explaining the meaning of a word to use the word in a way that is at variance with our intentions while thinking that he is using it in conformity with them. No matter how much we do for him there would always be the possibility that he may need some further explanation. No matter how many explanations we give him the possibility that he may need more can never be ruled out. The *possibility* cannot, but in most cases the need can be: 'That is not to say that we are in doubt because it is possible for us to imagine a doubt' (*Inv.* §84).

There is need for an explanation where there is some doubt or misunderstanding. But where there is no doubt or misunderstanding left any further explanation would be idle and even senseless. As Wittgenstein puts it: 'An explanation may indeed rest on another one that has been given, but none stands in need of another—unless *we* require it to prevent a misunderstanding. One might say: an explanation serves to remove or avert a misunderstanding—one, that is, that would occur but for the explanation; not everyone that I can imagine' (§87). An explanation that does not avert or remove a misunderstanding, or secure the understanding sought, may in itself be incomplete or inadequate. So there is still something further that needs to be explained. But where it does remove the misunderstanding for which it was called, or secure the understanding sought, there will be no need for any further explanation: 'The sign-post is in order—if, under normal circumstances, it fulfils its purpose' (*ibid.*).

These points hold both for explanations of particular events and for the justification of inductive claims. In the passage I have quoted Hume was more concerned with the explanation of the principles and laws used in explaining particular anomalies or accidents and specific regularities. These constitute part of the knowledge and assumptions which we bring into our practical inquiries. Obviously it makes sense to ask for these to be made intelligible. A doctor, for instance, who is explaining how a particular drug relieves pain may use and take for granted various principles of chemistry—e.g. that certain elements and chemical compounds react in certain ways in certain circumstances. This does not mean that one is barred from asking for an explanation of these principles themselves. One will then find that other principles, more general still, are being referred to and used. 'To us [wrote Newton] it is enough that gravity does really exist, and acts according to the laws which we have explained, and abundantly serves to account for all motions of celestial bodies, and of our sea.' Hume must have been thinking of Newton when he wrote: 'Elasticity, gravity, cohesion of parts, communication of motion by impulse—these are probably the ultimate causes and principles which we shall ever discover in nature; and we may esteem ourselves sufficiently happy if we can trace up the particular phenomena to, or near to, these general principles.'

However, what are the most general laws and principles in one period of scientific inquiry may at a later period be capable of being presented as a limiting case of more general principles in what are regarded as special circumstances. This, for instance, is the case now with classical mechanics. As Einstein says of his theory of relativity: 'This more general theory does not contradict the classical transformation and classical mechanics. On the contrary, we regain the old concepts as a limiting case when the velocities are small' (*The Evolution of Physics*, p. 202). Thus the ultimacy of the general laws and principles of explanation in any science is relative to what has been achieved in it and to the form of that achievement. It would be very misleading, however, to put this point by saying that we can never know the ultimate springs and principles of natural phenomena—as if these were there from the start, existing independently of the developments in that science, only waiting to be discovered.

Yet I believe that it was just this point that Hume was drawing attention to when he said that 'nature has kept us at a great distance from all her secrets and has afforded us only the knowledge of a few superficial qualities of objects, while she conceals from us those powers and principles on which the influence of these objects entirely depends' (*Inq.* Sec. IV, Pt. II).

If Hume had been alive now and had seen the developments that have taken place since his time in chemistry, for instance, he would have had to admit that our knowledge of the properties of chemical substances is now less superficial than it was when he wrote his *Inquiry*. But he would have every right to hold on to the logical point he was making and so deny the ultimacy of what we know. Chemists not only know a great deal more about the reactions of chemical substances than they did in Hume's time, they have also developed theories and principles of classification which enable them to explain these reactions in terms of the internal constitution of the substances entering into these reactions. But there are still, and inevitably, assumptions from which their explanations begin and which cannot themselves be explained in these theories.

What are these general principles and assumptions that enter their explanations and cannot themselves be explained? What role do they play in these explanations? We have seen that scientific theories may be compared with systems of co-ordinates and that they help us to relate the phenomena we study to many others, not at once obviously related, thus transforming our vision and apprehension of them. As Ernst Mach puts it: The system of resemblances that are thus brought to our attention transforms the phenomena being studied 'into an old acquaintance . . . and enriches it with features which we are first induced to seek from such suggestions' ('On the Principle of Comparison in Physics', *Popular Scientific Lectures*). Writing on the theoretical account the chemist gives of what took place in the laboratory, Wisdom said: 'Fantastic as is his story, it serves its purpose, for like the engineer's, it connects the incidents before us with thousands of others with which we should never have connected it but for his myth of the molecules' (*P.P.A.*, p. 186).

In the engineer's account one movement is related to another in terms of a material connection of wheels and levers between

the two moving parts. But Hume asked how the material connection can account for the relation between the two movements.
He urged, rightly, that to establish that there is a material
connection between the two parts of the machine and to establish
that there is a causal connection between their movements are
not the same thing, and that there is a step taken by the mind
when from having established the former we claim the existence
of the latter, which can be justified, if at all, only in the light of
past experience, in the light of what we further know. He pointed
out, rightly, that the verification of the claim that there is a
material connection between these two parts of the machine and
the verification of the claim that there is a causal connection
between their movements differ profoundly. The material connection may not of course be at once visible as the machine
may be covered. Or it may be so intricate that though all the
relevant parts of the machine are open to view it may still be
difficult to take the links in at a glance and may call for some
careful watching. All the same the existence of the connection
does not depend on anything that cannot be noticed here
and now. Whereas, as Hume pointed out, the verification of
the existence of a causal connection would inevitably take us
outside the time in which it may be said to hold as the machine
runs before our eyes. As Wisdom puts it: 'Claims that on a
particular occasion there was a causal connection between one
thing and another are claims that have a certain feature which
we are reluctant to recognize, namely, that the verification of the
statement about a given time may involve logically what happens
outside that period of time' (*V.L.*). In other words, when from
the arrangement of the cogwheels we infer that if we move this
part of the machine then that part will move, the justification of
what we claim would necessarily take us to other movements in
other places and at other times. An inductive inference, a causal
inference, such as 'If A moves then B will move', cannot be
justified by considerations that confine themselves to those
movements alone.

The engineer tells us that the two moving parts, whose
movements seem disparate, are materially connected. The
material connection makes the sequence intelligible because by
connecting the two moving parts it connects them with other

similarly connected objects we have seen moving together on innumerable occasions. Hume pointed out that this is what 'making intelligible', 'explaining' comes to in these cases, though he was himself disinclined to use these expressions here —as he was also disinclined to speak of a 'connection' between events which we say are causally connected. This is, of course, part and parcel of the scepticism which we are studying.[1] Wisdom's point about the chemist's 'story of molecules and atoms hurrying, clinging, and separating' (*ibid.* p. 186) is that it makes the incidents we have observed in the laboratory intelligible in a similar way, for it too 'connects the incident before us with thousands of others with which we should never have connected it'. But, in another respect, it is 'quite different'.

The engineer's account makes the sequence of movements intelligible by referring to something that is not at the time visible. We need his account because the material connection which he speaks of is concealed from sight or so intricate that we fail to take it in. We need the chemist's account for a different reason. Perhaps we don't know what the powders and liquids he mixes together look like under a microscope. But even if we know this, and other things of this sort, we may still find unintelligible what happens when they are mixed together. For the connections between what we observe in the laboratory and the thousands of incidents chemists study are much more complicated than the connections between the movements of objects tied together by a piece of wire, those of objects connected by cogwheels, those of objects connected by a system of levers and pulleys. They are also more remote from the layman's experience who has not studied them. Nevertheless the connections between these incidents and those between moving objects materially connected are similar in one important respect: it is by virtue

[1] He denied that distinct events can be *connected*, that a proposition stating the occurrence of the one can be *inferred* from one stating the occurrence of the other, that knowing the truth of the former can give one *reason* for believing the truth of the former, that the occurrence of one such event can *account for* or *make intelligible* the occurrence of another. As we have seen, part of the reason why Hume was thus sceptical was that he was tempted to confine these expressions to the sense they have when we speak of 'necessary connections', 'formal inference', 'deductive reasons' and 'logical explanation' respectively.

of these that we have inductive reasons in each field for what we expect, it is by virtue of these that we are able to understand why they occur.

I asked what role the general principles used by the scientist play in the explanations he gives of natural phenomena. We have seen that their role is to bring other phenomena to bear on the phenomenon of which an explanation is sought. Seeing the incidents we are studying in the light of other incidents, familiar to us, enables us to see a pattern in them. It is in this way that the general principles in question make these incidents intelligible and open up new ways of studying them. We may, of course, ask for an explanation of the principles themselves. This may be because we find what is a feature of the many incidents thus brought to bear on each other itself unintelligible. In that case what is called for is a wider co-ordination of phenomena, perhaps along new lines. This in turn may be achieved by new assumptions and a more general theory. But whether or not the explanations in which these principles are used achieve their purpose is independent of whether or not those principles or theories can themselves be explained in terms of a still wider co-ordination of the facts and phenomena in question. Hume was right in so far as he maintained that all explanations of natural phenomena have an end—though as we have seen this end is not fixed once and for all. But he was wrong in thinking that the fact that our explanations come to an end makes them worthless. The idea that 'an explanation as it were hangs in the air unless supported by another one' comes from misunderstanding what is involved in giving an explanation.

Scepticism about the possibility of understanding the course of natural events, and about the possibility of understanding the step taken by the mind in inductive inference; scepticism about whether the former can be explained, the latter justified: I have suggested that these are closely connected, that they arise from common sources. One of these is the desire to find an explanation that will leave nothing unexplained, an explanation that will remove all possible misunderstandings. But the misunderstandings possible here are endless and do not constitute a system. It would therefore be impossible to anticipate them all, to meet them all at once. Besides, since all scientific explanations must make use of something that is understood, with every such explanation there is bound to be something that is not explained.

When one asks for an explanation, wishes something to be made intelligible, one's questions and difficulties must be fairly specific since they are difficulties in the light of what one has accepted and does not question. These too can be called in question but only in the light of something else that is not questioned. Hence there is nothing defective in an explanation that takes certain things for granted. Given the particular request for an explanation the chain of explanations comes to an end.

In the same way justification by experience too comes to an end. 'If it did not it would not be justification' (*Inv.* §485). I might, for example, say that I am justified in expecting an explosion any minute now and give you my reasons: rocks are being quarried and dynamited at regular intervals and I have just seen the men finish placing the charges. You may think that I have made a mistake or that my information is incomplete. You may question my reasons. This means that we have a common understanding of what counts as grounds for this kind of belief and what makes them good grounds. If we did not we could not even argue over this issue. If you ask me what justification I have for thinking that dynamite when detonated explodes, what can I tell you but that this is a truth I have learnt, a truth which anyone who knows anything about dynamite accepts. If you are still not satisfied and ask me why the fact that properly set charges of dynamite have exploded in the past should justify my expectation on this occasion I could only reply that this is what we *call* justification here (*Inv.* §486).

Wisdom might imagine someone asking: 'How do you know that this is an instance of what we call "justification"? What reasons have you for thinking that it is?' He would say that even if normally people do not need to be given reasons here this does not mean that reasons cannot be given. He says: 'The fact that a person doesn't need to reflect by no means proves that his statement [*viz.* "This is an instance of K—of justification"] doesn't call for reflection' (*V.L.*). He argues that reasons could always be given for the application of a general concept in a particular case and that this giving of reasons in the end takes the form of citing parallel cases—those cases, perhaps, in

G

connection with which we learnt the concept. He would further say that there is no end to this process of reasoning and justification: this process of citing parallel cases.

There is no conflict between Wisdom's claim that this process of justification is endless and Wittgenstein's remark that justification has an end. There is no conflict between Wisdom's claim that for every application of a general concept reasons can be given and Wittgenstein's remark that one does not have reasons e.g. for saying that this colour before one is red: 'How do I know that this colour is red?—It would be an answer to say: "I have learnt English" ' (*Inv.* §381). We have already seen that when we explain the meaning of a word to someone, no matter how many explanations we give him, the *possibility* that he may need more can never be ruled out, though normally the *need* for further explanation is met. If this were otherwise we would never learn to speak. We can imagine a person with whom this is not so, but he would be one whom it would be hopeless to teach. The possibility of his learning from his parents and teachers depends on their reaching instances where he needs no further explanation—instances to which as a matter of course he reacts as we do, that is without further guidance or explanation (*Inv.* §185).

If a definition, example or explanation can always be misunderstood how can it show one what one is to understand? Wittgenstein's answer is that interpretations by themselves do not determine meaning, that there is a way of grasping a definition, rule or explanation which is not an interpretation and which is exhibited in what we call 'observing the definition', 'obeying the rule' and 'going against it' *in actual cases* (*Inv.* §§198, 201). He writes a little later:

How can he *know* how he is to continue a pattern by himself [or use a word in its accepted sense]—whatever instruction you give him?—Well, how do I know?—If that means 'Have I reasons?' the answer is: my reasons will soon give out. And then I shall act, without reasons (*Inv.* §211).

He had said earlier: 'No course of action could be determined by a rule, because every course of action can be made out to accord with the rule' (§201). So he imagines someone asking: 'How am I then able to obey a rule? What is my reason, my justification, when I am given a rule, for going one way rather than any other way?' What is my reason, my justification, when I am given an explanation of the meaning of a word, for using it in one way rather than in any other way? Wittgenstein's answer is:

If I have exhausted the justifications I have reached bedrock, and my spade is turned. Then I am inclined to say: 'This is simply what I do' (*Inv.* §217).

This is just as true of the justifications of our beliefs and expectations. If there is always a further explanation needed to secure understanding, a further justification to secure conviction, then there is no explanation or justification at all. There must be circumstances in which we accept something as true or understand the meaning of an illustration or definition, and act as a matter of course without needing justifications or explanations. But this doesn't make what we do arbitrary. For to use a word without justification is not to use it without right (*Inv.* §289), to act without justification is not to proceed anyhow (*Rem.* I, §4).

CHAPTER 7

'CAN INDUCTION BE JUSTIFIED?'

Hume asked for 'the nature of that evidence' which assures us of any inductive conclusion and answered that all inference to such conclusions 'arises entirely from experience'. He then asked for 'the foundation of all conclusions from experience' and answered that all such conclusions are founded on 'the supposition that the future will be conformable to the past'. We saw how empty this is *as a supposition* (chapter 4) and also why Hume thought that past experience alone is not enough to justify an inductive conclusion (chapter 5). We saw further that there must be an end to the buttressing of an inductive conclusion if there is to be any inductive reasoning and justification (chapter 6). I want to suggest now that the foundation of inductive conclusions is experience and that there is no further foundation to be sought.

To ask whether someone has reasons, or good reasons, for supposing that the merchandise he has been offered for sale is defective, or for believing that his car will not be able to take the proposed journey, is to ask a perfectly sensible question. But to ask this after it has been admitted that he has the kind of reasons which *count* as good reasons is no longer to ask a sensible question. As Wittgenstein puts it: 'If anyone said that information about the past could not convince him that something would happen in the future, I should not understand him' (*Inv.* §481). Thus one could say that the foundation of all conclusions from experience is experience. To ask what would justify a conclusion that is justified by experience is to ask an unintelligible question.

When Hume says that what we call 'good grounds' are not enough to justify an inductive conclusion, Wittgenstein asks him what more he wants. 'What do you expect to be told, then? If you say these are not grounds, then you must surely be able to state what must be the case for us to have the right to say that there are grounds for our assumption' (§481). Hume's answer is that *if* it is the case that like causes are always followed by like effects, that nature is uniform, that the future is conformable to the past, then our experience from the past can justify an inductive conclusion and so give us the right to believe it. Since, however, the words in which Hume answers Wittgenstein's question do not rule out any state of affairs they satisfy Wittgenstein's demand only in semblance. We have seen that he would not have been able to tell Wittgenstein what more he wants to be told and convinced of except in words that turn out to be empty.

Hume knew, of course, that we talk of some inductive conclusions as justified and some others not. He knew how we draw the distinction, in other words what it is we look for before we consider an inductive conclusion to be justified, and he recognized that the distinction in question is not an idle one, that it has a role in our life. Yet, for reasons we have examined, it seemed to him that we are not justified in drawing this distinction. He thought that the differences on which it rests do not justify us in using the language of justification, that our standards of inductive reasoning and justification are themselves in need of justification. I tried to point out that it was not for nothing that he thought so. But I must now insist that in what he was seeking he was misguided, since it makes no sense to ask for a justification of induction as a whole, nor of the standards we appeal to when we call an inductive inference 'justified' in contrast with others.

'No doubt we do in fact speak of certainty in connection with inductive conclusions. But is this not a loose way of speaking? I want to know whether we have any justification for speaking in this way.' 'No doubt we call this sort of statement about the past a ground for such predictions. But I want it explained to me why we do? Is what we have here anything more than a human convention?' I want to suggest that these questions come from confusion. That we draw inductive conclusions in the ways we do, that we distinguish between those that are well founded and those that are not, that we speak of certainty in connection with those that satisfy certain conditions, that we act on such conclusions, regulate our behaviour in the light of these distinctions—these are facts about the way we live and act. The terms 'certain' and 'justified', for instance, serve us to compare and contrast beliefs and conclusions of a certain sort with others of the same sort with respect to the evidence on which they are based, the surrounding information we already have relevant to the conclusion, etc. But are we justified in comparing and contrasting them in these ways? The fact is we do. If we want to know what these comparisons achieve for us we have to consider the activities in the course of which they are made and the difference they make to the way these are carried—for instance, the evaluation of data in scientific research. We have to consider the actual use of the words to which these comparisons are tied and the actions that surround their application:

What is *called* a justification here?—How is the word 'justification' used? Describe language-games. From these you will also be able to see the importance of being justified (*Inv.* §486).

In this way we shall see 'the point' of our concept of being justified here—what it does for us, what purpose it serves. But neither this common use of the concept, nor what gives it the point that it has, can be either justified or unjustified.

You may ask someone why he thinks that what he said is true, what reasons he has for believing it to be the case. You may ask: 'Why do you think this?', 'Why do you say that?' You may also question the propositions which state his reasons. Or you may question the connection between these and what he believes, question their status as reasons. But it makes no sense to ask of the criteria used in answering these questions whether they themselves are true or justified. You may ask me to exhibit the significance or importance of these criteria and of the concepts whose use they govern. Or you may ask what underlies the existence of these criteria, in which case one will come down to various institutions, customs and practices that hang together in various ways.

But it doesn't make sense to ask for a justification or foundation of these, to ask if their various features correspond to any reality. For our notions of reality and truth are dependent on these features and cannot be divorced from them. With regard to them we can say no more than 'This is the way it is with us.' We can do no more than note these features of our own ways of acting and living:

The question is not one of explaining a language-game by means of our experiences, but of noting a language-game (*Inv.* §655).
Our mistake is to look for an explanation where we ought to look at what happens as a 'proto-phenomenon'. That is where we ought to have said: *this language-game is played* (§656).
The danger here, I believe, is one of giving a justification of our procedure where there is no such thing as a justification and we ought simply to have said: *that's how we do it* (*Rem.* II, §74).

We cannot ask for a justification of the standards and criteria that govern our judgments and our behaviour. For the standards and criteria are themselves what we appeal to when we wonder whether this particular judgment or that piece of behaviour is justified. To ask for a justification is to ask how one's reasons, evidence or behaviour in this or these cases compare with accepted standards of good reasons, evidence or behaviour. The need for justification arises when there is some suggestion of a discrepancy with the appropriate standards in question. With the different things to be justified—e.g. different kinds of assertion, belief, conclusion, action, principle or policy—the standards to which we appeal will vary and so too the kind of justification we seek. We can ask for a justification only where it makes sense to speak of reasons or evidence, and so where there are ways of discriminating between good and bad reasons, adequate and inadequate evidence, where there are standards of good and bad behaviour, right and wrong procedures. Where there are no such standards it does not make sense to ask for a justification. If it were not possible to distinguish between a right and a wrong way of doing something no question of justification could arise. But this does not mean that everything here is unjustified. For to speak of a statement or procedure as unjustified is to claim that a standard has been violated. The existence of standards means that within the practice individual procedures are compared with one another in certain ways.

There are of course many different practices and many different kinds of standard that we appeal to—for instance, solving simultaneous equations, diagnosing diseases, making weather forecasts, developing scientific theories. Different kinds of inquiry have different standards of right and wrong, correct and incorrect, certain and probable, true and false. We have already seen that the existence of a practice means the possibility of distinguishing between right and wrong, proper and improper ways of doing certain things. The kind of distinction in question is the kind of practice that goes on. What counts as right and wrong, proper and improper, the standards of what is correct and what is not, are internal to the practice in question and give it its distinctive character and identity.

It is only where there are such standards, where there is a practice, a mode of inquiry, that we can intelligibly ask for a justification, only within the practice that a question of justification can arise. When it does arise, to try to answer it is to proceed with that inquiry, to appeal to the standards that are internal to it. But what sense could there be in asking whether those standards themselves are justified, reliable or trustworthy? I am not saying that those standards are fixed once and for all and never change. They do, and with them the very questions which such an inquiry pursues, the concepts in terms of which answers, knowledge and understanding are sought by those who pursue the inquiry. Thus modes of justification change, new modes of justification come into existence.

Certainly it makes perfectly good sense to ask whether this or these inductive inferences are justified, and it may well be that the answer is 'No'. But if it is, this is an answer that is reached by applying *inductive* standards. The negative answer means that there is no inductive justification for this or these conclusions, that by inductive standards the reasons for this or these conclusions are inadequate. What is more, if the answer to our question is 'No', it could have been 'Yes'. Otherwise what would the negative answer mean? Yet, is this not what one is denying when one says that induction cannot be justified, that no inductive inference can be justified?

That is why the sceptical view that induction cannot be justified is incoherent. Yet in so far as it claims that there cannot be a justification of a whole mode of reasoning and of the standards and criteria that are internal to it, what it claims is correct. There is nothing sceptical about such a claim. Secondly, a philosopher who says that induction cannot be justified may be trying to point out, though perhaps in a confused and confusing way, that inductive inferences cannot be justified in the way that deductive inferences are justified. If they were so justified they would be deductive inferences. This truth has in fact been partly responsible for the way many philosophers clung so tenaciously to the assertion that induction cannot be justified. In so far as they were stressing that induction cannot be reduced to deduction and that all attempts at doing so are doomed to failure they were saying something that is necessarily true and unexceptionable. But once more there is nothing sceptical about this claim.

It becomes sceptical when it is coupled with the assumption that only deductive reasoning is really reasoning. It is this that is largely responsible for the craving of the sceptic about induction to find here conditions that are satisfied in the case of deductive reasoning (see chapter 5 above). Hume pointed out *rightly* and very forcefully that this craving can never be satisfied. But in doing so he suggested *wrongly* that scientific understanding and explanations (see also Mach) and inductive knowledge (see also Locke), reasons and certainty (see also Russell) are only the semblance of understanding, explanations, knowledge, reasons and certainty. Because he was unable to remove this craving behind the views he was opposing he remained the greatest opponent of those after him who shared that craving but found his bold scepticism repugnant.

The assumption that only deductive reasoning is really reasoning is thus often implicitly made by both those who maintain that induction cannot be justified and those who oppose this claim. It is this assumption that makes the claim that induction cannot be justified exciting to those who put it forward and disturbing to those who oppose it. It makes adhering to the claim tantamount to accepting that there is something wrong and untrustworthy about inductive and scientific methods of reasoning in the way that there may be something wrong and untrustworthy with certain methods of treating cancer, for instance, even though they are widely accepted. And it is right that one should wish to oppose this. This has, in fact, been the main argument of the present chapter. On the other hand, simply to deny the claim is to accept what the sceptic rightly rejects, namely that inductive reasoning can be reduced to deductive reasoning, that the differences between them are more apparent than real. One cannot oppose it, therefore, without bringing to daylight the assumptions that drive the sceptic to seek a justification of induction. If on examining them for their adequacy one can give them up one will be able to accept what the sceptic forcefully brings to our attention, without having to swallow with it the suggestions that one wished to resist from the start.

SUMMARY

We have examined Hume's and Russell's search for the foundations of inductive reasoning and their attempt to base it on a very general principle which can be justified by an appeal to reasons which cannot themselves be questioned.

We have seen how naturally one who embarks on such a search will tend to raise fears in our hearts and how inadequate Hume's attempts to pacify those fears were. The fears in question come from confusion, for the whole attempt to find foundations for a mode of reasoning is misguided.

This search, however, is one that is very persistent in philosophy. It stems in the end from misunderstandings about what it is to give reasons for what one claims or concludes in different fields of human inquiry. We find it difficult to appreciate that in every field of discourse and reasoning there are and must be things which we are prepared to say and accept without justification. One source of confusion here is the idea that unless the use of a word on a particular occasion has a justification it is arbitrary. In his discussion of what it is to follow a rule Wittgenstein shows what is wrong with this idea.

To ask whether someone has reasons or good reasons to suppose that something is the case or will be so when one has already admitted that he has the kind of reasons which we consider good reasons for beliefs or conclusions of this sort is to ask an unintelligible question. Yet this is what Hume did when he asked: 'What is the foundation of all conclusions from experience?' Hence Wittgenstein's remark: 'If anyone said that information about the past could not convince him that something would happen in the future, I should not understand him' (*Inv.* §481).

Misled into asking this question Hume answered that experience or information about the past would be grounds only on the supposition that the future will be like the past. We have seen how empty this is as a supposition and so how little Hume is able to meet Wittgenstein's challenge 'to state what must be the case for us to have the right to say that there are grounds for our assumption' (§481): 'If *these* are not grounds, then what are grounds?' Positive instances, experience, information about the past: these are what we call grounds here (§480). Compare with: What makes you say that the colour you see is red? I have been taught to call it red. How do you know that in working out the series '+ 2' you must write '2004, 2006' and not '2004, 2008'? I know how to add; I was taught it at school.

We have seen that Hume's assumption is no assumption about nature, as he thought, but more akin to a principle of reasoning. It belongs to the form or grammar of the reasonings he was concerned with.

We have seen too that one of the sources behind the misguided search for foundations is the idea that all forms of reasoning must have a common essence and that this is best exemplified in deductive reasoning. The centre of attraction here are the strict rules and definite criteria that govern deductive inferences, and the way these can be abstracted from the surroundings and subject-matter of these inferences. They thus seem to stand out as something distinct from our judgments and hence as something objective; their strictness seems to leave no room for the fallibility of human judgment. Thus where we cannot find them we think that something is missing which leaves our inferences and judgments defective, arbitrary, and without justification. We have seen that it is a mistake to think so. It is a mistake, however, which is very deeply rooted in our thinking. To eradicate it we shall have to look more closely at what is involved in deductive reasoning and what the existence of strict rules which may be appealed to in justifying a formal inference amounts to. This will be the topic of our discussion in Part II of this book.

Part II

DEDUCTIVE REASONING

Part 5

CHAPTER 8

WITTGENSTEIN'S THEORY OF FORMAL INFERENCE IN THE *TRACTATUS*

The nature of logic, its relation to our talk and thought has always been central to Wittgenstein's interest. In the *Tractatus* it is a mark of a logical proposition that it is a tautology—for instance 'TTTT (p,q)'. In thus representing logical propositions as tautologies Wittgenstein showed both that they do not bring any new content to an argument and also that they are related to propositions that do. For both the 'significance' of empirical propositions and the 'senselessness' of logical propositions are symbolized in the same T–F notation.[1] This is meant to exhibit the application of logic to ordinary language. As he put it later: ' "A tautology (e.g. 'p v p̄') says nothing" is a proposition referring to the language-game in which the proposition p has application' (*Remarks* III, §14).

If logical propositions 'do not say anything' they still have 'a connection with the world' through the language of which they are a part: 'they are part of the symbolism, just as "o" is part of the symbolism of arithmetic' (4.4611). If they are 'senseless' this is not to say that they show nothing about the world. On the contrary Wittgenstein speaks of logic as mirroring the world (5.511); he thinks of logic as 'a mirror-image of the world' (6.13). In other words, logic sets limits to the way we conceive things; logical propositions show what is intelligible, conceivable or thinkable. This is closely connected with what he would have said later, namely that a grammatical proposition exhibits a feature of our use of language, one that goes through a large area of our thought; it exhibits a form or style of thinking, one that may be at the centre of our conception of a wide range of things.

When Wittgenstein said that logical propositions are 'devoid

[1] With acknowledgment to R. Rhees.

of sense' he meant to contrast them with empirical propositions. In reserving the term 'significant' for the latter propositions only he did not mean to suggest that logical propositions are useless or trivial. He said of mathematical propositions which are equally 'devoid of sense', though they are not tautologies, that we make use of them in our calculations (6.211). He said further that an investigation of their role 'in inferences from propositions that do not belong to mathematics to others that likewise do not belong to mathematics' would lead to 'valuable insights' (*ibid.*). But such an investigation was to await changes in his conception of language. If at the time he wrote the *Tractatus* he had been able to look at language as an instrument he would have said that mathematical equations are as much tools of the language we speak as are the non-mathematical, empirical propositions whose connections they exhibit and help us to grasp. This is just as true of logical propositions such as the *modus ponens*. If, as we shall see, Wittgenstein regarded them as redundant (5.132, 6.122) he never suggested that they are of no use. He never meant to deny that they may be of great help to us in our reasonings. Their role may be very different from the roles of empirical propositions, but they are both tools of our language.

In *this* sense Wittgenstein did not mean to deny the significance of mathematical and logical propositions. When he said that they are not significant propositions he meant that they are not significant in the way that empirical propositions are. He was opposing a chain of philosophical confusions into which it is easy to be dragged when reflecting on the nature of logic—on what logical propositions say or mean, what logical constants symbolize, what sanctions or justifies the logical inferences we make, what logical or necessary truths are based on, how we know or recognize them, in what way they differ from and how they are related to each other. A great deal hangs on the contrast between logical (and mathematical) propositions and empirical ones for the kind of view of logic Wittgenstein was developing in the *Tractatus*. The significance of the latter is independent of their truth; to recognize their sense, to understand them is not yet to know that they are true (4.024). To find out whether or not they are true one has to carry out an investigation into something that exists independently of them. Whereas we recognize the truth of logical propositions 'from the symbol alone' (6.113). 'This fact [Wittgenstein said] contains in itself the whole philosophy of logic' (*ibid.*).

If the truth of a logical proposition were thought to depend on something other than the symbol this would have many inevitable consequences for one's whole view of logic—consequences, for instance, for one's view of the part played by logical principles in the formal inferences we make, for one's view of the kind of generality to be found in logic, for one's view of what gives meaning to our logical constants and how they are related to each other, for one's view of the source of the necessity of logical principles and formal inferences, for one's view ultimately of the way one learns to reason, think and speak at all. When Wittgenstein says that we recognize the truth of logical propositions 'from the symbol alone' he is denying that logic is 'a kind of ultra-physics' (*Remarks* I, §8). Any view, he said in the *Tractatus*, which represents logical propositions as having content, which attributes to them 'the characteristics of a proposition of natural science' must have construed them wrongly. We have already noted that Russell thought of logic in this way: 'Logic is concerned with the real world just as truly as geology, though with its more abstract and general features' (*Intro. to Math. Phil.* p. 169).

In what way does the truth of logical propositions and the validity of formal inferences depend on the symbol alone? Wittgenstein begins to answer this question in the theory of formal inference he develops in the *Tractatus*. He held, as we shall see, that logical propositions symbolize the general pattern of transitions in formally valid arguments (see chapter 9). The validity of each formal inference depends wholly on the sense of the propositions involved or on their logical structures, in other words on how they stand to the elementary propositions of which they are truth-functions. Thus the validity of the inference lies wholly in what can be gathered from the expression of the propositions concerned. It is sufficient for one to see clearly what it means to assert the premises and conclusion of a formal argument to know that one would be justified in inferring the latter from the former. If this is not at

H

once obvious one would have to analyse these propositions, ask oneself what their truth-grounds are and try to see how these stand to each other. This is to 'calculate the logical properties of the symbol' (6.126), to reflect on what it means to assert the propositions concerned.[2] It would not be sufficient to do so if the relation between the premises and the conclusion were not a connection of meanings, if there had to be a 'material connection' to sanction or justify the inference (5.136). It would not have been sufficient if the logical principles we may use in justifying such an inference were not 'devoid of sense' and 'superfluous' (5.132).

But in what way, according to the *Tractatus*, does the validity of a formal inference depend solely on the truth-functional structures of its premises and conclusion? The idea is a very simple one. The truth-value of all significant propositions is a function of the truth-values of one or more propositions belonging to a class of *logically independent* elementary propositions.[3] If we could know which of these propositions are true and which false we would know everything that is the case (4.26). True and false, they provide us with the basis for understanding everything that can be said (4.411, 4.52). Thus take elementary propositions p, q and r and three propositions l, m and n whose truth-values wholly depend on those of p, q and r (see p. 103).

Since in the *Tractatus* the sense of any proposition is given in the conditions under which it is true and those under which it is false, the senses of l, m and n are completely determined by the way their truth and falsity are related to the truth-possibilities of p, q and r—that is the eight possible combinations of their

---

[2] For in the *Tractatus* questions as to the context in which a proposition is used, the role it plays there, do not come into a consideration of what it says.

[3] It is essential to Wittgenstein's account here that these elementary propositions should be logically independent of each other. For his account of what it means for one proposition to follow logically from another or others is, as will be seen, in terms of the way their truth-grounds overlap. Since these are given in terms of the truth and falsity of elementary propositions, if these latter propositions could stand in logical relations to each other, these relations would remain unaccounted. That is there would be logical relations and forms of inference to which the *Tractatus* account does not apply.

	p	q	r		l	m	n
1.	T	T	T		T	F	F
2.	F	T	T		T	T	T
3.	T	F	T		F	F	F
4.	F	F	T		F	T	F
5.	T	T	F		F	T	T
6.	F	T	F		T	T	T
7.	T	F	F		T	F	F
8.	F	F	F		F	F	F

truth and falsity (first three columns of the table above). Thus l is a proposition that is True when the truth and falsity of p, q and r are combined as in lines 1, 2, 6 or 7 of the table (when, for instance, $\frac{p}{T}\frac{q}{T}\frac{r}{T}$—line 1) and False when the truth and falsity of p, q and r are combined as in lines 3, 4, 5 or 8 (when, for instance, $\frac{p}{T}\frac{q}{F}\frac{r}{T}$—line 3). Since 'a proposition *is* the expression of its truth-conditions' (4.431), l can be symbolized as 'TTFFFTTF (p,q,r)'—provided that we have agreed on a convention for ordering the truth-possibilities of two, three, four or more propositions.[4] The symbol for l, namely 'TTFFFTTF (p,q,r)', is thus an expression of the agreement and disagreement of the truth-values of l with the truth-possibilities of p, q and r (4.4). It represents the truth-conditions of l (4.41).

Hence if we know the truth-values of p, q and r we can *calculate* the truth-value of l. For instance, if $\frac{p}{F}\frac{q}{T}\frac{r}{T}$ (line 2 of the table) l is T (the corresponding letter in the row of Ts and Fs in 'TTFFFTTF (p,q,r)'. This is not an ordinary inference,

[4] According to the convention Wittgenstein adopts the Ts and Fs alternate singly in the first column, two by two in the second, four by four in the third, and so on, for each of the elementary propositions in parenthesis (p,q,r), in that order.

since p, q and r are not propositions we actually use as premises in arguments. But it shows what is meant by saying that l is a particular truth-function of p, q and r, and conversely that p, q and r are its truth-arguments. This terminology comes from mathematics, though the analogy is a limited one. Thus l $\equiv$ TTFFFTTF (p,q,r), i.e. l is a particular truth-function of p, q and r, in the way that $y = x^3$. For just as given that $y = x^3$ I can find out, by calculation, the value of y for any possible argument or value of x, similarly I can find out, by calculation, the truth-value of 'TTFFFTTF (p,q,r)' for any truth-value of p, q and r, its arguments. The values that we calculate here are truth-values, i.e. whether a given proposition, l, is T or F. Again, just as there are different functions in mathematics, two, three, four or more elementary propositions have each a different number of truth-functions. l, m and n are three out of 64 possible truth-functions of p, q and r—for there are 2^{2n} different ways in which 8Ts and 8Fs can be combined, including the possibilities of 8Ts and 8Fs. These form a system and can be arranged in a series (4.45).

Now if we turn to the relations between l, m and n, we shall see that since they are all truth-functions of *the same* elementary propositions, p, q and r, their relations to each other are wholly determined by their relations to p, q and r. They are members of the same system or series. In particular, if we consider the conditions under which they are true we shall see that the conditions under which l and m are jointly true, namely $\frac{p}{F}\Big|\frac{q}{T}\Big|\frac{r}{T}$ and $\frac{p}{F}\Big|\frac{q}{T}\Big|\frac{r}{F}$ (lines 2 and 6 under the first three columns of the table, corresponding to those lines under l and m where we have 2Ts[5]) are included or contained in the conditions under which n is true, namely $\frac{p}{F}\Big|\frac{q}{T}\Big|\frac{r}{T}$, $\frac{p}{T}\Big|\frac{q}{T}\Big|\frac{r}{F}$ and $\frac{p}{F}\Big|\frac{q}{T}\Big|\frac{r}{F}$:

l.m is T only when $\frac{p}{F}\Big|\frac{q}{T}\Big|\frac{r}{T}$ or when $\frac{p}{F}\Big|\frac{q}{T}\Big|\frac{r}{F}$

n is T only when $\frac{p}{F}\Big|\frac{q}{T}\Big|\frac{r}{T}$ or when $\frac{p}{T}\Big|\frac{q}{T}\Big|\frac{r}{F}$ or when $\frac{p}{F}\Big|\frac{q}{T}\Big|\frac{r}{F}$

---

[5] A joint assertion l.m is T only when both conjuncts are true and F when either conjunct or both are false.

This means that when l and m are jointly T, n is necessarily T
—though the reverse does not hold, since when $\frac{p}{T}\Big|\frac{q}{T}\Big|\frac{r}{F}$ n is T
but l and m are not jointly T. In other words, when l, m and n
are related in this way the inference from l.m to n is valid, and
we have the right to infer n from l.m. So Wittgenstein says that
the truth of a proposition n follows from the truth of several
others together, l and m, when all or some of the truth-grounds
of n are among the truth-grounds which l and m have in common
—in other words, when the truth-grounds which l and m have
in common are contained in the truth-grounds of n (5.11). (The
truth-grounds of a proposition l are the conditions under which
it is true, i.e. those truth-possibilities of its truth-arguments
which make it true—5.101.)

Rewriting

l.m as 'FTFFFTFF (p,q,r)'

and   n as 'FTFFTTFF (p,q,r)'

we see that (l.m) ⊃ n is 'TTTTTTTT (p,q,r)', in other words
a tautology.

That is, to say that whenever the common truth-grounds of l
and m are contained in the truth-grounds of n, l and m jointly
entail n, is to state a logical truth. This means that we can
appreciate the truth of 5.11 by reflecting on what it says. The
present discussion has been just this kind of reflection.

The conditions under which one proposition follows logically
from a conjunct of propositions (5.11) constitute a *special* case
of the conditions under which one proposition follows from a
compound proposition—for the compound proposition need not
be a conjunct of propositions. These latter conditions—the
general case—are given by Wittgenstein in 5.12: 'The truth of a
proposition p follows from the truth of another proposition q
if all the truth-grounds of the latter [i.e. of q] are truth-grounds
of the former [i.e. of p].' We have here a non-elementary proposition q (say '(r ⊃ s).s̄') which entails another proposition
(say 'r̄'):

q entails p
(r ⊃ s).s̄ entails r̄

r	s	r⊃s	s̄	q:(r⊃s).s̄	p:r̄	q⊃p
T	T	T	F	F	F	T
F	T	T	F	F	T	T
T	F	F	T	F	F	T
F	F	T	T	T	T	T

We see from this table that all the truth-grounds of q (the premise or antecedent) are also truth-grounds of p (the conclusion or consequent), though not the other way round. We can describe what we have here by saying that the truth-grounds of q, the antecedent, are contained in the truth-grounds of p, the consequent (5.121). In other words, every state of affairs that verifies the antecedent necessarily also verifies the consequent, or makes it true. Hence when the logical conditions specified alternatively in 5.12 and 5.121 are fulfilled, then once one has satisfied oneself about the truth of q one has necessarily and by that alone also satisfied oneself about the truth of p.

Wittgenstein has another formulation of these conditions: 'If p follows from q, the sense of p is contained in the sense of q' (5.122). Here one should remember that the sense of a proposition is its truth-possibility, what is the case if it is true, the circumstances under which we would say it is true (see 2.201, 2.221, 4.022, 4.063—p. 47, para. 3). Take the previous example, namely that q (i.e. (r ⊃ s).s̄) entails p (i.e. r̄). What is the sense of q, i.e. what conditions must be satisfied for q to be true? The following: q is T only when both r and s are F—i.e. q says r̄.s̄. What is the sense of p? p is T when both r and s are F or when r is F and s is T—i.e. p says either r̄.s̄ or r̄.s. Which of these conditions is the *more stringent* one? Those for the truth of q, the antecedent. For more is required for q to be true than is required for p to be true—since for q to be true r̄.s̄ must be true, whereas for p to be true it is sufficient that either r̄.s̄ or r̄.s should be true. In other words, q *excludes more possibilities* than p does, and therefore is *more informative* or *claims more* than p. As Wittgenstein puts it: 'If one proposition follows from another, the latter says more than the former, and the former less than the latter' (5.14).

In short, according to the *Tractatus*, whenever

   (i) the truth-grounds of q are included in the truth-grounds of p

or (ii) the sense of q includes (or contains) the sense of p then q entails p. Again, one could show this to be a logical truth by using a truth-table:

Write down two columns of Ts and Fs for any two propositions q and p in *any* way that will make the truth-grounds of p include those of q:

q	p	q ⊃ p
F	T	T
T	T	T
F	F	T
F	T	T

If q does really entail p then 'q ⊃ p' must be a tautology. For it to be a tautology $\frac{q|p}{T|F}$ must be excluded, since 'q ⊃ p' ≡ 'TFTT (p,q)' and the F here corresponds to the second line of the truth table for q ⊃ p, namely $\frac{p|q}{F|T}$, which is of course the same as $\frac{q|p}{T|F}$. But this possibility is excluded by the condition that the truth-grounds of p should include those of q.

Or alternatively:

p	q	(i)	q ⊃ p	(i) ⊃ (q ⊃ p) (i.e. 5.12)
T	T	T	T	T
F	T	F	F	T
T	F	F	T	T
F	F	F	T	T

To fill in column 3 under (i)—the antecedent in 5.12—we ask: When is it true that the truth-grounds of q are included in the truth-grounds of p? The answer is: Only when $\frac{p|q}{T|T}$.

In a similar way we can show that '(ii) $\supset$ (q $\supset$ p)' is a tautology—i.e. that 5.122 is a logical truth.

This means, again, that we can appreciate the truth of 5.12 and 5.122 by reflecting on what Wittgenstein says there.

But, of course, Wittgenstein says more in 5.11, 5.12 and 5.122 than I have attributed to him in the above proofs. For he does not merely claim that when the conditions set out there are satisfied one or more propositions entail another—which is what I have proved. He also claims that *whenever* one or more propositions entail another the conditions in question must be satisfied. He intends (i) and (ii) above to be each different ways of saying that q entails p—i.e. that 'q entails p' $\equiv$ (i) v (ii). In other words, he intends to provide a *definition* of entailment, an account of what it means for *any* deductive inference to be valid. This, however, presupposes that all propositions that enter our deductive arguments, as premises and conclusions, are truth-functions of elementary propositions. Wittgenstein later came to question and reject this assumption.

He came to see that there are many formal inferences to which the account in the *Tractatus* does not apply. For instance, if q says that S is red and p says that S is green then from q one can infer that p̄. Yet one cannot represent the relation between these two propositions as in 5.121, one cannot say that the truth-grounds of the antecedent q are contained in those of the consequent p̄. One cannot represent $\sim$ (q.p̄) as a tautology—as for instance 'TTTTTTTT . . . (r,s,t . . .)'. This means that the theory of formal inference in the *Tractatus* has a restricted scope. Reflection on what lies at the source of this restriction led Wittgenstein to modify his views of language and its relation to reality in ways that changed his whole approach to the problem of understanding what makes a formal inference valid, what enables us to make deductions *a priori*.

Still Wittgenstein was right in insisting that 'all deductions are made *a priori*' (5.133) and, given the framework of the *Tractatus*, his theory of formal inference is important for work-

ing out an ingenious model for the way two or more propositions
may be so connected solely by virtue of what they say so that
one can justifiably infer one from the others. What this model
brings out is that the connection between the premises and the
conclusion of a deductive argument is a 'connection of sense',
an 'internal relation'. Its existence 'is an immediate result of
the existence of the propositions' in question (5.131). It is by
virtue of this alone, and nothing else, that p follows from q. In
short, the line between valid and invalid inferences and arguments is not an arbitrary one; it is determined by the language
in which we speak, reason and argue.

I have argued that Wittgenstein's model of the way one, two
or more propositions entail another is not defective in itself. I
have tried to show that when the conditions he sets out in 5.11,
5.12 and 5.122 obtain then we do really have a valid deductive
argument. I have suggested that his account of formal inference
is part of a general view of logic developed in the *Tractatus* in
the course of which a chain of misconceptions is rejected. I
hope that the considerations in the next two chapters will put
this account of inference in perspective and so help us to appreciate its importance. However, as I have pointed out, it does suffer
from a serious limitation. For not all deductive relations are
truth-functional. Besides where this account is applicable there
are deeper questions which it can neither open nor answer.
Wittgenstein could only ask these when he began to move out
of the framework within which he had worked out the theory of
formal inference we find in the *Tractatus*. I hope to consider
some of these in the last chapter of this book.

CHAPTER 9

JUSTIFICATION OF A FORMAL INFERENCE

Russell thought that each particular inference that we make is valid only if it is in accordance with a general law of logic. The general law, the *modus ponens* for instance, is needed to justify the inference. Without it the inference is not justified. A person who does not know the law cannot make the inference and be justified. This is an instance of Russell's idea that the whole of logic can be derived from a limited number of general primitive propositions. They constitute the foundations of logic in that they are the final support of whatever principles we appeal to in our deductive reasonings, in the justifications we offer of the formal inferences we make, and in the deductive proofs we develop. They are our final court of appeal. Even if we do not in fact need to appeal to them they are nevertheless presupposed in our proofs, justifications and inferences. Without them the proofs would not be proofs, the justifications would have no force, the inferences would not be valid. For Russell a logical proposition is valid only if it can be derived ultimately from these general primitive propositions, and an inference is justified only if it accords with a general principle which can itself be derived from them. Thus the principles or logical propositions which sanction the deductive steps we take in our proofs and arguments form a hierarchy. Those that have the greatest generality lie at the foundations of the edifice. They are self-evident, or 'obvious to the instructed mind', and state some very general truth about the world. (The parallel with Russell's views on inductive inference is striking. See chart at the end of this chapter.)

Wittgenstein was opposed to this conception of the way logical propositions are related to each other and to the deductive steps we take in our arguments. He claimed (i) that every logical proposition is its own proof (6.1265) and (ii) that the premises and conclusion of a formal inference are themselves the only possible justification of the inference (5.132). He denied that logical propositions constitute a hierarchy:

All the propositions of logic are of equal status: it is not the case that some of them are essentially primitive propositions and others essentially derived propositions[1] (6.127).
It seems scarcely credible . . . that the infinite number of propositions of logic (and mathematics) should follow from half a dozen 'primitive propositions'.
In fact all the propositions of logic say the same thing, to wit nothing (5.43).
In logic there can be no distinction between the general and the specific (5.454).

He argued against the notion of both primitive signs and primitive propositions in logic. Russell's and Frege's 'primitive signs', he argued, are 'interdefinable' (5.42). 'If logic has primitive ideas, they must be independent of one another' (5.451). And then the question would arise: Why are there just these primitive ideas and no other ones? (5.453). This would make their existence contingent on something that could be otherwise. Whereas, says Wittgenstein, 'it is self-evident that v, ⊃, etc. are not relations in the sense in which right and left, etc. are relations' (5.42).

'Where there is a system by which we can create symbols [he writes], the system is what is important for logic and not the individual symbols' (5.555). The only thing that Wittgenstein regards as primitive in logic is *the repetition of an operation.* He works with the operation of simultaneous negation, symbolized by the Scheffer stroke (5.5). By means of it we can construct every truth-function of one, two, or more elementary propositions—however many. In other words, given any number of elementary propositions and nothing else we can, by repeating this operation, construct all their combinations and all the propositions that can be inferred from any of these combinations.

[1] Russell did not think of the 'primitive propositions' in *P.M.* as being essentially primitive in any very strict sense. He thought that what propositions 'must be assumed without proof . . . are to some extent a matter of arbitrary choice' (*P.M.* p. 12). But he did think of logical propositions as forming a hierarchy.

The point is that in this we do not rely on any of Russell's primitive ideas, we do not presuppose any of his primitive propositions. The only thing that is presupposed is the operation of simultaneous negation and our ability to repeat it endlessly. 'It is clear [he says] that this [i.e. the construction of such a system of signs] is not a question of a *number of primitive ideas* that have to be signified, but rather of the expression of a rule' (5.476).

Once a notation has been established, there will be in it a rule governing the construction of all propositions that negate p, a rule governing the construction of all propositions that affirm p, and a rule governing the construction of all propositions that affirm p or q; and so on. These rules are equivalent to the symbols; and in them their sense is mirrored (5.514).

Wittgenstein's treatment of the question of the way logical propositions are related to each other needs separate discussion. But it is closely connected to his treatment of the question of the way logical propositions are related to the formal inferences we make, and I now turn to a consideration of what he says in the *Tractatus* on this latter question. He writes:

The nature of the inference [from q to p] can be gathered only from the two propositions. [We have seen how in the previous chapter.] They themselves are the only possible justification of the inference. 'Laws of inference', which are supposed to justify inferences, as in the works of Frege and Russell, have no sense, and would be superfluous (5.132).

These laws have no sense; they are themselves tautologies, in the way that 'q entails p', or 'p follows from q', or 'p can be validly inferred from q' is a tautology. That is, the law of inference which is supposed to be necessary for the justification of the inference from q to p is on the same footing with the inference—with the claim that q entails p. It cannot, therefore, give us what we do not already have in the particular inference. As I said, if one has the right to infer p from q this means that 'q entails p' is a tautology; and there is no need to bring in anything else to show this.

The point in question, namely that if p can be inferred formally from q such an inference is not in need of support from a general proposition, that to think that it is the function of the laws of logic to give it such support betrays a misunderstanding of what logic is, was illustrated beautifully by Lewis Carroll in a piece called 'What the Tortoise said to Achilles'. I shall quote Winch's summary of it:

Achilles and the Tortoise are discussing three propositions, A, B, and Z, which are so related that Z follows logically from A and B. The Tortoise asks Achilles to treat him as if he accepted A and B as true but did not yet accept the truth of the hypothetical proposition (C) 'If A and B are true, Z must be true', and to force him, logically, to accept Z as true. Achilles begins by asking the Tortoise to accept C, which the Tortoise does; Achilles then writes in his notebook:

A
B
C (If A and B are true, Z must be true)
Z.

He now says to the Tortoise: 'If you accept A and B and C, you must accept Z.' When the Tortoise asks why he must, Achilles replies: 'Because it follows *logically* from them. If A and B and C are true, Z *must* be true (D). You don't dispute *that*, I imagine?' The Tortoise agrees to accept D if Achilles will write it down. The following dialogue then ensues. Achilles says:

'Now that you accept A and B and C and D, *of course* you accept Z.'

'Do I?' said the Tortoise innocently. 'Let's make that quite clear. I accept A and B and C and D. Suppose I *still* refuse to accept Z?'

'Then Logic would take you by the throat, and *force* you to do it!' Achilles triumphantly replied. 'Logic would tell you "You can't help yourself. Now that you've accepted A and B and C and D, you must accept Z." So you've no choice, you see.'

'Whatever *Logic* is good enough to tell me is worth *writing down*,' said the Tortoise. 'So enter it in your book, please. We will call it (E): If A and B and C and D are true, Z must be true. Until I've granted *that*, of course, I needn't grant Z. So it's quite a *necessary* step, you see?'

'I see,' said Achilles; and there was a touch of sadness in his tone.

The story ends some months later with the narrator returning to the spot and finding the pair still sitting there. The notebook is nearly full.

The moral of this [Winch goes on] is that the actual process of drawing an inference is something which cannot be represented as a logical formula; that, moreover, a sufficient justification for inferring a conclusion from a set of premises is to see that the conclusion does in fact follow. To insist on any further justification is not to be extra cautious; it is to display a misunderstanding of what inference is (*The Idea of a Social Science*, pp. 55–7).

One is inclined to think that the truth or necessity of a proposition which is established by deductive proof is contingent on the truth or necessity of the general principles used in the proof, and perhaps explicitly mentioned. Wittgenstein thinks that this way of thinking betrays a misunderstanding of the nature of logical propositions and the kind of generality they have, and also of what it is to give a formal proof. He argues that logical propositions do not say anything (6.1, 6.11) and so do not add anything to the propositions or inference in question. When Z follows from A and B, to say C—If A and B are true, Z must be true—is not to add anything to what is already there. This point holds however general C may be. The logical truth exemplified in the inference from q to p, namely 'q entails p', is on an equal footing with the general principles of inference. What gives one the right to make the inference lies in the propositions themselves, in the sense they have. One who understands the propositions will see the connection; seeing the connection, drawing the inference is an expression of one's understanding.

It is true, of course, that one may have what would count as an understanding of the propositions in question and yet fail to see that one follows from the other. Obviously we do not require that a person should see every implication of a proposition before we say that he understands it. Wittgenstein would have said later that the implications of a proposition do not form a closed class and that we do not have rules which determine them once and for all. When we discover a new proof we lay down a new track in language and so alter or develop the sense which the proposition had so far. Where someone gives us a proof which brings to our attention a connection between two propositions which we had not previously seen, our understanding of the propositions *changes*. We come to see that there was more to the sense of the propositions than we realized. But Wittgenstein's views when he wrote the *Tractatus* were different. There the sense and so also the implications of a proposition are held to be perfectly definite and determinate, to be fixed once and for all in advance of any actual situation in which the proposition may be asserted. It is thus possible to calculate every possible implication the proposition has. Still Wittgenstein allowed that a person who understands the proposition may fail to see some of its implications. This he generally attributed to a lack of perspicuity in the symbolism in which the proposition is expressed. He thought that it should always be possible by analysis to make these implications and connections clear.

The connections which a formal proof makes us see are a function of the sense of the propositions in question, just as much as the sense is a function of these connections. They exist on their own account: 'their existence is an immediate result of the existence of the propositions' (5.131). The inference we make is valid in its own right. It is valid by virtue of these connections. Our recognition of them comes from our understanding of the propositions involved; it *is* a part of that understanding. One does not have to know anything else in order to be able to infer one proposition from the other. To know the general principles of inference is not to know anything over and above, for instance, that this inference here is valid. To know the principles *is* to be able to draw logical conclusions, to be able to judge validity. Hence Wittgenstein regards logical principles as dispensable, redundant or superfluous: 'We can actually do without logical propositions [he says]; for in a suitable notation we can in fact recognize the formal properties of propositions by mere inspection of the propositions themselves' (6.122). Wittgenstein is here emphasizing that the relation between logic and language is not external. He is not saying that the propositions of logic are useless.

In his unpublished lectures on 'Proof and Explanation' Wisdom illustrates this point by an example. A child is confronted with an *a priori* question: There are six airlines from England

to France, and for each of these, six ways of going to France by
one airline and coming back on that airline by a different airplane. How many ways are there of going to France on one airplane of a given line and coming back on a different airplane of
that line? He is bewildered. His mother asks him to consider
very simple examples which bear on this complicated case of the
airlines. 'You have two boxes and in each box two beads. How
many beads have you?' The child can easily see the answer to
this question. The mother thinks up other examples, each a
little more difficult, each a little nearer the case which bewilders
him. Having answered the simpler question each time the child
is able to see the similarity in the slightly more difficult one and
so is able to answer it himself, until upon reaching the original
question he is also able to answer it. The child is thus brought
to see that when there are six airlines etc. (when q is true) then
there are six times six ways of going to France by one airplane
and returning by a different one (then p is true). He sees that p
follows from q. He has been brought to see this through a
consideration of other instances, other propositions which are
similarly related. He has been brought to see a deductive connection where he had not seen one; he has been convinced that
q entails p. Yet there has been no appeal to a general principle.
Does this mean that no proof has been given?

Wisdom compares what we have here with the case where
general principles are invoked and appealed to: 'And now
suppose that his father takes a hand. He says, "Look here, if
there are N things of sort X, and for each of these there are N
things of sort Y, then there are N times N things of sort Y.
Therefore if there are six airlines to France, and if for each of
these there are six ways of going to France by one airline and
coming back by a different one, then there are six times six ways
of going to France on one airplane and coming back by a
different one." Short, conclusive, the father's procedure. That's
more what one might call proof.' Wisdom then imagines the
child asks his father how he knows this general principle, on what
grounds he is so confident of it. Is the instance on which it
sheds light among these grounds? If it is, says the child, then the
argument is circular, and if it is not then the argument is not
conclusive. Wisdom points out that deducing the principle from

one yet more general will not change the situation, for the child could ask the same questions with regard to the more general principle. When he can no longer go in this direction the father says: 'This principle is self-evident. You have only to consider what it means to see that it is true. Take an instance . . .' He now resorts to the mother's procedure. He supports the general principle by a consideration of instances—those which the mother used or might have used. 'What the father does [says Wisdom] is to bring to bear upon the case in question all the cases covered by the principle except the case in question. It's not that his procedure is of no use—on the contrary, it's most useful, convenient, though less vivid, than the other one. It does as much as mother's procedure, *but no more*. And that is what I mean by saying that father's procedure comes in the end to proof by parallels. And this is true for any proof that an argument is valid.'

In other words, the general principles are dispensable, since it is possible to do the same job without using any general principles. A consideration of the nature of the kind of connection established or of the nature of these principles would show this. In his later writings Wittgenstein sometimes spoke of these principles as *rules* which we observe in keeping to the sense of our utterances. Wisdom spoke of them as rules which we can extract, as mnemonics, from logical practice—that is from the procedures we follow when we make inferences and evaluate arguments (see *Philosophy and Psycho-Analysis*, p. 105). It is worth noting that a rule too, like a tautology, does not say anything: it is something that we can observe or break.

Logical practice is constituted by what we do on particular occasions when we move from one proposition to another, from one thought to another, and the rules we observe in doing so are an expression of the practice. They do not justify the practice as such. If the step that someone takes on a particular occasion when he makes an inference is said to be justified when it accords with an accepted rule, this means that it is justified if it agrees with what is general practice. This, in turn, means that the step is justified if it agrees with the steps we take in those simple cases like those in which we first learned to take such steps when beginning to speak and reason. These are cases

I

where there is overwhelming agreement that a deductive step is justified. They may be regarded as paradigms of valid inference. In other words, in a given instance we are justified, our inference is valid, when what we do accords with other instances in which we recognize the procedure as justified—where we have been taught to call the inference 'valid'. Obviously unless there are such instances the question of whether this inference here is valid cannot arise, it cannot mean anything to us.

Wisdom's point was that when in an attempt to justify a particular inference, to prove its validity, we appeal to a general principle, the function of this principle is to help us compare the inference which we don't recognize as valid with others which we do. We are justified in making that inference, i.e. our inference is valid, if it accords with these undisputed cases of valid inference where the deductive relation can be read off from the structure of the propositions concerned. The complex case of inference is valid if the relation between the structures of the propositions involved there is the same as the relation in the simpler cases where it can be taken in at a glance. The general principle which the father uses in his proof is a means of bringing out this identity. It is in this sense that logical propositions such as the *modus ponens* may be said to symbolize general patterns of transition in arguments that are formally valid.

The term 'valid' is a technical word and we do not normally learn to use it until we take a course in logic, long before which time we have learned to draw logical conclusions and evaluate arguments. In this respect logic differs from arithmetic. In arithmetic we have various techniques which we employ in very many situations in our daily life and we learn them at school. We are specifically taught to count, to do sums, to subtract, divide and multiply. Whereas we master the techniques of logic as we learn to speak. This is not surprising since to learn to make sense with words is to learn to recognize what our utterances commit us to, how they bear on each other, what logical force they have in conversation. Thus if, using words in their normal sense and meaning what you say, you utter a proposition, you commit yourself to certain consequences for the future. This is what keeping the meanings of one's words and meaning what one says comes to. If what you say or do next is not in accordance with what your words led us to expect, we would say that you didn't *mean* what you said, or that you meant it but changed your mind, or that you were being inconsistent. If none of these is the case then we have failed to understand you, we do not know what you meant. The point is that the connections between propositions is part of their sense, and that how a person observes the implications of his utterances —which is an important part of his practice with words—is a criterion of whether he understands them or not, of whether or not they make sense. In other words, logical practice is inseparable from the practice of using words intelligibly, and the rules or principles of inference are inseparable from the rules governing the use of words.

In Wisdom's example when the father was asked on what grounds he is so confident of his general principle, he at first derived it from one more general still. In other words he claimed that the more general principle was his ground. When he was pressed far enough in this direction he said, 'You have only to consider what it *means* to see that it is true', and illustrated its meaning by means of particular examples. The instances made explicit its meaning and by virtue of that alone provided reasons for accepting it; and also at the same time did so for the particular inference which the father was trying to justify. My point is that elucidating the meaning of a logical truth *is* providing reasons for accepting it. As Wittgenstein puts it: 'It is the peculiar mark of logical propositions that one can recognize that they are true from the symbol alone' (6.113); 'we "prove" a logical proposition by calculating the logical properties of the *symbol*' (6.126). (Also see 6.2321.) Wisdom's example was: 'There are six airlines from England to France, and for each of these, six ways of going to France by one airplane and coming back on that airline by a different airplane.' This *means* that there are six times six ways of going to France by airplane. One can know this by reflecting on what one has been given in the original description, by reflecting on its sense.

We ask: (i) What makes R (the father's general principle) true? (ii) What makes 'q entails p' true? In both cases what is in question is a logical truth. We have seen that what makes R true is what it means to assert R, and also why this is so. We have

seen that what makes 'q entails p' true is the sense of q and the
sense of p. This is precisely why Wittgenstein says that R does
not justify 'q entails p' in the way that Russell thought. For 'q
entails p' can be justified, shown to be valid, without appealing
to R. One could do this, as Wisdom has shown, by instances
which make clear the senses of q and p and so how they stand
to each other. It is not that an appeal to R is not a justification,
but that it is not anything more than referring or appealing to
instances which make the senses of q and p explicit. Where
what one proves is a logical proposition (say that q entails p),
and not a contingent one, the proof consists in making clear the
senses of p and q. This is to the point, it is what is called for,
because the connection between q and p which one is trying to
establish is an internal one. As Wisdom puts it in 'Proof and
Explanation': 'We said that the point about deduction was this,
that an attempt to prove a conclusion C from a premise P was
valid only when every investigation and every comparison required for the establishment of C is also required for the establishment of P. The point is that if C follows from P, then any
distance from another particular case which is required for the
truth of C, will also be required for the truth of P. It may nevertheless be much easier to carry out the comparisons when our
conclusion is stated in the form of C.' (Compare with 5.124.)
In other words, if p follows from q, then whatever is required
for the verification of p is equally required for the verification of
q—though more may be required for the verification of q—and,
of course, what the verification of a proposition requires is a
matter of what it means to assert it. Put it differently: Given the
senses of p and q, when what is a reason for accepting q is also a
reason for accepting p, we say that p follows from q. In other
words, the kind of relation we have here is a connection of
reasons, a connection of meanings, an internal relation—one
whose identity depends on the identity of the propositions
concerned, and vice versa. That is why one doesn't need to appeal
to anything external to establish its existence. If we appeal to a
general principle of logic this is not to appeal to anything
external; and therefore we could dispense with doing so.

In fact instances which make clear the senses of q and p and
so how they are related and thus bring home to one who does

not see this at once that q entails p are among the examples we would give in explaining what it means to hold R. But accepting R as a principle of inference is to see what it means to hold it—and one can see this best in particular instances of formal inference. Therefore, since the proof of R involves the proof of 'q entails p' the latter can be proved without appealing to R. We see again thus that R is dispensable.

We have seen that in justifying an inductive inference, in establishing that A and B are causally connected, we have to appeal to instances, other cases. We have seen that this appeal to instances is an essential part of giving an inductive justification, and that there being a causal connection here, in this instance, is a matter of the sequence observed here holding true in other instances at other times and in other places. But this is very different from our appeal to instances in justifying a formal inference, in establishing a deductive connection, in trying to convince someone that p does really follow from q. In this latter case the point of appealing to instances is to bring out the *sense* of asserting the propositions in question. We are asking a person what he would *say* in these cases, with a view to getting him to see *that he ought to say the same here too.* Obviously whether the examples we ask him to reflect on are actual or only imaginary makes no difference. In inductive justification, however, it is essential that the instances we appeal to should be actual ones. For A and B here are causally connected only if other instances of A and B at other times and at other places do *really* follow the sequence they exhibit here and now; and what we are concerned with is *not* what we mean by 'A' and 'B'.

To put it briefly, there being a causal connection here logically depends on a regularity or repetition in the sequences we observe; but the identities of A and B do not depend on there being such a connection between them. Whereas there being a deductive connection between q and p depends on there being a regular use of the expressions in q and p; and the identities of q and p depend on the connection that exists between them by virtue of the regular use of these expressions. Thus what we are trying to do in the case of deductive justification is to get a person to see and honour the commitments that go with using certain words in their meanings and meaning what one says with them.

We are showing him what consequences operating with a rule, which he is familiar with elsewhere, has here, in this case. While an appeal to instances is fundamental to both deductive and inductive justification, this appeal is directed to different ends, and the instances play a different role in the two cases.

The question of the relation between the validity of an inference that I draw on a given occasion and the principle of inference with which it accords is a particular case of the relation between the steps that a man takes in accordance with a rule and the rule itself. We say that the steps are determined by the rule and that each actual step is right if it accords with the rule. Wittgenstein has given much thought in the *Investigations* to what this comes to. He doesn't question the adequacy of this way of speaking, he wishes to understand what it means: 'We use the expression: "The steps are determined by the formula . . ." *How* is it used?' (§189). In particular he is concerned to combat the idea that the rule and the man's understanding of it is external to the steps he actually takes. This idea finds expression in the thought that the rule exists independently of what men actually do in particular cases, that it can be grasped apart from instances of its application, and that it is this grasp or understanding that makes people take the actual steps which they do take. The justification of the steps taken then becomes an appeal to something independent of the steps, something over and above them—something psychical, perhaps, that exists in the medium of the understanding.

Wittgenstein argues that the rule exists *in* the actual practice that people carry out, that it cannot exist apart from such a practice. Hence his rejection of the possibility of a 'private' rule. He argues, too, that a man's understanding of a rule shows itself *in* what he actually does on particular occasions. He cannot have the understanding and continually fail to take the correct steps— that is the steps which most people call 'correct'. If his understanding of the rule is something that shows itself in what he actually does, if what he does over a stretch of time is our criterion of whether or not he understands it, or of how he understands it, then that understanding cannot determine what he actually does at different times in the way that the genetic structure of a seed, say, is said to determine the growth of the plant and its subsequent characteristics. Hence when a rule is said to give us the criterion of a correct step on a particular occasion, when the claim that the step is correct is justified by showing that it accords with the rule, what one is referring to are other steps taken at other times which people regard as correct.

One may be tempted to wonder if they may not be all wrong. People are disturbed by Wittgenstein's move to make what the majority of people say on innumerable occasions the final court of appeal in these situations because it does not seem to put such a court at a sufficient distance from our actions. If the court of appeal is to be objective, they think, it must stand over and above each and every of our actions and be able to pronounce on them. They imagine the rule itself to be just such a court of appeal. But the trouble is that removing the rule in this way from the face of the earth, with a view to preventing the possibility of universal error, empties it of any content. For what gives it content is what people say and do in actual cases. On this they agree overwhelmingly. It is this agreement that fixes the meaning of the rule. As Wittgenstein puts it:

Not only rules, but also examples are needed for establishing a practice. Our rules leave loop-holes open, and the practice has to speak for itself (*On Certainty* §139).

'We do not learn the practice of making empirical judgments by learning rules', he writes (§140). Again he considers the remark that if someone multiplies 12 by 12 and obtains 144 then he *cannot* have made a mistake. Does this follow from a rule? His answer is: 'We did not learn this through a rule, but by learning to calculate' (§44). In the former case he speaks of learning *judgments* and their connections with other judgments, and in the latter case he speaks of *training*. He then asks how we satisfy ourselves of the reliability of a calculation. He answers that no rule emerges when we describe how we do so. This is not to say that we may not appeal to a rule, but that 'the rule is not needed', and if no rule is mentioned 'nothing is lacking'. That 'we do calculate according to a rule' is not in question (§46). The point is that when asked what it is to apply this rule here, in carrying out the calculation, the explanation takes the form of giving instances and pointing to the way they are alike. It is hoped that this will be grasped directly, without the need for further explanation. Thus when asked what makes this calculation, or a step in it, correct one can point to instances where this is obvious and not doubted, and not mention any rule. Since it is the instances that have to be mentioned in explaining what the rule is, since it is what people do in the particular cases that give meaning to the rule, Wisdom speaks of this procedure (which he sometimes calls 'mother's procedure') as being more fundamental: All *a priori* proof and justification (he says) in the end comes down to 'proof by parallel cases'.

I have tried to point out how much what Wittgenstein says about the redundancy of logical principles in the *Tractatus* anticipates his later discussion of the sense in which the steps in a calculation are determined by the rules of calculation. What does not come within the purview of the *Tractatus* is a discussion of the way when someone utters a sentence to say something he *commits himself for the future* if he means what he says. It could not have done so since in the *Tractatus* Wittgenstein does not attach any special significance to the fact that words and sentences are instruments which we *use*, and that this means that what we do with them at different times and on different occasions has a certain regularity. Thus in turning his attention to what we do with words and sentences, to the consistency with which we must employ them if we are to be able to say anything, and to the way we do so in the weave of other actions and behaviour, Wittgenstein was able to deepen his views of the relation between logic and language. There is much in his earlier views on logic that he did not go back on. What he says on the redundancy of logical principles is one of them. We have already seen that it is connected with other things that he maintained in the *Tractatus* and did not give up later.

RULES AND CASES

Principles, commitment to principles, and what
men do in particular cases. (Connection between
the arguments of chapter 3 and chapter 9.)

I. Belief in a general law
of induction or principle of
the uniformity of nature
→ Inductive conclusions
based on various kinds of
evidence (great variety)

Such beliefs as that fire will
burn me if I touch it

'The squirrel does not infer by induction that it is going to need
stores next winter as well. And no more do we need a law of induction to justify our actions and our predictions' (*Cert.* 287).

II. Regard for, adherence to
logical laws

→ Deductive conclusions

Knowledge of what to say
in particular cases—when
one has already asserted
certain propositions

To know the general principles of inference is not to know anything
over and above, for instance, that this inference here is valid. To
know the principles is to be able to draw logical conclusions, to be
able to judge validity. One learns the general principles as one
learns to make formal inferences; one learns logic as one learns to
speak.

III. Rule, mathematical formula

→ Results arrived at by
calculation

Steps that I learn to take in
specific situations—steps on which
there is wide agreement

The rule and my understanding of it are not external to the steps I
actually take. The rule does not exist independently of what men do
in particular cases and it cannot be grasped apart from instances of
its application. What gives the rule content is what people say and
do in particular cases. The understanding of the man who follows it
is exhibited in the steps he actually takes. The rule exists *in* the
actual practice that people carry out.

IV. Regard for moral values

Moral conclusions and
decisions based on moral
reasons, arrived at by moral
reasoning and deliberation

Particular moral convictions and
affective reactions in specific
situations

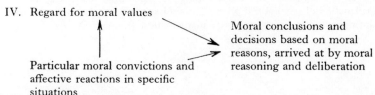

CHAPTER 10

LOGICAL CONNECTIONS AND CAUSAL TIES

Both Hume and Wittgenstein insisted that there can never be a necessary connection between distinct facts, events or actions. In Part I we have discussed the sceptical view that when we reason inductively we are not really reasoning at all. The reverse of this, namely the view that when we infer one set of facts from another distinct set of facts, as we often do, if we are reasoning at all then our inference must really be deductive, holds an equal sway over our thoughts. We tend to think that either when we reason from fact to fact we are not really reasoning at all or there are necessary connections in nature, ties of necessity between distinct facts.[1]

This is an idea which Wittgenstein opposes in the *Tractatus*, and continued to oppose in his later work. In the *Tractatus* he denied, like Hume, that distinct events could be connected by logical ties or bonds of necessity. He said that one cannot infer formally one fact or situation from another (5.135), that where one does make a formal inference 'there is no causal nexus to justify such an inference' (5.136). 'The only necessity that exists is logical necessity' (6.37). Unlike Hume, however, he was primarily concerned with the notion of a logical connection, not a causal one. When he said that 'belief in the causal nexus is *superstition*' (5.1361) he did not mean to deny that events can be causally connected. Of course there is a difference between events which we say are causally connected and those which we say are not. Neither did Hume deny this when he said: 'All events seem entirely loose and separate. One event follows another, but we never can observe any tie between them. They seem *conjoined*, but never connected.'

---

[1] Another version of this antinomy is that either there can be no explanation of any natural phenomenon or scientific explanations are like those we find in logic, geometry, mathematics.

What they denied was that causality is 'an *inner* necessity like that of a logical inference' (5.1362). If Wittgenstein called this a superstition he meant that it is a *grammatical* superstition, in other words a superstition concerning what is meant by 'establishing a causal connection'. When he says that causality is not 'an *inner* necessity' he means that if we have two events such that one is the cause of the other, the statement of the occurrence of the first cannot entail the statement of the occurrence of the second. Thus if q states that billiard ball A hits billiard ball B and p states that billiard ball B moves then 'if q then p' cannot be justified *a priori*. One who understands q and p and knows q to be true does not *that far* know that p is true. He does not know that 'if q then p'. He cannot know this 'from the symbol alone', for the connection in question is external to q and p. The superstition that Wittgenstein is opposing is the idea that in the kind of example I have mentioned 'if q then p' can be justified *a priori*. Conversely, and more importantly, he is combating the idea that a necessary connection is a 'material' connection, in other words the kind of connection that is established *a posteriori*. This is what he has in mind when he says that a belief in the causal nexus to justify a formal inference is *superstition*.

Locke held such a belief:

I doubt not but if we could discover the figure, size, texture and motion of the minute constituent parts of any two bodies [he wrote] we should know *without trial* several of their operations one upon another, as we do now the properties of a square or a triangle. Did we know the mechanical affections of the particles of rhubarb, hemlock, opium, and a man, as a watch-maker does those of a watch, whereby it performs its operations; and of a file, which by rubbing on them will alter the figure of any of the wheels; we should be able to tell *beforehand* [that is, in advance of experience, *a priori*] that rhubarb will purge, hemlock kill, and opium make a man sleep: as well as a watch-maker can, that a little piece of paper laid on the balance will keep the watch from going till it be removed. But whilst we are destitute of senses acute enough to discover the minute particles of bodies, and to give us ideas of their mechanical affections, we must be content to be ignorant of their properties and ways of operation; nor can we be assured about them any further than some few trials we make are able to reach (*Essay Concerning Human Understanding*, Bk. IV, Ch. III, Sec. 25).

Clearly Locke thinks here that it is possible for us to succeed in establishing a causal connection in a purely *a priori* manner, in the way that we may come to see a geometrical connection. This thought is not foreign to our thinking. A man has a headache. He takes an aspirin. Five minutes later he faints. We suspect that the two incidents may be causally connected: perhaps he has an allergy to taking aspirins, or perhaps the aspirin had gone bad. We do not need Hume to tell us how such a hypothesis is investigated, how we find out whether or not there is a casual connection between his taking the aspirin at 5.40 p.m. and his fainting at 5.45. We know, for instance, that we should ask him if in the past he ever fainted after taking aspirin. We know that it would be to the point to analyse other tablets of aspirin from the same bottle and, if there is anything unusual in their composition, to try and ascertain if there is any past record of the effect of such samples on men and animals. Yet, however familiar we may be with this mode of procedure, it may strike us as rather indirect and roundabout. We may think that it is only because the aspirin tablet in question has dissolved and gone that we have to resort to such a roundabout way of establishing whether the aspirin taken at 5.40 had a causal effect on the man who took it, whether his fainting at 5.45 was the effect of that tablet of aspirin. If it had such an effect, we think, it must be because of what took place between 5.40 and 5.45 that afternoon; and it seems that all our investigations of what takes place with other tablets of aspirin and other men and animals at other times and other places must be second best. So we may feel, as Locke did, that if only we had more knowledge about the chemistry of the aspirin tablet and the physiological constitution of the man at the time he took it then we should know whether his fainting was caused by the aspirin *more directly*, that is without trial and experimentation. In other words, we may ourselves be inclined to think that our consideration of other events in other places and at other times is an *accidental* feature of the procedure for establishing the existence of a causal connection.

A man, perhaps a child, discovers that there is a causal connection between the hands of the clock on the wall reaching certain positions and its giving definite numbers of chimes. He need not have seen the mechanism inside the clock, or know anything about it. His discovery is not dependent on his having any such knowledge. However, had he seen or known about the mechanism he might have been able to infer or guess such a connection without having had to listen to the chimes and observe the position of the hands time after time in the way he did. Further if, subsequent to such a discovery, he were shown the mechanism and allowed to examine it he might come to understand something that he did not understand before. He might then say that he understands, for the first time, why the clock chimes when its hands reach certain positions. But does this mean that we can discover a causal connection 'without trial'? Does it mean that when we have seen and examined the mechanism responsible for a causal sequence we understand why events take this course and no other in the way that we understand why, for instance, the angles of a triangle add to two right angles, no more and no less?

I tell you that I have a piece of mechanism which consists of two cogwheels in mesh. I ask you what would happen if I rotate one of the wheels clockwise. Perhaps you picture it to yourself and tell me that the other wheel would rotate counterclockwise. I ask you how you know this when you have not examined the mechanism in question, have not actually tried to rotate one of the wheels to see what happens. You tell me that it *stands to reason.* In other words it seems that you can answer my question *a priori*, by mere reflection. You tell me that if the parts of the mechanism fit together in the way described then they *must* move as you tell me, that they *cannot* move any other way. You say that you do not need to wait and watch before you can know this. In the same way if I tell you that I have the figure of a triangle on the blackboard and its two base angles add to 135° you will tell me that its interior angle at the apex must be 45°. Here too it seems that I am able to make a formal inference from one or more facts to a further fact—these facts being independently identifiable.

This analogy is worth considering. The statement '*If* that figure is a well-drawn triangle and the sum of its base angles is 135° *then* its top angle is 45°' is indeed established or known *a priori*. But for that very reason it cannot conflict with the results of measurement. If, upon measurement, the base angles are found to add to 135° but the top angle turns out to be only 42°, this would not show that the statement we made *a priori* is wrong. Rather that statement would show that we had made a mistake *somewhere*, though locating the mistake would have to wait on experience—observation and measurement. It may be that we have made a mistake in our measurements and so we might have to check them again. It may be that our instruments, e.g. protractor, are inaccurate or faulty. Or it may be that the figure we have is not a good triangle, its sides not being quite straight. If prior to any further examination we suspect a mistake some-where that is because of the role we assign to the geometrical statement in accepting it *a priori*. To adhere to it *a priori* is to refuse to count a three-cornered figure a proper triangle when its three angles do not add to 180°. In other words, the proposition we assert *a priori* is a *criterion* of what is to count as a triangle, and any three-cornered figure that does not conform to it will not be *called* a perfect triangle.

Our hypothetical proposition states that *if* the figure on the blackboard is a proper triangle and *if* its base angles add to 135° *then* its top angle must be 45°. In the particular instance before us the second antecedent clause, namely that the base angles add to 135°, is satisfied but not the consequent clause, namely that the top angle is 45°. This, provided that no mistakes have been made, guarantees that the first antecedent clause is falsified, the clause that says that the figure is a well-constructed triangle. More briefly, what falsifies the consequent clause necessarily falsifies one of the two antecedent clauses. That is why the full hypothetical proposition cannot be falsified by any measure-ment. Is it any wonder that it is necessarily true, known *a priori*? Put it like this: One of the antecedent clauses is an identification clause. The truth of that clause *requires* that both the second antecedent clause and the consequent one be true, i.e. that the sum of the three angles be equal to 180°. This is precisely why nothing can falsify our hypothetical proposition.

However, whether or not the three angles of the figure we have on the blackboard add to 180° is an empirical question and has to be decided by measurement. They may not add to 180°. If in fact they do not then what we have before us is not a well-constructed triangle, if they do then it is. We can, on that basis, *predict* other results—such that, for instance, its exterior angles at the apex will upon measurement be found to be 135°. Further measurements, however, may falsify these predictions. Our *predictions* may turn out to be incorrect while our *calculations* are impeccable.

It is important to recognize that we have two distinct results here which it is easy to confuse: the results of measurement and the results of calculation. The question 'If that figure is an accurate triangle and its base angles add to 135° what is the size of its top angle?' is an *a priori* question, a question of pure geometry. It is answered by reason, reflection, calculation. On the other hand, the question 'In that three-cornered figure the sum of the base angles is 135°, what is the top angle?' is an empirical question. It can only be answered by measurement. If one confuses these two questions, if one fails to distinguish them, then one may think that one is answering a question of fact, inferring one fact (i.e. the size of this top angle) from another distinct fact (i.e. the sizes of these two base angles), yet doing so by pure reflection, *a priori*.

That this angle is this size and that angle that size are distinct facts and we cannot logically infer one from the other. That this angle is this size means that if we measure it in this way, for instance, by means of a protractor, we shall obtain such a result. Geometry has nothing to say on this question, though we can use geometry to predict this result. As Wittgenstein puts it: We make use of geometrical propositions in inferences from propositions that do not belong to geometry to others that likewise do not belong to geometry (6.211). The geometrical proposition in question says that the sum of the angles of a triangle equals two right angles or 180°. But it does not tell us that the figure on the blackboard is a triangle—a well-constructed one. This may not be obvious because geometry does provide a definition for 'triangle': a three-angled figure bounded by straight sides. It also provides definitions for 'angle' and 'straight line', but it is not concerned with the application of these terms. In other words, it tells us *in general* that if a three-angled figure is bounded by straight lines it is a triangle. But it does not tell us that these conditions are satisfied *in a particular case*.

We can of course establish that the figure on the blackboard is a well-constructed triangle, but our claim that it is such a triangle will necessarily be open to the challenge of the future. In other words, it is always imaginable that further observation and measurements will conflict with it. This does not mean that our identification clause is an hypothesis that can never be confirmed with finality, but it does mean that when from the size of the base angles I infer the size of the top angle of the figure on the blackboard my conclusion has implicit in it the proviso that such-and-such and such-and-such are not the case. My inference is that if the base angles add to 135° then *necessarily* the top angle is 45° *unless* any of a number of possible circumstances shows that the figure in question is not a well-constructed triangle. Obviously the 'unless' in the above inference cancels the force of the 'necessarily'. Until we can enumerate *exhaustively* the conditions that must be satisfied for the figure on the blackboard to be a well-constructed triangle, until we can say that *nothing else* would be relevant to our right to make the inference under consideration, the step in question cannot be a deductive step, however well assured it may be.

In geometry we have deductive steps precisely because accidents are excluded so that the data of a problem in pure geometry includes *everything* that is relevant to the solution of the problem. Finding the solution consists in rearranging the data. One does not need to go outside what one has been given in the statement of the problem to find its solution. As Rhees once put it: Mathematics, so to speak, works in a closed vessel. Whereas when you have sequences taking place in time, that the same sequence will take place again is a contingent matter. When one repeats an experiment, as scientists do, one tries to 'approximate' such an ideal. But it is always on the cards that things may go wrong. The laboratory may burn down before the experiment is completed. One might want to say: If one could repeat *all* the conditions that held when the result was obtained the first time then one should get the same result again. But these conditions do not form a closed class so that the attempt to produce a closed system is always limited in real life.

When I reason about the figure on the blackboard, then, I rely on an implicit identification clause about the truth of which geometry has nothing to say. *If* I have correctly identified this figure as a well-constructed triangle then, indeed, given the size of the base angles my conclusion *must* be correct. That is the truth of my conclusion does not follow deductively from the data about the sizes of the base angles *alone*. But the additional data that I need to have for my conclusion to follow deductively can never be sufficient until it includes the conclusion itself in one form or another. In the case of pure geometry this is ensured by the way 'triangle' is defined. In other words, so long as one is not concerned with whether this is *in fact* a well-constructed triangle, so long as one can merely suppose that it is, for argument's sake, then one's reasoning from the size of the two base angles to the size of the third angle will be deductive. In the case of an *actual* figure, however, it is always possible that what I find on measuring the third angle will not tally with the conclusion I reached *a priori*. Geometry itself cannot rule out this possibility.

We are in a similar situation with the two cogwheels in mesh. If someone, like Locke, says that 'it stands to reason, if one of the cogwheels turns clockwise the other must turn counterclockwise' he is indeed enunciating an *a priori* truth, one that belongs to kinematics or the geometry of movements. Kinematics too, like geometry, has an application; it is of great help to those who study, design and construct actual machines. We may thus reason on paper or in our head and on the basis of this reasoning construct a piece of mechanism whose various parts we mean to move in certain narrowly specified ways.

But our reasonings and diagrams, however impeccable and accurate they may be, *do not logically guarantee* that the parts of the mechanism will move to plan. For the cogs may be soft and slip, the parts may bend or twist, they may 'slip, slide or perish'. Our reasoning on paper does not allow for this sort of thing. Indeed, in reality, it can be prevented to a large extent. A great deal of inductive know-how and theoretical knowledge may be brought to bear on preventing slipping, bending, metal fatigue, and so on. But the kind of assurance that one can justifiably have is and must be inductive in character. Accidents cannot happen in logic, but even the best designed, the most carefully constructed machines may break down. In any case they are subject to wear and tear.

Our *a priori* reflections on the relations of the movements to

K

one another presume that the moving parts are *perfectly rigid*, just as our geometrical reasonings, when for instance we use a drawing in giving a proof, presume the drawing to have *perfectly straight* edges. Here too we have two distinct propositions which are easily confused. One is that *if* the parts of this mechanism are perfectly rigid then when one wheel turns clockwise the other one *must* turn counterclockwise. This is an *a priori*, necessary proposition. Reflection alone will show that given the antecedent condition the consequent one must be satisfied. The other proposition is that in this piece of mechanism when one wheel turns clockwise the other one *will* turn counterclockwise. This may be a pretty safe and reasonable prediction to make, and you may, if you are an engineer and have tested it, be justifiably so certain that you are willing to bet your last penny on it. But it is nevertheless a prediction and it may be falsified.

The rigidity of the parts of the mechanism, like the straightness of the edges of the figure on the blackboard, has to be established by observation. In the case of the straightness of the edges of the figure one looks closely, puts a rule alongside it, and so on. But one may be mistaken, and one can check and check again one's measurements. I intend this as a grammatical statement: I mean that one's second measurement, which necessarily comes later in time, can give one reason for retracting the result of one's first measurement. The giving of a geometrical proof too takes time, and if an actual figure is used, it is presumed that the figure does not alter during the proof. Wittgenstein points out that 'if it were otherwise, if for instance one mathematician was convinced that a figure had altered unperceived . . . etc.—then our concept of "mathematical certainty" would not exist' (*Inv.* p. 225). In other words, that presumption is a feature of the grammar of mathematics. The figure about which this presumption is made (i.e. that it has straight edges and continues to have straight edges during the demonstration) is used as a model in the proof. The proof establishes a paradigm in comparison with which other figures are to be judged and described. The figure on the blackboard is used as a model which has certain determinate features, e.g. straight edges. What the proof establishes takes this for granted. Whether this is in fact true does not matter as far as the proof is concerned.

Similarly, the conclusion arrived at by purely *a priori* reflection that given this arrangement of parts, i.e. two cogwheels in mesh, then when one wheel turns clockwise the other one must turn counterclockwise, presumes that the parts are perfectly rigid and remain so throughout the actual movement. This is taken for granted in our *a priori* reflections. If we reason in terms of a movable model then it is a feature of the model that its parts are rigid. For purposes of reasoning we *disregard* any shrinkage, slipping, wear and tear.

In reality, however, how do we establish that the cogs won't bend, break or slip, that the parts of the mechanism are strong and rigid? By subjecting them to certain forces to see whether they give way or bend? (A) If this is how the proposition 'These parts are rigid' is established, and it can be established that way, then we must remember that the proposition 'These parts have not given way to pressure' does not entail the proposition 'These parts will be rigid throughout the movement.' In other words, the step from what we have established, our evidence, to what we presuppose in our *a priori* reasoning is an inductive one. (B) If, on the other hand, we are using the words 'These parts are rigid' to mean 'These parts will remain rigid throughout the movement' then we have here a proposition which cannot be established once and for all, by subjecting the parts to certain forces. In other words, that the condition we presuppose in our *a priori* reasoning about the movements of the cogwheels holds can only be established inductively. The condition in question is subject to the vagaries of nature. Inevitably the move from any observation or set of observations to the truth of the presupposition in question involves an inductive step. In other words, it is impossible to reach any conclusion about how this cogwheel will turn if the other one is turned clockwise by purely *a priori* reasoning. It seems otherwise because the inductive step that one takes here is so very reasonable, so well justified that one takes it for granted and so forgets its presence. So it seems deceptively that here we have an occasion on which it is possible to make a formal inference from the existence of one situation (e.g. wheel A will be rotated clockwise) to the existence of another situation (e.g. wheel B will rotate counterclockwise). Wittgenstein denies this (5.135).

Let me put it differently. There is here, indeed, a proposition which we know or reach *a priori*—a proposition about the relation of movements, about the possibilities of movement in given conditions. It states: 'If these parts are perfectly rigid and this wheel turns clockwise then that wheel must turn counterclockwise.' But here 'these parts are perfectly rigid' means more than 'they did not bend under certain pressures.' Its being an *a priori*, necessary proposition depends on this. It will not be an *a priori* proposition, the antecedent clauses will not entail the consequent clause, until the consequent clause has become a criterion of the rigidity of the parts. This is, of course, a matter of how the words 'are perfectly rigid' are used, i.e. of what they mean in the *a priori* proposition, the proposition that states a truth of reason. When those words are so used and meant that we shall not say that the parts of our mechanism are perfectly rigid until they actually move so-and-so then is it any wonder that we can formally infer that the parts will move so-and-so when the premises from which we infer this includes the premise that the parts are perfectly rigid? For here, to use the language of the *Tractatus*, 5.12, the truth-grounds of the premises are included in the truth-grounds of the conclusion.

The reasoning we wish to be clear about takes the following form: If p.q then r. Here q asserts that cogwheel A will be moved clockwise, and r that cogwheel B will move counterclockwise. Locke thought that this, namely if q then r, can be known *a priori*, that it is evident to reason. I suggested that when this is so there is an implicit premise p which states that the parts are perfectly rigid. We have seen that so long as the truth-grounds of that premise p are results of trials (such as at t_1 the parts were subjected to pressure and did not bend, at t_2 . . . etc.) then the inference is necessarily inductive, and can never be anything else. Only when the words which state p are so used that p is true only when r is true will the inference become a deductive one. In other words, nothing short of the statement which you wish formally to infer can entail it. To put it differently, by the time you have a formal inference the situation which you are inferring is no longer distinct and entirely different from the situation at hand.

Put it yet another way: I put the piece of mechanism before

you. You merely look at it and perhaps also actually move it or merely imagine it moving. Note that for the present purpose it makes no difference whether you actually move it or merely imagine it moving. You then tell me that if this part moves this way then that part *must* move that way. What you tell me has the inevitability of a geometrical conclusion and yet it seems to be a statement about this piece of mechanism. We have seen that you have in fact used the piece of mechanism before you as you would use an actual figure or drawing on the blackboard in giving a geometrical proof. You need not say or write anything else. You look at the picture and see, for instance, that any triangle inscribed in a semi-circle must be a right triangle. Or, to take a simpler instance from Wittgenstein, I prove to myself the commutative law of multiplication thus:

$$\begin{matrix} \cdot & \cdot & \cdot & \cdot & \cdot \\ \cdot & \cdot & \cdot & \cdot & \cdot \\ \cdot & \cdot & \cdot & \cdot & \cdot \\ \cdot & \cdot & \cdot & \cdot & \cdot \end{matrix}$$

'The mere picture [writes Wittgenstein] regarded now as four rows of five dots, now as five columns of four dots, might convince someone of the commutative law. And he might there-upon carry out multiplications, now in the one direction, now in the other' (*Remarks* III, §17). A little way below he writes: 'And that brings me to the fact that a picture may very well convince us that a particular part of a mechanism will move in such-and-such a way when the mechanism is set in motion. The effect of such a picture (or series of pictures) is like that of a proof . . .' (*ibid.* §21). 'When I work the mechanism its movement proves the proposition to me; as would a construction on paper' (V, §51).

When the piece of mechanism is used to reason geometrically about the relations of its movements, when one movement is derived from another in sequence, it is being used as a model or paradigm, it 'serves as a measure' (*Remarks* II, §§21–2). The possibility that its parts may bend, stretch or shrink is dis-regarded, it does not come into our use of the mechanism as a model. This is not an assumption we make about the actual piece of mechanism. For if it were an assumption that the parts of this mechanism are 'perfectly rigid' this would mean that they would not stretch, bend or twist *under any condition*. But how can one intelligibly give any content to this expression? How can one intelligibly maintain that something will continue to exist or happen come what may unless one means to lay down a requirement of sense or to comment on one that already exists? The mechanic could tell us that it will not bend or stretch under *such-and-such conditions*. But that would be different. That would be an intelligible assumption and there might be very good inductive grounds to support it.

The point is that when the actual piece of mechanism is treated as a model to demonstrate that when one of the wheels is rotated in one direction the other one *must* turn in the opposite direction we are making no assumption about the mechanism before us. And if we were making an assumption about it, as the mechanic might, this would not give us what we want. As Wittgenstein puts it: 'When we say: "Kinematics describes the movements of the mechanism on the assumption that its parts are completely rigid", on the one hand we are admitting that this assumption never squares with reality, and on the other hand it is not supposed to be in any way doubtful that completely rigid parts would move in this way. But whence this certainty? The question here is not really one of certainty but of something stipulated by us' (*Remarks* I, §120).

When I move the mechanism or merely imagine its cogwheels turning, I derive one picture from another and they form a series—see figure on opposite page.

It is *stipulated* and understood that the parts are completely rigid, that the relation of each part of each cogwheel to one another *remains the same*. This is a rule that is employed in the derivations. It gives us the correct way to draw the series of pictures. I start with Picture I, then I ask myself: If wheel A is rotated 90° clockwise so that the cross on it now occupies its lowest position, where should I put the cross on wheel B when I redraw Picture I accordingly? The position of the cross is determined by the rule in question. When I say 'If wheel A is rotated 90° clockwise wheel B must rotate 90° counterclockwise' I am following a rule. That is the way in which the movement or

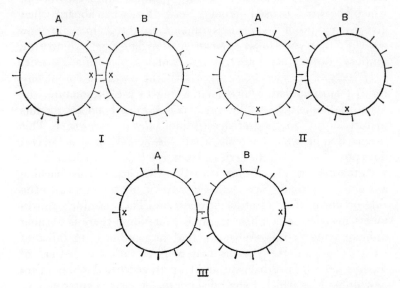

and so on . . .

successive positions of wheel B are determined *in our picture* by the movement or successive positions of wheel A is quite different from the way these are determined *in our actual mechanism.* 'The movement of the machine-as-symbol [writes Wittgenstein] is predetermined in a different sense from that in which the movement of any given actual machine is predetermined' (*Remarks* I, §122).

The position of the cross on wheel B in Picture II is strictly determined and determined in advance by our adherence to a rule, in the sense that any position other than the correct one (as shown above) will not be in accordance with the rule. I cannot at one and the same time be said to follow this rule and also to draw or think Picture II differently. But what is the connection between the picture and the rule? Wittgenstein talks of the machine-as-symbol. It becomes a symbol in the proof when it is used in accordance with a rule. Its identity as a picture, model or symbol is not external to and so cannot be separated from the rule in question—just as the identity of a concept, what the word for that concept means, cannot be separated from the way in which the word is used. What I draw on the blackboard when giving you a proof is a *sign* or symbol. I use it to help me express what I am trying to say. *Drawing* the figure is like writing numerals down when I am trying to explain a piece of arithmetic.

If I say 'I am going to assume that the parts are completely rigid' I am stipulating how I am going to use the picture, the machine-as-symbol. In Wittgenstein's words: I am taking this picture as my 'method of description' (*Remarks* I, §121). This means that if what happens when the actual machine moves does not square with the series of pictures I derive in accordance with the rule stipulated then I *say* that the parts of this machine are not quite rigid. *Saying* this is part of my adherence to the rule or norm of description in question. The machine's movements may fail to conform to my expectations; there is nothing unimaginable in this. What we find impossible is to think of what happens here in terms that conflict with the method of description we have been brought up to accept. But this raises new difficulties which I shall discuss in the next chapter.

In this chapter I have argued that the idea which Wittgenstein opposes in 5.135 to 5.1362 in the *Tractatus*, namely the 'superstition' that causality is 'an *inner* necessity like that of logical inference', comes from our confusing the movements of the machine-as-symbol with the movements of the actual machine. 'The difficulty in all these cases [writes Wittgenstein] arises through mixing up "is" and "is called" ' (*Remarks* I, §127). Confusing these we take the propositions of geometry and kinematics as material propositions as though they themselves offered descriptions of objects and their movements. We fail to recognize that they are rules of grammar for expressions which may be used in describing objects and their movements.

We have seen that when we actually predict the movements of a machine the rigidity that we assume its parts to have is indeed a material property and that such a prediction is based on an assumption about the machine. When, however, we use the machine-as-symbol and derive *a priori* a certain sequence of movements the rigidity in question is a stipulation. Here we are not predicting what will be the case but fixing possibilities. We confuse these two and it seems that one movement determines another with the inevitability of the steps of a formal inference or mathematical proof. As Wittgenstein puts it: 'The connection which is not supposed to be a causal, experiential one, but much stricter and harder, so rigid even, that the one thing somehow already *is* the other, is always a connection in grammar' (*Remarks* I, §128). 'There are no causal connections in a calculation [he writes], only the connections of the pattern' (V, §15). In its negative contention this is the same as what he says in the *Tractatus*, namely that there is no causal nexus to justify a formal inference (5.136).

CHAPTER 11

LOGICAL NECESSITY

I

We speak of necessity in connection with logical and mathematical truths and in connection with formal inferences and mathematical deductions. We say that a logical proposition expresses a necessary truth, that it is necessarily true, and we describe the connection between the premises and conclusion of a valid deductive argument as a necessary connection. Thus we use such locutions as 'if things stand so-and-so then *necessarily* such-and-such is the case', 'if angle C is 90°, a is 8 inches and b is 6 inches, then c *must* be 10 inches'.

Part of what we mean is that what is in question does not depend on anything that could be otherwise; nothing that may come up or change can falsify what is being expressed. Hence the idea that everything that we can think of is subject to change and decay except the truths of logic and mathematics which are *timeless* and *eternal*. Another part of what we mean is that propositions of logic and pure mathematics cannot be false without being unintelligible. We cannot both imagine them to be false and understand what we are imagining or, in short, we cannot think or imagine them to be false. There is no alternative to what is in question; any alternative is both impossible and unthinkable. Hence the idea of necessity and the suggestion that our thoughts cannot go against or contravene the truths of logic and mathematics. They almost seem to *compel* our assent: once we understand them we have to admit that they are true and unexceptionable.

There is something mystifying in the ideas of timeless truths and propositions that compel our assent. In the *Tractatus* Wittgenstein tried to dispel this mystery while retaining what he thought is obviously correct. He argued that logical and mathematical truths are independent of everything that is the case and could be otherwise in that the former are tautologies and the latter equations which express identities. It is in this sense that they are necessarily true or unfalsifiable. They cannot compel us in what we say, think or infer, since they are not external to our speech and thought. A formal inference, for instance, is a transition that has no external justification;[1] principles of inference like the *modus ponens* do not provide the inference with any backing, sanction or justification that is not already contained in the premises of the inference—in what it means to assert those premises.

Thus logic does not give us truths that are additional to those that are contingent. It provides a method for making explicit what we have committed ourselves to in saying this or that; it gives us the measure of what it would be correct to say in view of what we have already said. The norms it thus provides are implicit in our speech; we could not say anything if we did not observe them.

Once we understand a logical proposition we *have to* admit that it is true only in the sense that the truth of such a proposition is not anything over and above its sense and can be read off 'from the symbol alone'. Once we have asserted an empirical proposition we *have to* admit that what logically follows from it is true only in the sense that the latter is a part of what we have asserted. In neither case are we forced to admit anything. But if we do not acknowledge the truth of a logical proposition then this *means* that we have not understood it;[2] and if we refuse to admit that what follows from an assertion we have made is true this *means* that we are going back on what we said, or at any rate amending it. If we express a transition to which there is no alternative in our language and thought, in the form of a proposition thus: if p and q are true then r *must* be true, then this proposition says nothing—it is a tautology (*Tractatus*), a rule (*Remarks*).

A tautology's truth is certain or necessary (4.464) in the

---

[1] As I have argued in chapter 9 this is not to say that how we infer in *other* cases does not bear on the validity of *this* inference. Of course it does. But equally how we use on *other* occasions the words we have uttered now bears on what we mean by them *now*.

[2] Our not understanding it is something that would show itself in the fallacies we commit in reasoning about various matters of fact and logic.

sense that it is fixed or determined by the nature of the symbolism
—so that one can recognize that it is true from the symbol alone
(6.113). Thus given, for instance, that p ≡ q̄ is T and also that
p is T, it follows *necessarily* that q is F. That this follows is a
tautology. We can write it as:

$$[(q \equiv \bar{p}).p] \supset \bar{q}$$

p	q	q ≡ p̄	p	(1) (q ≡ p̄)·p	(2) q̄	(1) ⊃ (2)
T	T	F	T	F	F	T
F	T	T	F	F	F	T
T	F	T	T	T	T	T
F	F	F	F	F	T	T

and, therefore, also as: (TTTT) (p,q).

Looking at the above table we see that (q ≡ p̄) is T means that
p is F and q is T or that p is T and q is F. (q ≡ p̄) is T *and* p is
T means p is T and q is F. The conclusion q̄ is T means that
q is F.

> The premises together say: p is T and q is F
> The conclusion says: q is F

Thus we can see 'from the symbol alone', that is from a consideration of what the premises and conclusion *mean*, that if
what the premises say is T what the conclusion says *must* be T.
The proposition which states this is a tautology—(TTTT) (p,q).
In other words it is T for all combinations of the truth-values of
p and q that are possible—namely:

p	q	proposition which states that the above conclusion follows from the above premises
T	T	T
F	T	T
T	F	T
F	F	T

Obviously the truth or falsity of any elementary proposition other than p and q is not relevant to whether it is true or false and, therefore, cannot falsify it. But we have just seen that none of the possible combinations of the truth-values of p and q can falsify it either, since it is true under all these conditions. Hence *nothing at all* can falsify it. According to the *Tractatus* this is what is meant by saying that it is *necessarily* or *unconditionally* true (4.461), this is what is meant by saying that in a valid deductive argument the conclusion *necessarily* follows from the premises, this is what is meant by saying that if the premises are true then the conclusion *must* be true. This is what the force of the logical MUST comes to.

Necessity in the *Tractatus* is not, of course, confined to tautologies since mathematical propositions whose truth is equally necessary are not tautologies but equations. They too are said to say nothing and are characterized as 'pseudo-propositions' (6.2). This is true of any formula which expresses such transitions as we make in mathematical calculations and proofs. Thus if y is the cube of x, for instance, then any value one assigns to x will automatically determine the value of y:

Given that $y = x^3$, if $x = 3$ then *necessarily* $y = 27$.

Compare with:

Given that $\bar{p} \equiv (FT)(p)$, if p is T then *necessarily* $\bar{p}$ is F.

The value of x determines the value of y, and the truth-value of p determines the truth-value of $\bar{p}$, for in each case the values in question are connected by a rule or formula—namely, $y = x^3$ and $\bar{p} \equiv (FT)(p)$. The latter rule gives us the meaning of the negation sign.

I used the locution 'given that $y = x^3$' and suggested that this is an expression of one's acceptance of an equation, of one's commitment to a rule. This in turn implies that we have a choice in the matter. But, of course, when we are solving a mathematical problem or calculating, what equation is the correct one to use, what formula we ought to apply at this point or that, is strictly determined by the way the problem has been set. It is determined in just the same way as in the above example when we assign a value to x what value y will have is strictly determined. We may have a choice in what value we assign to x and we may have a choice in what problem we wish to solve. But once we have made that choice we have committed ourselves to a particular result, and the calculation is a process of making our commitments explicit.

The same is true of the expression 'given that $\bar{p} \equiv$ (FT) (p)' above. This is the rule which gives meaning to the bar above the propositional variable p—a meaning which corresponds to that of the expression 'it is not the case that . . .' as used in English. Of course we can adopt a different rule, define the bar (-) differently. But if we do so we would have given a different sense to '$\bar{p}$'; what it means would not be the same as what we mean by 'it is not the case that p'. We have a choice, of course, in what we say. But once we say something, once we utter the words 'It is *not* raining', for instance, and mean them as they are normally meant, we have committed ourselves to the rule '$\bar{p} \equiv$(FT) (p)'. We cannot mean them as these words are normally meant and refuse to be guided by the rule '$\bar{p} \equiv$ (FT) (p)', since meaning the word 'not' in this context as we normally understand it *means* accepting the above rule.

We are free to say what we wish and, since what words in a given language mean is a purely contingent matter, we are also free to change the meanings of words.[3] But given what we mean by them our use of them on a particular occasion limits what further words we can use in that connection provided that we wish to stand by what we have said. We may, of course, not wish to do so. We may wish to revise our judgment or retract our comment. But if people never stood by what they said, they could not be speaking at all—and then neither would the possibility of revising or retracting a judgment be open to them.

We see that once we have said something or made a comment we have committed ourselves for the future, and then there are some things we cannot say without going back on what we have said. This is what Wittgenstein was thinking of when he said that there is something in ,the different languages that people speak that is not arbitrary, something that is not open to choice,

[3] I do not mean, of course, that we can keep changing their meanings from one occasion to the next as we wish. For their having a meaning at all depends on our using them in the same sense on different occasions.

namely 'that when we have determined one thing arbitrarily something else is necessarily the case' and that this is bound up with what it means to speak (3.342). It is precisely this which constitutes the domain of logic. As he put it:

Logic is not a field in which we express what we wish with the help of signs, but rather one in which the nature of the natural and inevitable signs speaks for itself (6.124).

The idea of the 'inevitable signs' is interesting. There are different ways of saying the same thing. In different languages the same thought is expressed in different ways. Wittgenstein speaks of the differences here as being purely conventional. Conventions are open to choice, and they are arbitrary, optional or accidental in the sense that whether we adopt one convention or another does not affect what we say. There is nothing 'inevitable' about conventions and what accords with them. But there is something about what we say which is independent of the conventions we observe in saying it and which we could uncover by logical analysis. *This* could not be otherwise without our saying something different and hence committing ourselves differently (3.34). It is what all the different ways of saying the same thing have in common. A symbolism which is able to reveal it would thus reveal what is *essential* to the proposition expressed (3.341). Logic comes in at this level, not at the level of what is accidental to the language we use.

Thus in the *Tractatus* the answer to the question 'Why do we follow just these principles of logic, why can we not even conceive of others?' is simple and unequivocal. They constitute the absolute measure of what is intelligible in *any* language; they determine once and for all the limits of sense. There cannot be anything relative about what is logically necessary. The tautologous character of logical propositions shows that logic is neither a kind of ultra-physics nor a set of human conventions. What is logically or necessarily true, is independent both of the facts of this world and of the conventions of this or that language. Logical necessity is bound up with what is essential to any language.

It is Wittgenstein's contention in the *Tractatus* that what is essential to different ways of saying the same thing is provided by what different languages have in common. It can be reached by the *analysis* of anyone of the ways of saying it and it can also be *constructed* from the elementary propositions that are relevant to its sense. For it is a member of the system or series of truth-functions of these propositions.

These (Wittgenstein tells us) can be arranged in a series (4.45, 5.1). Thus given two elementary propositions p and q we can determine *a priori* all their possible truth-functions—16 in number. These stand to one another in *internal relations*. This is shown by the fact that they can be constructed from the elementary propositions by the successive application to them of a single operation. Wittgenstein calls it 'simultaneous negation' and represents it with a capital N or the Scheffer stroke ·/·.

We can now see that the link between logic and mathematics is to be found in Wittgenstein's notion of *the repetition of an operation*. It is by the repetition of the operation N (ξ) that language is constructed from elementary propositions: 'Suppose that I am given *all* elementary propositions: then I can simply ask what propositions I can construct out of them. And there I have *all* propositions, and that fixes their limits' (4.51). It is in this way that the boundaries between sense and nonsense are determined—by the repetition of an operation. It is this same idea that Wittgenstein regards as fundamental for the understanding of mathematics:

The general form of operation . . . is the most general form of transition from one proposition to another (6.01).
And *this* is how we arrive at numbers . . . (6.02).
A number is the exponent of an operation (6.021).

In other words, just as truth-functions are generated out of elementary propositions by the repetition of an operation and thus form a formal series, so are numbers generated by the repetition of an operation and they can be arranged in a formal series.

We are in a better position now to appreciate what Wittgenstein meant when he said that logical necessity 'derives from the *essence* of notation' (3.342). How does what is essential to any language determine the boundaries of sense? How does it rule out certain combinations of signs as senseless? The way it does so, according to the *Tractatus*, is very close to the way, for instance, anything other than 5 is ruled out as a value for x in the equation x = 2 + 3. A contradiction is ruled out as unintelligible, as necessarily false, in the sense that there is a general rule for constructing all significant propositions:

It now seems possible [writes Wittgenstein] to give the most general propositional form: that is, to give a description of the propositions of *any* sign-language *whatsoever* in such a way that every possible sense can be expressed by a symbol satisfying the description, and every symbol satisfying the description can express a sense, provided that the meanings of the names are suitably chosen (4.5).

Those combinations which conform to this general description will be possible values as significant propositional forms. Wittgenstein would agree that 'description' is a misnomer here. What is in question is a rule or general criterion of sense. He makes this clear when he says that 'the general form of a proposition' is 'the general form according to which one proposition can be generated out of another by means of an operation' (6.001–6.01). The operation determines in advance what are and what are not significant propositional forms in the sense that what is a significant combination of elementary propositions is precisely what can be constructed by the repetition of this operation—by the successive application of it on elementary propositions as the initial bases. It is in this way that in the *Tractatus* Wittgenstein thought the limits of language or sense are determined, in this way that certain combinations of signs are ruled out as not expressing sense. The situation is similar in mathematics.

But how does a formal operation determine all the possible values of a system? What Wittgenstein has to say on this question in his later writings is foreshadowed in the *Tractatus*. Let us take a simple example from arithmetic: y = x + 2. Starting with 0, if x = 0 then y = 0 + 2 = 2, if x = 2 then y = 2 + 2 = 4, if x = 4 then y = 4 + 2 = 6, and so on. The repetition of this operation yields a formal series: 0, 2, 4, 6 and so on. Each member of this series is determined in advance by the

L

operation. Each step of the operation can be symbolized in the following way: If $y = x + 2$ and $x = 2$ then *necessarily* $y = 4$; if $y = x + 2$ and $x = 4$ then *necessarily* $y = 6$, and so on. At each step the correct result is the only possible one. Incorrect results are ruled out: 'If $y = x + 2$ and $x = 4$ it is *impossible* that y should be anything other than 6.'

We have already seen the sense in which mathematics works in a closed vessel (chapter 10) and the statement of a mathematical problem includes all the factors that are relevant to its solution. Therefore nothing that can turn up can interfere with that solution. When one repeats an experiment it is otherwise; all sorts of things can go wrong and influence the result. The scientist tries to find out what could influence the result and by trying to keep these factors constant attempts to secure uniformity in the results obtained in repeating the experiment. But, as we have seen, this attempt to produce a closed system is always limited in real life. Whereas the necessity that belongs to the result of the repetition of an operation is not subject to any sort of interference. One of the characteristics of a formal method is that *accidents are excluded*.[4]

When considering the example of the two cogwheels in mesh we saw why we cannot exclude accidents. There we can at best have good *inductive* reasons for not expecting shrinking, slipping, bending, metal fatigue. Whereas, in contrast, in the model of the mechanism accidents played no role since they were excluded by the symbolism. Given the model we derive the successive movements or positions of the second cogwheel as the first one goes through a certain sequence *in accordance with a rule*. Here there can be no accidents in the sense that certain positions simply do not constitute the application of the rule in question.

Supposing that one were to draw the successive movements wrongly and develop the sequence as shown in the figure on the opposite page.

If this happened with an actual machine we should say that the cogs are slipping. But where these are successive pictures you

---

[4] The content of the above paragraph comes almost wholly from Rhees whom I have heard elaborate and discuss this point in Seminars in Swansea. Though I would like to acknowledge my debt to him, I should not like to make him responsible for my rendering of his ideas.

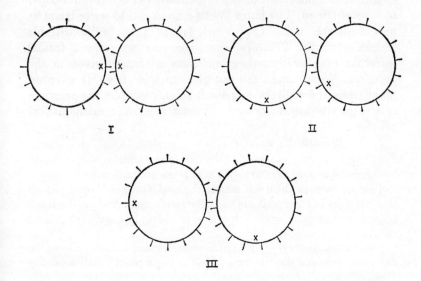

have drawn, we should say that you were not following the rule
in question, that you had failed to do so, that you had misunderstood the picture. 'If you and I were operating with the same
model then you could not have developed the sequence as above.'
For the criterion of your operating with the same picture, the
same rule as I, is the agreement of your results and mine. It is
in this sense that our results are determined in advance and are
immune to accidents. This does not mean that you and I cannot
make a slip. We can. But our attitude towards such a slip is
very different from our attitude towards a slip of the cogs. We
talk of them in different terms. Our slip is a mistake, it may be a
defect in our understanding. The slip of the cogs is a defect in
the mechanism.

This is, I think, implicit in Wittgenstein's remark in the
Tractatus that 'calculation is not an experiment' (6.2331). The
immediate point is that in a calculation all accidents are excluded,
that they are not regarded as part of the calculation. If I make a

mistake and obtain the wrong result this does not mean that the calculation yields the wrong result. It is the result that *I* have obtained, not the result of the calculation, i.e. the result I *ought* to have obtained. The latter (Wittgenstein was to write later) 'is part of the calculation' (*Remarks* I, §112). This is in line with his insistence in the *Tractatus* that whenever we have a formal inference or transition the conclusion is already given in the premises. Wittgenstein did not give up this view. He gave up his analysis of *how* the conclusion is already given in the premises of a deductive argument or in the statement of a mathematical problem.

In his *Remarks* he writes:

A proof shews us what OUGHT to come out . . .
That is: we reproduce not merely the *conditions* which once yielded this result (as in an experiment), but the result itself. And yet the proof is not a stacked game, inasmuch as it must always be capable of guiding us. . . .
'Proof must be surveyable': this aims at drawing our attention to the difference between the concepts of 'repeating a proof', and 'repeating an experiment'. To repeat a proof means, not to reproduce the conditions under which a particular result was once obtained, but to repeat every step *and the result*. And although this shews that proof is something that must be capable of being reproduced *in toto* automatically, still every such reproduction must contain the force of proof, which compels acceptance of the result (II, §55).

'To repeat a proof means . . . to repeat every step *and the result*.' Hence if you repeat every step but get a different result then you will not be said to have repeated the proof in question. Is it any wonder that you cannot repeat the proof and obtain a different result! Whereas you can repeat an experiment—set up the same apparatus, use the same materials, regulate the relevant conditions so that they are the same as they were when you performed the experiment previously—and obtain a different result. But then 'to obtain a result' means something different in the two cases. In the case of the formal proof, you go through a certain process, that is you repeat or reproduce the steps one by one. But if you do not repeat the result then you have not repeated the proof. In the example of the kinematic diagram, for instance, if you do not obtain the same result as before, the same result as others, this means that you are not proceeding in accordance with the rule in question, that you are not operating with the same diagram. If you were, this could not have happened in the sense that the criterion of your operating with the same diagram, the same rule as we were, or as you were before, is the agreement of your results at different times with one another, the agreement of your results and mine. It is in this sense that here 'process and result are equivalent' (6.1261, also *Remarks* I, §82).

You turn one of the cogwheels to see what happens; you put a penny in the slot to see what will come out. Here the process and the outcome are distinct, logically independent, they can be identified in separation from each other. Hence something unforeseen may happen which will interfere with the process so that you get a different result. An accident: so the result may be surprising—it was not what you expected. Whereas where you are repeating a proof, reasoning geometrically, developing a formal series, the result or results that you arrive at constitute the criterion of the identity of what you have been doing—of how the process you have carried out is to be identified. Are we going to say that you have repeated the proof? That you were applying such-and-such a rule or formula? This depends on the steps you took *and* the result you arrived at; it cannot be judged independently of the latter. It is in this sense that you cannot make mistakes here (5.473), that the proof, rule or formula determines its result in advance (5.47).

We have already seen that this does not mean that one cannot make a slip or mistake here. We can say that someone *meant* to apply a certain formula, that he *knew* how to apply it, judging by his past applications, but that he made a mistake, judging by his present result. In this sense, of course, one can make mistakes in logic and mathematics. What we cannot say is that he *did* apply the formula and yet arrived at a different result. If he did apply it then he could not have arrived at the result which he actually obtained. It is in *this* sense that a mistake is impossible in logic (5.473).

Neither does it mean that one is compelled by the formula— in the way that Achilles suggests we are in what he says to the

Tortoise. As I said, someone may set off to apply a formula, to solve an equation, to carry out an inference or a multiplication. He may be competent, and still he may fail, he may arrive at the wrong result. Logic itself cannot guarantee that this will not happen. There cannot be a deductive guarantee that it will not happen. But if it were to happen, we would not say that he had in fact succeeded in carrying out what he had set out to do. There is no constraint or restriction on what one writes down or says. But there are standards and criteria about how what one does, says or writes in these circumstances ought to be described, limits to what could be correctly said in specific circumstances. Hence, if, for instance, you wish to multiply 289 by 382 and obtain 7,348 instead of 9,248 we should say that you did not really succeed in carrying out the multiplication, that you tried to do so but failed.[5]

If you accept premises which entail a certain conclusion you would have committed yourself to that conclusion. This means that you could not correctly be said to accept the premises if you refuse to accept the conclusion. You can, of course, refuse to do so, in which case you will have been inconsistent. Logic itself cannot prevent you from being inconsistent. The necessary connection holds between the premises and the conclusion; it cannot hold between what you utter now and what you utter next—any more than it can hold between one movement of the machine and another movement which follows the first. It is a contingent matter whether or not having asserted the premises on one occasion you will go on to assert the conclusion, whether or not you will accept it if questioned.

When Wittgenstein says that we cannot think illogically (3.02, 3.03, 5.4731, 5.61, 6.361) he is not saying that we are compelled to think logically. His point is that there are limits to what counts as a thought (or proposition): it is of the essence of thought that

[5] We may say 'You multiplied wrongly'. But this is no answer to the philosophical question 'Did he or did he not carry out the multiplication —when he came up with the wrong result?' The point is that the correct answer is not determined by what generally happens when we multiply these numbers, but by standards or norms of multiplication. These standards define what we mean by multiplication. (And what gives them content are what people who have received a particular training agree in doing in particular cases where they carry out multiplications.)

it should be the thought of something and an 'illogical thought' cannot have this relation to anything and so cannot be a thought. If the moves we make do not conform to certain norms then they do not constitute a thought—they do not express any thought. Just as an investigation that is not methodical or 'subject to law' (6.361) is no investigation. Later Wittgenstein said: 'The laws of logic are indeed the expression of "thinking habits" but also of the habit of *thinking*. That is to say they can be said to shew: how human beings think, and also what human beings call "thinking" ' (*Remarks* I, §131). In the *Tractatus* he agrees with the last part of this remark. When he speaks there of 'the impossibility of illogical thought' (5.4731) he means this: that the laws of logic 'show what human beings call "thinking" ', that they 'bring out the essence of human thinking' (*Remarks* I, §133). (When in the *Investigations* he speaks of the mistaken 'conception of thought as a gaseous medium' (§109) his point is that if thought were a gaseous medium, then an inquiry into what is and what is not a possible thought would be a scientific, empirical inquiry—in the way that an inquiry into the possible combinations of the carbon atom is a scientific inquiry. So he says: 'It was true to say that our considerations could not be scientific ones. It was not of any possible interest to us to find out empirically that, contrary to our preconceived ideas, it is possible to think such-and-such—whatever that may mean.' This is as much a remark on the concept of a thought—on how 'the grammar of the word "think" differs from that of, say, the word "eat" ' (*Inv.* §339)—as a remark on logic, on the notion of a possibility or an impossibility in logic, on the relation between logic and thinking, on the sense in which the laws of logic are 'laws of thought'.)

When Wittgenstein says that 'there can never be surprises in logic' (6.1251), that we can know the answer or solution of a logical or mathematical problem in advance (5.47, 6.125), he does not mean that we cannot make discoveries in logic or mathematics, that taking a logical step or giving a mathematical proof is a futile operation. As he puts it quite explicitly in the *Remarks*: 'The proof is not a stacked game, inasmuch as it must always be capable of guiding us . . . This reproduction must once more be *proof* of the result . . . Every such reproduction must contain the force of proof, which compels acceptance of the result' (II, §55). In other words, it must be capable of showing you something you did not see before; it must be capable of securing conviction. One reason why he denies here that the proof is a stacked game is because he thought of the process of proof as a process of stacking the cards, i.e. of forming a new concept or modifying an old one. This idea does not come into the *Tractatus*, however, and he would have said there that there is a sense in which the proof is a stacked game, though obviously how the cards are stacked cannot be apparent to one who needs the proof. When he denies that there can be surprises in logic he means that when we come to see something we had not realized we see that it could not have been otherwise. We are not surprised by its being so, but by our not having seen it before.

I have argued that in these remarks in the *Tractatus* Wittgenstein is commenting on those features of a formal method which distinguish it from empirical methods of inquiry. He is furthering his elucidation of the sense in which in a mathematical problem or a purely deductive argument what we have been given or start from *determines* the solution of the problem or the conclusion of the argument. It is this determination that we acknowledge when in drawing the conclusion we say that it MUST be so.

II

In the *Tractatus* logical propositions are represented as devoid of content and the necessity that belongs to a formal inference is elucidated in terms of truth-functional analysis. The position with regard to mathematics is similar, except that the steps of a calculation corresponds to equations rather than tautologies. If one could accept Wittgenstein's truth-functional account of language one would have to admit that he had managed to avoid a conception of logic that makes it into a kind of ultraphysics without falling into any form of conventionalism.

While he held that it would be nonsense to look for a justification of logic,[6] the way he characterized it left it with no feature that anyone could possibly think might need justifying. For although its relation to the language we speak was internal it had

[6] 'Logic must look after itself' (5.473).

nevertheless a universality which transcends any particular language. Thus in the *Tractatus* logic has an absolute character in that there is nothing in it that is relative to time, place and culture, and it is so to speak self-authenticating in that all its propositions have the same form, namely (TTTT . . .) (p,q . . .). There is no multiplicity of primitive signs or ideas in logic and nothing about what is logically necessary that may be said to rest on our intuition (5.4731, 6.1271).

When, primarily through reflection on our colour concepts, Wittgenstein came to see that the calculus of truth-functions gives only *part* of the grammar of the logical constants 'and', 'or', 'not', etc., he had to modify his whole conception of logic and abandon his earlier criterion of a logical proposition or necessary truth. For $\sim$ (f(green).f(red)) is as much a necessary truth as $\sim$ (p.p̄) without being a tautology. The same applies to 'Orange is between red and yellow', 'There is no colour between red and green', 'White is lighter than black', and a host of others. Once the earlier way of distinguishing between what is and what is not a logical proposition is given up and ever newer forms admitted into the class of necessary truths, it can easily come to seem that where we draw the line is an arbitrary matter. For once a variety of systems of rules of syntax is recognized one will be inclined to ask 'How do we know that these rules of syntax are the right ones, that they are not arbitrary?' (Rhees, 1963). The difficulty is heightened when rules of syntax or grammar are compared with rules of games (see *Zettel* §§134, 320). When Wittgenstein was further to admit that new language-games can develop and so new grammars come into existence and old ones become obsolete (*Inv.* §§18, 21), when he argued that while the steps in mathematical calculations are logically necessary, what has become established in mathematics does not logically bind us to accept extensions which are suggested by new proofs, the difficulty became even more acute. We shall see that Wittgenstein faced these difficulties squarely and still managed to avoid conventionalism.

He would say that propositions like 'A surface cannot be both red and green all over at the same time', 'There is no colour between red and green', 'There are four primary colours' are *grammatical* propositions. They are *rules* of our language-game with colours; they characterize the language-game (*Rem.* V, §§23, 28). This sounds odd at first. We want to protest: 'Given what we mean by "red" and "green" there cannot be a colour between red and green as there is between red and yellow. Anyone who is acquainted with these colours in particular instances can see it *a priori*. It stands to reason. This is not a fact that human beings create or can alter; nor can we imagine it to be otherwise. Therein lies the necessity of the proposition. It expresses a truth; it does not state a rule.'

In this protest truth and falsehood are mixed together. First, although acquaintance with red and green requires normal sight, so that a blind person cannot be acquainted with these or any other colours, it also presupposes the framework of our language: 'Do not believe that you have the concept of colour within you because you look at a coloured object—however you look' (*Z.* §332). If we wish to say that the proposition under discussion can be derived from the *essence* of the colours in question, that its truth flows from those essences (*vide* Locke), then we must remember that the essences themselves are fixed by grammar. The proposition that red and green are discontinuous expresses those essences: '*Essence* is expressed by grammar' (*Inv.* §371). (See *Rem.* I, §105.)

We want to say: 'Given what we mean by "red" and "green" it follows that there can be no colour between red and green. If by "red" and "green" we mean these colours—the colour of blood and grass—then there cannot be a colour between them.' But that proposition is part of what gives the words 'red' and 'green' their familiar meanings. They have their meanings in our language-game with colours, and the proposition in question characterizes that language-game. Hence its truth or necessity cannot be said to derive from the meanings of 'red' and 'green'.

What we see on looking at a drop of blood and a blade of grass has nothing to do with what language we speak. But when somebody introduces the word 'red' or 'rouge' by pointing to a drop of blood, how we understand the pointing depends on what we already know. We can see what is meant only 'when the overall role of the word in language is clear' (*Inv.* §30). The pointing and the seeing cannot by themselves tell us how we are to use this and other colour words—what we are going to call simple colours and what mixed or composite, how we are going to compare colours, what is going to count as light and what as dark, etc. How we are to go on with our use of these words cannot be derived from or seen in what we see when we look at coloured objects. Grammatical propositions, which need never be formulated, set this out in words: how we are to go on in our use of colour words and the limits to what is permissible. They give content to the words we begin to teach children by pointing to coloured objects.

When we think of what we see on looking at blood and grass we find it impossible to imagine a colour intermediate to what we think or see—although we can easily imagine the continuous ripening of an apple turning from green through lime to yellow and then through orange to red.[7] We find it impossible to do so because thinking of what we see on looking at blood and grass is thinking within our language-game with colours. We cannot both remain within this language-game and imagine an inter- mediate colour—make sense of the expression 'a colour between red and green', or more briefly 'reddish green'. The grammatical propositions which characterize our language-game with colours, and so give content to our colour concepts, go together and form a system—though not a deductive one. Nest is the simile which Wittgenstein used in another connection (*Cert.* §225). While we hold fast to the nest we find it impossible to give up an individual proposition that forms part of the nest.

Giving it up means departing from our everyday language- game with colours. Much else, outside that language-game with which our familiar use of colour words is connected, holds it in place for us. To give it up would upset us in all sorts of ways since it would interfere with many procedures we carry on in our lives and find convenient. If we are imaginative we could, like Wittgenstein, imagine variations on our language- game with colours. But the further we depart from our actual language-game the greater becomes the possible changes we

[7] If we can walk in a straight line from A to B and again in a straight line from B to C, this does not mean that A, B and C lie in a straight line. Nor, in the above example, does it follow that the change from green to yellow is continuous (or in the same direction) with the one from yellow to red.

have to imagine outside that language-game if it is to make sense
to us. Soon it begins to lose sense; we are unable to fill the words,
sentences and behaviour we are imagining with personal content
—we find ourselves unable to understand the people we imagine
speaking these. What we are up against here are the limits of
our own language and life. These are not fixed once and for all
and can be extended bit by bit in different directions in different
ways—e.g. by contact with different cultures.

We are inclined to say that a reality corresponds to the
proposition that there is no such colour as reddish green.
Wittgenstein does not deny this; he points out that it does not
lie where we look for it.[8] What he denies is that the proposition
in question says anything like 'There is no substance that is both
magnetic and non-metallic' (see *Z.* §362). It is a rule of grammar;
but it has a 'basis' in 'very general facts of nature' (*Inv.* p. 230).
For instance, that given a certain training we proceed like *this*
and not like *that* in a new situation, that we get stuck in certain
cases and find it natural to go on in certain ways in others (*Z.*
§355). Given such orders as 'Bring me something whose colour
is between black and white, blue and red, red and yellow, red
and white, green and yellow' most of us would bring something
grey, purple, orange, pink and lime green. But asked to bring
something between red and green most of us get stuck. Asked
such questions as 'Which two colours is grey between? or purple?
orange? pink? lime green?' most of us answer 'black and white,
blue and red, red and yellow, red and white, yellow and green'.
With olive green, however, we get stuck. That given a certain
experience and education we are not willing to acknowledge
anything as a colour intermediate between red and green is a
fact that lies at the basis of our grammar of colours (*Z.* §359).
That we are not able to recognize straight off a colour that has
come about by mixing red and green as one that is produced in
that way is another such fact (*Z.* §365). That if we mix red and
green we get a dirty colour that is difficult to remember is yet
another one (Wittgenstein). We have here a mixture of facts—
facts about mixing paints as well as facts about us. These in
part explain why we speak about colours, compare and arrange

[8] 'Has nature nothing to say here? Indeed she has—but she makes
herself audible in another way' (*Z.* §364).

them in the way we do. But they neither justify that way of speaking, nor do they rule out of court the possibility of different language-games. ('I am not saying: if such-and-such facts of nature were different people would have different concepts—in the sense of an hypothesis'—*Inv.* p. 230).

I have mentioned facts about what we are inclined to say, how given a certain training we react naturally, as a matter of course, what we find easy to remember. These lie at the basis of our language-game with colours. I have also mentioned our use of colour concepts in the weave of different activities which we carry on in our lives. The grammar in which we speak of colours must have developed in harness with these other features of our life and language. We are not the arbiter of its various features. Thus the truth of propositions in which we remark on these features[9] is independent of our wishes and thoughts. They constitute the framework within which we think and so form the boundaries of what we find intelligible. If we have some freedom of choice regarding conventions, in the sense that we can reject or modify them at will, we must remember that the possibility of any choice presupposes a framework within which there are intelligible alternatives. Therefore the nest of grammatical propositions which bound an area of thought and language is not itself something that we can frame, choose, adopt or reject. We can at best play a part in modifying a small part of it—as with great innovations of thought in physics, mathematics and the arts. (Even then this happens only when much historical preparation that transcends any one individual has made it possible. Innovations, however deep going, presuppose a tradition within which they take place.)

When Wittgenstein said that rules of grammar are arbitrary he did not wish to suggest that they are man made in the way that rules of traffic or chess are—although some people have read him that way. He wanted to deny that it makes sense to justify rules of grammar:

One is tempted to justify rules of grammar by sentences like 'But there really are four primary colours.' And the saying that the rules of

[9] What 'truth' means here I shall examine in section IV below in connection with mathematical propositions.

grammar are arbitrary is directed against the possibility of this justification, which is constructed on the model of justifying a sentence by pointing to what verifies it (*Z.* §331).

One cannot compare grammar or grammatical propositions with an independent reality and find it adequate or inadequate to it. Certainly the sceptic is misled when he denies the existence of a reality that is independent of us—independent of what we think, wish and say. The propositions we assert, if they say anything, must be checkable against a reality that is independent of them. But that reality is not independent of the grammar within which those propositions are asserted and checked. The standards we employ in comparing them with reality come from the grammar in question; they belong to that grammar.

Thus while it is important to recognize that if we can assert a proposition to say something what makes it true or false is something that is independent of it, that reality is not independent of the grammar in which the proposition says what it says. One could say that the proposition has the same grammar as the reality with which it is compared. If that were different the proposition would say something different, something of a different order. Hence Wittgenstein characterizes propositions which are used to remark on features of this grammar as 'autonomous'. For they constitute the speaker's conception of reality —the reality against which those who speak the language measure the truth and adequacy of what they say. They state rules of the language-game in which the speakers communicate with each other; rules without which the language-game would be different. In this respect the rules are like those of a game: 'If you follow other rules than those of chess you are *playing another game*; and if you follow rules other than such-and-such ones, that does not mean you say something wrong, no, you are speaking of something else' (*Z.* §320).

So Wittgenstein contrasts them with what he calls 'empirical rules'—for instance, rules of cookery. The latter are not arbitrary in that what rules we develop, learn to follow, and consider best, depends on what we aim to achieve and on certain facts about cooking.[10] These aims are certainly intelligible apart from our

[10] In a sense this is true of the rules of chess too—though they are still

methods or rules of cooking. With speaking and rules of grammar it is otherwise. The speaker may have various aims—to communicate something, to express a feeling, to evoke a memory. But his aims come from the language with which he grew and which he now speaks. Without it he could not have those aims; they are not intelligible apart from the language: 'In so far as I do intend to construct a sentence in advance, that [intention] is made possible by the fact that I can speak the language in question' (*Inv.* §337). If a poet, for instance, *can* aim to communicate something, 'struggle with words and meanings', find what he writes unsatisfactory and rewrite his lines to improve them, there must be a language he speaks and a poetic tradition in which he writes. If he finds that his words and similes do not quite match what he aims to say, his standards of comparison come from the language. What it is possible for the poet or speaker to aim at saying is thus determined by the language he speaks, the grammar in which he tries to attain clarity of thought and adequacy or accuracy of expression: 'The rules of grammar may be called "arbitrary" [writes Wittgenstein] if that is to mean that the *aim* of the grammar is nothing but that of the language' (*Inv.* §497).

Propositions that are necessarily true are thus statements of rules of grammar. Given what we have already said or accepted what logically follows from it is determined by these rules in the way that the steps we take in developing a pattern are determined by the rule of the pattern. We may appeal to such rules in justifying steps in a deductive argument or calculation. But the rules cannot themselves be justified; nor do they need justifying. If anyone who speaks the language should ask that such a rule, or the proposition stating it, be justified it would be enough to show him how it is involved in the language he speaks. One could do this by means of examples. These would be intended to show him the role of the grammatical proposition in the language he speaks, and so what it comes to or *means*. Hence

---

different from rules of cookery: 'Is there nothing in the object of the game which determines these rules?' (Wittgenstein). Similarly for styles of painting: 'Is even our style of painting arbitrary? Can we choose one at pleasure? Is it a mere question of pleasing and ugly?' (*Inv.* p. 230).

one could still say, in the language of the *Tractatus*, that one recognizes its truth from the symbol alone, though what this means would be quite different now. For it is no longer thought of as an analytic proposition and there is nothing self-authenticating about its truth. Besides, 'from the symbol alone' would now mean 'from its use in the language'. Thirdly, in those cases where the rule introduces a new concept-formation we are not committed to it, and any 'proof' would have the character of 'persuasion'.[11]

I said that a man may not understand or recognize the statement of a grammatical rule (e.g. 'There is no such colour as reddish green' or 'There is no colour between red and green') and his reaction to it may take the form of asking for a justification: 'What makes you think that there is no such colour? Can you justify your claim that there is not?' The justification that we give him, if it can be called that, would consist of bringing out, by means of examples, that it is involved in the language he speaks. It is not a matter of providing him with reasons for accepting what he is reluctant to accept, but of showing that he does accept it. Hence Wittgenstein does not call it justification:

Logical inference is a transition that is justified if it follows a particular paradigm, and whose rightness is not dependent on anything else (*Rem.* V, §45).

The paradigm itself is not responsible to anything more fundamental, though it is involved in the way we do a great many things. This may explain why we treat it as unimpeachable, but it does not justify it.

In a logical inference the premises commit one who accepts them to a particular conclusion, and its justification is the process of bringing this out. But nothing in this sense commits one to rules of grammar or principles of inference. One accepts them in the sense that one learns to speak and to use words in certain ways. Nor does a language-game commit one to a grammar since taking part in the language-game *is* speaking in a particular

---

[11] I shall return to this point in section III below.

grammar. It isn't as if one who takes part in the language-game is unable to escape certain grammatical requirements. As Wittgenstein puts it:

Do not say 'one cannot', but say instead: 'it doesn't exist in this game'. Not: 'one can't castle in draughts' but—'there is no castling in draughts' . . . (*Z.* §134).

One can follow different rules, only then one would be 'speaking of something else' (*Z.* §320).

One might say that rules of grammar or the propositions which express them are not themselves necessary *in the same way* that the logical steps we take in a deductive argument are necessary. For they do not have a deductive justification; they determine what steps we take in particular cases but are not themselves determined by rules that are more general. But this would be to forget that what gives substance or content to any such rule are the logical steps that we take in innumerable cases. The inexorability of the rule is nothing but the inexorability which these steps have in particular cases for all those who speak the language.

When he compared rules of grammar with the rules of a game Wittgenstein did not mean to deny this inexorability. If anyone thought that he meant to deny it he would have said that the rules of chess are arbitrary in a way that rules of grammar are not, and in saying this he would not be going back on what he has said. As he put it: The rules of grammar are 'akin both to what is arbitrary and to what is non-arbitrary' (*Z.* §358). In fact he contrasted the rules of chess with the theory of chess (1939). Thus whereas one can modify the game of chess and play in accordance with different rules, if one played with the accepted rules then, for instance, one could not mate one's opponent with two knights. This is a necessary truth *within* chess, or better within the theory of chess, which takes for granted the rules of chess. It is fixed or determined, and is not in that sense arbitrary, in the way that each step in the development of a formal series is determined by the rule of progression. But, of course, there is nothing binding about the rules of chess themselves in the way there is about principles of inference or

M

mathematical axioms or other rules of grammar. Wittgenstein did not deny this; on the contrary he insisted on the contrast.[12]

So we have to ask: What makes rules of grammar and the steps we take in accordance with them inexorable for us? What makes the propositions in which they are stated necessary? In what respect are rules of grammar 'akin to what is non-arbitrary'? Wittgenstein's discussion of this question is very closely related to his later discussion in *On Certainty* of what makes propositions which have the form of empirical propositions but which belong to the 'scaffolding of our thought' *beyond question* for us. In both cases he insists that we regard them as unquestionable, indubitable, unassailable. That we regard *some* things in this way is part of speaking, reasoning and judging. *What* in particular we so regard is part of our natural history. It is *both* dependent on the kind of beings we are, the kind of environment in which we live, *and* also makes us the kind of beings we are. We do not *choose* what we are to regard as unassailable. As Wittgenstein puts it:

Thinking and inferring (like counting) is of course bounded for us, not by an arbitrary definition, but by natural limits corresponding to the body of what can be called the role of thinking and inferring in our life (*Rem.* I, §116).

In other words, what we regard as unassailable, what paths we follow in our calculations and deductions, the very character of the language we speak and the mathematics we develop, depend to a large extent on certain natural, matter-of-course reactions which we exhibit in particular situations—reactions that are widely shared among those who speak the same language. There is a two-way dependence between the language we speak and the kind of life we live and our culture. This means that what we regard as unquestionable and untouchable will *also* depend on the various activities that have a prominent place in our life, in the weave of which we use language,[13] and on the interests we develop in the context of these activities. In these

[12] See his criticisms of the formalist view of mathematics.

[13] For instance, the diverse connections in which we use colour concepts or mathematical concepts.

respects rules of grammar, principles of logic and mathematical axioms differ from rules of games, and they are akin to what is not arbitrary.

As early as 1939, contrasting chess with its theory, Wittgenstein said that the theory is not arbitrary in the sense that it has an obvious application; whereas chess does not. That's why it is a game.[14] In fact Wittgenstein constantly stresses the significance of the *application* of logic and mathematics for their very character:

> We should presumably not call it 'counting' if everyone said the numbers one after the other *anyhow*; but of course it is not simply a question of name. For what we call 'counting' is an important part of our life's activities. Counting and calculating are not—e.g.—simply a pastime. Counting (and that means: counting like *this*) is a technique that is employed daily in the most various operations of our lives. And that is why we learn to count as we do; . . . that is why it is inexorably insisted that we shall say 'two' after 'one', 'three' after 'two' and so on (*Rem.* I, §4).

If mathematics did not have an employment 'in civil life' then indeed it would be no more than a game or pastime, the various transitions and transformations within it would not have the force of calculation, mathematical propositions would not express necessary truths for us. It is not logical inference for me to make a change from one formation to another if these formations do not have a linguistic function apart from this transformation (*Rem.* IV, §2). Thus the formations or sentences do not merely occur in formal proofs and systems in which deductions are made from one to the other. They occur in contexts in which they are used to say something, and the deductions themselves are also carried out in such contexts. In other words the concepts which are mentioned in the rules which govern these deductions are used in propositions which are true or false (IV, §41) and the rules themselves have a use or linguistic function in 'civil life'.

It is this that enables us to refer to the statement of these

---

[14] Lectures on the Philosophy of Mathematics, Cambridge 1939. I am indebted to Rhees for letting me see his notes of these lectures.

rules as 'propositions' and to attribute 'truth' to them. They are thus at once rules of linguistic practice characterizing different language-games and also instruments of language used in those language-games—no more or less so than propositions that express contingent truths: they are 'a different part of speech' (III, §5). Their unfalsifiability is a matter of their role in our language and their necessity comes from our having come to depend on this role in so much of our talk and thought. Propositions which express necessary truths for us are grounded in the many activities we carry on in our lives—and also (as we have seen) in certain very general facts of nature which influence the form of these activities and the concepts we develop in connection with them. This is one reason why they are unassailable: they are so anchored in all our questions and answers that we cannot touch them (*Cert.* §103).

To be able to imagine any such proposition as false, to contemplate a different possibility, means giving up so much of what we take for granted in our understanding of anything that we find it impossible to do so. No doubt we succeed in formulating a sentence which would express an alternative to a necessary truth. But we fail to make any sense of it. As Wittgenstein puts it: We cannot fill it with personal content; we cannot really go along with it—personally, with our intelligence. He compares this with someone's inability to make sense of a particular sequence of notes, to sing it with expression. Such a man may say: 'I cannot *respond* to it' (*Rem.* I, §116). This sequence of notes goes against the grain of his whole understanding of music. To be able to sing it with expression he would have to give that up. But that would preclude his singing it, or any other sequence of notes, with expression. It is the same with the logical step I am trying to reverse, the grammatical proposition I am trying to imagine as false. For my intelligence is bound up with my commitment to the norms of intelligibility with which it belongs; and these go through most aspects of my life. When I try to reverse what is in question the whole mechanism of my understanding jams.

We cannot understand this by concentrating on the structure of a necessary proposition—as Wittgenstein did in the *Tractatus*. We have to consider their role, the way this goes through much of our lives, and their connection with other such propositions. Their role as rule, norm or method of description makes them unfalsifiable, invincible to facts, invulnerable to the challenge of the future. But this in itself does not explain our determination to give them this role, our inability to allow other propositions to take their place—even in our thinking. We have to understand *both* of these things if we are to understand what is meant by the *necessity* of a necessary proposition. I have argued that what makes the rules of the language-games we take part in inexorable for us, what makes the propositions that state these rules necessary, is to be found in the way these language-games are linked with each other into a natural language and enter into the many activities of our life, themselves connected with one another in many ways.

A proposition which is necessarily true is thus one which has a special position in our life and language. For different propositions to occupy such a position much in our life and language and, therefore, outlook and understanding would have to be different. Hence given our language, outlook, interests and matter-of-course reactions and also certain contingent features of the environment in which we live, we cannot countenance abandoning them and letting others occupy their place. It is here that the source of their necessity lies. The word 'must' expresses our inability to depart from a concept-formation. What holds the concept-formation fast for us is its employment in so much of our life and all those achievements in understanding bound up with it.

Wittgenstein says: When we say 'It *must* be like this' we see only one possibility (*Rem*. III, §31)—one that is internal to a particular concept-formation (V, §46). The concept-formation does not limit or shackle our understanding. On the contrary it makes what understanding we have of things possible. That what counts as a possibility for us depends on the life we live, the language we speak and so the concepts in terms of which we think about and comprehend things, does not mean that what we regard as logically possible and what as impossible is in any way subjective or man made. Neither our life and culture nor our language and concepts are our creations. It isn't even intelligible to suppose that any man or group of men should have invented or created them. Rather we are born into the life of a society where they are already in existence; we learn its language, assimilate its culture, and grow within their framework. There can be no independent understanding that could be shackled by any of this—which is not to say that there are no circumstances in which we can intelligibly speak of language or a tradition as having *become* like a cage or prison. But in those situations freedom would not mean an emancipation from language but the growth of language itself. Here we could have the revival of traditions, in literature, the arts and the sciences, even new concept-formations, to which gifted individuals contribute, but which gifts themselves presuppose a life and culture within which they develop and a heritage by which they are nourished.

III

Wittgenstein said that 'the mathematical Must is only another expression of the fact that mathematics forms concepts' (*Rem.* V, §46). He regarded mathematical propositions as giving us rules for the use of mathematical concepts which we employ in our thought and descriptions in innumerable situations.[15] These rules fix or determine the meanings of the words or expressions for these concepts. Pure mathematics is an enormous network of such rules and techniques for passing from rule to rule as well as for extending existing rules. It gives us an extremely attractive and convenient way of talking about all sorts of things and also at times induces us to modify current forms of description. It is, therefore, no more than a 'phraseology', which may be taken into language and change our ways of looking at things.

When I spoke of rules of grammar earlier I spoke of them as mnemonics which may be extracted from practices that constitute different language-games. Pure mathematics is itself a game (or a motley of games) in which transitions are made from rule to rule, old rules are developed, and new ones formulated. Hence the mathematical rules for the use of concepts that are employed outside mathematics have a certain autonomy, so to

[15] The case of mathematical concepts which have no such application raises questions which I shall not consider.

speak, in the sense that the game of mathematics can actually influence other language-games—though the reverse is equally true so that mathematical developments may be influenced by what happens outside mathematics. What I am trying to get at is that the mathematician does not merely do the sort of thing that a formal logician does—analysing forms of speech and linguistic expressions, formulating, classifying and arranging the rules we actually employ in our language. He also develops those rules, modifies them, and he makes up new ones; he plays a part in fashioning and refashioning our outlook on things. This activity is part of the established practice of pure mathematics.

Some mathematical propositions may in the first place have been suggested by observations and experience. But once, in the course of the development of knowledge, they are transformed into norms or rules they are thereby 'released from all responsibility in the face of experience' (*Rem.* III, §30). In this role no observation can contradict them since they give us a method for describing the observations we make in certain situations: 'If 2 and 2 apples add up to only 3 apples, i.e. if there are 3 apples there after I have put down two and again two, I don't say: "So after all 2 + 2 are not always 4"; but "Somehow one *must* have gone" ' (I, §156, italics mine). The 'must' here is an expression of the fact that mathematics forms concepts; it is an expression of my commitment to a particular concept-formation. That is to say, I use '2 + 2 = 4' not as an empirical proposition, as a description of what generally happens, but as a measure—a ruler against which I measure what actually happens in numerous situations so that I can see how they stand to each other in a quick and easy way. Hence in this situation there is for me something to look for, something to explain. I have not actually seen an apple disappear. Yet upon finding three I look for a fourth one. If the mathematical proposition had been an empirical generalization—(x) (2x + 2x = 4x)—I would also have to look for the fourth apple. But if I made sure that it hadn't disappeared I would have to admit that the generalization wasn't true in this case—and by further experimentation I might be able to restrict its scope.

If one said that '2 + 2 = 4' has *absolute generality* this would be misleading because it would suggest that the kind of generality it has is continuous with that of (x) (2x + 2x = 4x). Whereas the kind of generality '2 + 2 = 4' has is not a matter of how widely what it says is true. It is a matter of the inexorability with which we stick to it as a method of description, not making an exception to it in any situation—any situation where two pairs of things are counted or considered together. If in fact we find only three we say that one *must* have disappeared or that we *must* have miscounted. The 'must' here is an expression of our unwillingness to depart from the method of description in question. I do not mean that this is a piece of stubbornness on our part—as if we had alternative methods of description and simply refused to have anything to do with them. No, what is in question is 'an attitude towards the technique of calculation which comes out everywhere in our life'. This attitude is a feature of our life. 'The emphasis of the *must* [writes Wittgenstein] corresponds only to the inexorableness of this attitude both to the technique of calculating and to a host of related techniques' (*Rem.* V, §46). 'It is *we* that are inexorable in applying these laws' (I, §118).

I said earlier that there is a close parallel between what Wittgenstein says on the necessity of mathematical propositions and what he says in *On Certainty* on the invulnerability of propositions which have the form of empirical propositions but which belong to the 'scaffolding of our thought'. We take the latter for granted in our reasonings, we refuse to question them.[16] They are like the hinges on which our reasonings turn. Mathematical propositions too are like the hinges on which many of our reasonings on innumerable occasions turn. I am thinking of the *applications* of mathematics, not of pure mathematical reasoning. That there is such a thing as pure mathematical reasoning is, of course, important and interesting. It means that mathematical propositions do not all have the same status, that we can doubt a great many of them, that we may have to establish these latter, and that there is such a thing as making sure that they are true. This form of reasoning too revolves on certain truths that we regard as beyond question—for instance '2 + 2

---

[16] ' "But, if you are *certain*, isn't it that you are shutting your eyes in the face of doubt?"—They are shut' (*Inv.* p. 224).

= 4'. What distinguishes it from various kinds of empirical reasoning is that it establishes truths which are to be regarded as beyond question in other forms of reasoning. For the truths established are precisely those that are to be the hinges around which our non-mathematical reasonings revolve. It is this, their peculiar role outside mathematics, that makes them necessary: 'the fact that mathematics forms concepts' (V, §46) and that these concepts (or the words for them) 'have a meaning in non-necessary propositions' (IV, §42). The movements around these truths, outside mathematics, determine their immobility, make them invulnerable.

It may be thought that there is no need to bring in the application of mathematical propositions in elucidating their necessity: 'The propositions of arithmetic, say $2 + 2 = 4$, are members of a deductive system, and the reason why the falsity of $2 + 2 = 4$ is out of the question is simply that it is *inconsistent* with the truth of the other propositions.' But this offers no elucidation of the notion of necessity in mathematics. For it leaves unanswered the question of what makes the denial of one proposition in the system ($2 + 2 \neq 4$) inconsistent with any other (e.g. $2 + 8 = 10$). How is $2 + 2 = 5$ incompatible with $2 + 8 = 10$? It is easy at first to suppose that their incompatibility comes from the meanings we have assigned to the symbols in question. But what gives meaning to the symbols in these equations and others in the system? What do we mean when we say: 'If $2 + 2 = 4$ and the symbols "2" and "+" are used *in the same sense* in "$2 + 2 = x$" as they are in "$2 + 8 = 10$", then x must be 4'? What is it that gives sense to the phrase 'in the same sense' in the above statement?

One could say that neither the ostensive definition of '2', nor the formal definition '$2 = 1 + 1$', in itself settles whether or not $2 + 2 = 4$. Rhees says that neither says anything about the result of $2 + 2$ (*Discussions*, p. 112). This is the same as the point Wittgenstein makes in *Investigations* §185. The pupil he imagines has learned the meaning of '$x + 2$' where $x < 1000$. When he reaches 1000 he goes on 1004, 1008, 1012. On being admonished he anwers: 'Yes isn't it right? I thought that was how I was *meant* to do it'; 'But I went on in the same way.' That is not the way he was meant to go on. But what makes the way he did actually go on different from the way he was meant to go on? So far there is nothing inconsistent in the way he does go on—no inconsistency between 0, 2, 4, 6, 8 and 1000, 1004, 1008, 1012, 1016. A sense could be given to 'x + 2' in which what he writes down is correct; a sense could be given to his words 'but I went on in the same way' in which it is perfectly true that he did go on in the same way. This is not what *we* mean by 'x + 2', not what *we* mean by 'going on in the same way after 1000'. But what we mean lies in what we do, in what given a certain kind of training, such as Wittgenstein describes, we call 'the same' naturally, as a matter of course. Without this kind of agreement in deed or practice the words 'same' and 'consistent' are empty.

So if a philosopher says that if $2 = 1 + 1$ then provided that we use '+' and '2' in the same sense $2 + 2$ *must* give 4, there is much that he takes for granted—much that a discussion of logical and mathematical necessity needs to bring out into the open. For what is it that determines that '+' and '2' are used in the same sense in '$2 = 1 + 1$' and in '$2 + 2 = 4$'? The meaning of these symbols, the identity of their meaning in different equations, lies in what we do with them in arithmetic. The formal definition itself does not commit one who accepts it to agreeing that $2 + 2 = 4$. The commitment lies in the actual arithmetic as we have developed it and practise it. What gives content to its rules is what those who have been trained in it actually do in particular cases. If we do agree that $2 + 2 = 4$, as in fact we do, then we have extended the rule that $2 = 1 + 1$, we have taken a new step, developed the meaning of '2'. We have agreed, as we naturally do, that when we write down '$2 + 2 = 4$' we are using '+' and '2' in the same way as in the formal definition of '2'. This identity comes from the technique or practice; it does not give direction to the technique. The meaning of our arithmetical symbols is given by the arithmetic in which they are used. That is why Wittgenstein says that 'it is not possible to appeal to the meaning of the signs in arithmetic, because it is only arithmetic that gives them their meaning' (*Rem.* IV, §16).

It is worth emphasizing here that for Wittgenstein necessary propositions are not analytic. Mathematical propositions do not analyse the meanings of mathematical terms. They synthesize them. These meanings cannot 'be got out of their concepts by means of some kind of analysis' (III, §42). What is more they contribute to our vision of things in a way that what Locke called 'barely verbal propositions' do not. Hence Locke characterized them as 'trifling'. Mathematical propositions are far from being, in this sense, 'trifling'. But how do they contribute to our comprehension of things?

This is part of what Kant was seeking to understand when he asked: 'How are *a priori* synthetic judgments possible?' It is part of what Wisdom tried to understand when he asked: 'How can *a priori* reasoning (whether deductive or non-deductive) guide us in our apprehension of contingent truths?' Wittgenstein's answer with regard to mathematical reasoning is that it guides us in our apprehension of contingent truths by forming concepts —'and concepts help us to comprehend things' (V, §46). Mathematical reasoning can thus alter our apprehension of what we are considering. It can give us a new grasp of it: it can make us see something about it which we had not seen before. For instance, if I know that $26 \times 26 = 676$ then on having counted 676 nuts in a bag I shall know that I can arrange these nuts in 26 rows of 26 nuts. That equation will give me a new perspective on the nuts before me once I have counted them—just as when I know the amount of money in my pocket and the cost of the things I want to buy, upon performing a simple operation, I can see whether I have enough money to buy these things. I can *see* the money in my pocket *as* sufficient to buy such-and-such groceries. Our perspective on these situations is so familiar that we find it hard to imagine what it would be like if we had not developed the elementary techniques of arithmetic. (We could still have counted and compared different amounts of things, but without any simple way of doing so or any perspicuous way of representing these results.)

A mathematical proof, Wittgenstein argues, creates a new concept, or modifies an old one, it establishes a new paradigm of comparison, and through it opens up a new possibility, reveals a new aspect of things—one which may be important to us. It can make us see something in mathematics, a possibility, which is not at once obvious, or it can open up a new possibility—

'make new connections and create the concept of these connections' (II, §31). This in turn can make us see something new outside mathematics, through the application we make of it. But there is no sharp line between the first and second case. Let us consider examples.

The first one comes from Wittgenstein. We are given two congruent parallelograms and two congruent right triangles and are asked to fit them together into a rectangle. We juggle them about one way, then another, but to no avail. Then someone fits them together thus:

This position [writes Wittgenstein] is as it were excluded from space. As if there were e.g. a 'blind spot' in our brain here.—And *isn't* it like this when I believe I have tried all *possible* arrangements and have always passed this one by, as if bewitched?[17]

Can't we say: the figure which shews you the solution removes a blindness, or even changes your geometry? It as it were shews you a new dimension of space. (As if a fly were shewn the way out of the fly-bottle.) (I, §44).

The solution is extremely simple. But it doesn't occur to us to look for it where it is found. We do not expect to find it there. Hence it comes as a surprise (I, §69). Wittgenstein asks why we say that the figure which shows the solution to this puzzle makes us *realize* something any more than the one on the following page. For the latter figure too shows that two bits like that can fit together to make up a rectangle. ' "But that isn't interesting", we want to say. And why is it uninteresting?' (I, §70).

[17] When in the *Investigations* he speaks of the bewitchment of our intelligence by language (§109), when he speaks of a picture holding us captive (§115), what he is speaking of has a close affinity to what he is discussing here. It is no accident that in both cases he has used the simile of the fly in the fly-bottle (§308).

The answer, I think, is that there is nothing that makes us want to say 'impossible' before we see the solution. Secondly, the two bits that make up the rectangle do not connect with anything in our perception or experience. With the triangles and parallelograms it is otherwise. Their fitting together into a rectangle is like taking perfectly ordinary words and arranging them into a line of poetry. In both cases one comes up against a limitation in oneself, and one learns something. I am inclined to say: 'One knew a lot about these familiar figures; but not *this*. And what the proof teaches one is taken into one's concept of them.'

But was it not already in our concept of these figures? Here I would not like to press strongly for an answer Yes or No, except to point out that what is in our concept of them is to be seen in what we normally do with these figures, what we say about them, and our natural reactions to them. If the 'blind spot' in question is fairly common, then to that extent the proof that removes it may be said to change our concept.

Take the case of Pythagoras' proof that in a right triangle the square on the hypotenuse equals the sum of the squares on the other two sides. Presumably if, before Pythagoras, one had constructed squares on the three sides of right triangles and compared their areas one would have obtained results that come fairly near to what Pythagoras stated. But this does not mean to say that where in a particular case this did not turn out to be true one would refuse to count the triangle in question as a right triangle. This is what Pythagoras induced us to do with his proof. Hence this proof changed our concept of a right triangle.

The proof establishes a new connection between the sides and the angles: A right triangle is one in which this connection holds.

Where it does not hold, where $\sim (c^2 = a^2 + b^2)$, the angle formed by a and b cannot correctly be described as a right angle. Before the Pythagorean proof there was no such standard of correctness. To accept this proof means to refuse to accept certain measurements together as correct—for instance a = 3 inches, b = 4 inches, and c = 4.75 inches. We say: 'They *cannot* all be correct; one at least *must* be wrong.' So the proof gives us a new measure or criterion of what is and what is not a correct result here. Before the proof we had no such criterion. But that doesn't mean to say that we were blind or ignorant. (Hence Wittgenstein would say that the Pythagorean proof does not *explore* the essence of a right triangle; it expresses what is to be counted as belonging to its essence—i.e. what is going to be regarded as essential or necessary to a right triangle—*Rem*. I, §32. It 'creates *essence*' and what it creates is deposited 'among the paradigms of language'.)

Imagine a people who in the course of their lives often come across a great many-sided polygonal figures, never few-sided ones—so they can never take in the number of sides or angles at a glance and without counting. Sometimes they count the sides of such a figure and sometimes the angles, but very rarely both. They count them in the way they count a great many other things—which they count as *we* count them. After one of them has laboriously counted 157 sides to a polygon we ask him to tell us how many angles (or corners) it has. He counts the angles. This is the way they normally respond. Should we say that they are ignorant of certain facts of nature—certain facts about these common figures in their environment? That they have not made or noticed a correlation? Or should we say that they are ignorant of a geometrical truth, namely that an n-sided polygon has n angles? Or that their geometry is not as developed as ours, that their concept of a polygon is not quite the same as ours, in that the relation between its number of sides and angles is not fixed? (Is there any inherent impossibility in such a concept?)

We reason with one of them thus: Take a triangle which is the same kind of figure as you so often meet—it is a three-angled polygon. You can see at a glance that it has three sides. This is not an accident. An angle is formed by two lines meeting at a point. Therefore to make three angles you need 3 × 2 sides—

in other words 6 sides. But in a closed figure, such as a triangle, each angle has one line in common. That is each side figures twice in the constitution of an angle; it is used twice over in making an angle. Hence to form three angles only $\dfrac{3 \times 2}{2} = 3$ sides are needed. Therefore a closed figure with *three* angles can have no more and no less than *three* sides. Next take a four-angled figure—a square, rhombus or rectangle. Given again that each side figures twice in the constitution of an angle, to make up four angles you need no more and no less than $\dfrac{4 \times 2}{2}$ $= 4$ sides. With a pentagon, where you have five angles, you must have $\dfrac{5 \times 2}{2} = 5$ sides. For a hexagon . . . 6 sides, *and so on*. In other words, in *any* polygon the number of angles and the number of sides *must* be equal.

If these people go along with our reasoning, which may be called a proof, then if ever they need to know both the number of angles and the number of sides of a many-sided polygon they will find it sufficient to count either the sides or the angles— they will not count both as before. They can be said to have adopted a *new* method for determining how many sides and angles a many-sided polygon has. Our proof has thus changed their way of thinking about these figures. They had the concept of a polygon before we reasoned with them, but the equality of the number of sides and angles was not a part of it—as shown in their use of the concept, in their talk and behaviour. We did not extract what we got them to accept from *their* concept of a polygon; this was not implicit in their thinking. There need not have been anything inconsistent in their thinking or behaviour if they refused or were unable to go along with us.

For let us modify our example. These people do count, add and subtract, but only with an abacus. They express the number of the things they are concerned with as follows: 'There are as many soldiers as there are beads on the first row of the abacus.' 'There are as many more guests than seats as there are pots in the cupboard.' They do not have a pure arithmetic; they do not share the kind of theoretical interest that flourishes among us. They are not taught to count with care and each time they are interested in the number of anything it is for a 'rough' comparison.[18] Hence when the results of counting a group of things obtained by two people or on two different occasions diverges by a small number—by only a 'few' beads on the abacus—they consider both results correct. Such discrepancies are ignored; they make no difference to their actions.

Now if we tried our previous form of reasoning or proof on these people they would probably not be able to go along with it. And if one of them was able to follow every step and raise no objections, it would still be for him no more than a curious intellectual exercise. I don't think that he would see the force of our *must* in the conclusion we try to steer him to: 'In an n-sided polygon there *must* be no more and no less than n angles; and conversely in an n-angled polygon there *can* be no more and no less than n sides.' It is unlikely that our reasoning would induce him to accept a new measure, a new method for counting the sides or angles of polygonal figures. My point is that in the surroundings I have hinted at the kind of reasoning I have imagined turns into an exercise and the force of our *must* disappears. This links with the earlier point that nothing follows from definitions (e.g. $2 = 1 + 1$) until actual practice gives them content. That is why every new step (e.g. $2 + 2 = 4$) that we take is an extension of the definition and adds to its content: 'If $2 = 1 + 1$ then surely $2 + 2 = (1 + 1) + (1 + 1)$, and so $2 + 2$ *must* be 4.' Yes, but only within the practice. That is why Wittgenstein says that a proof makes a new connection—one that did not exist before. It induces us to go along with it. If the connection is taken into language—e.g. the language of mathematics—and is established in practice, it becomes binding. When we observe such a connection in our arguments or calculations we say that assuming that what we have been given in the premises or the statement of the problem is true, our conclusion *must* be true.

---

[18] I put 'rough' in inverted commas to indicate that it is a characterization that *we* would give. They would not say that their comparisons are only rough.

The fourth example I want to consider is the proof that $a^0 = 1$:

$$a^m \div a^m = a^m/a^m = 1$$
$$a^m \div a^m = a^{m-m} = a^0$$
$$\therefore a^0 = 1 \text{ for all values of } a$$

Here we have a piece of deductive reasoning, but it is used to give meaning to the expression 'a^x' in the particular case where $x = 0$. To be sure the expression 'a^x' does already have a meaning: 'an exponent x is the number of times an expression a is used as a factor'. Thus, on this definition, $a^3 = a.a.a$—where 'a' is used three times as a factor. Similarly for other values of x—$a^2 = a.a$, $a^1 = a$. But what about a^0? What would it be for 'a' to be used 0 times as a factor? This is not clear. So the definition does not help us to give sense to 'a^0'. What the proof does is to utilize existing rules governing the use of exponential expressions to make up a new rule, or at least to take a new step. There would be no inconsistency, however, if we refused to take this step. For to refuse to take it is to refuse to give a certain meaning to the rules of exponential operations: 'I didn't mean it like that' (*Inv.* §125). The rules do not have that meaning until it is the practice with us to take that step (see *Cert.* §139). (Hence Wittgenstein's remark that 'the further expansion of an irrational number is a further expansion of mathematics'—*Rem.* IV, §9.)

The point in question may be put as follows: A person may use certain words correctly to make statements but *never* draw certain inferences which those who speak the language normally draw. We can say that he does not recognize some of the implications of his words, that in that respect his understanding of their meaning is limited. The implications in question are there in the way these words are normally used. When he is shown them he comes to see something he had not recognized. We could even say that *his* concepts (or perhaps conceptions) change—for they did not quite coincide with those of the people who speak the language. If he had merely failed to take note of these implications on a particular occasion we could not say even this much. We could get him to recognize them by a piece of deductive reasoning. In mathematics this would take the form of a calculation.

In contrast, if neither he nor anyone speaking the language

N

ever drew these inferences, if this is not part of their practice, if it is not a move in their language-game, then we cannot say that they are all blind to or ignorant of certain implications or connections of meaning. For where could these exist except in their language-game, in their actual practice? What *we* 'see' in their concepts is the possibility of certain developments which may or may not be acceptable to them. It is not part of what *they* mean by the words for these concepts. The people I have imagined earlier have an arithmetic and a geometry, but these are not the same as ours although at points their geometry and ours coincide. What is more the geometry they have is not incomplete in the way that a deductive system that we develop— a well-established practice in formal logic and mathematics— may be incomplete.

In the present section of this chapter I have examined the relation between formal proofs, such as we have in mathematics, and concept formation. I have argued that such a proof makes a connection and induces us to make it part of our reasoning. It becomes binding only if it is actually taken into language. The step which the proof induces us to take may be a perfectly natural one in view of the rules and techniques we already use; but it is not one to which we are as yet committed. It becomes established by acquiring a role in mathematics so that other steps we take there come to depend on it and much mathematical reasoning begins to revolve around it. Or it does so by proving useful outside mathematics, in the application of certain mathematical techniques. We cannot understand the sense in which that step becomes binding on us, so that we speak of logical necessity, if we merely concentrate on the rule which determines it and leave out its role and position in the practices we have developed.

Wittgenstein asks us to look at a formal proof which a mathematician may discover not as a procedure which *compels* us, but rather as one which *guides* us: 'Can I say [he asks] that a proof induces us to make a certain decision, namely that of accepting a particular concept-formation?' (*Rem.* III, §30). If Wittgenstein speaks of 'decision' here we must remember that it is in a very *special* connection that he does so. He is not saying generally, as Mr. Dummett reads him, that the necessity of a necessary proposition or statement 'consists always in our having expressly decided to treat that very statement as unassailable'.[19] We have already seen that our decision to treat a statement as unassailable, or as a rule, would not be sufficient to make it binding; it would not explain the 'inexorability' of such a statement or proposition. The role of such a proposition as a rule, norm, or method of description makes it unfalsifiable, invincible to facts, but it does not explain our determination to give it this role, our inability to allow another proposition to take its place (see pp. 168–9 above). Even with a formal proof, whether or not we accept it, whether or not the proposition it introduces is going to express a necessary truth for us depends on developments within and outside mathematics. What developments take place there is largely determined by the present state of mathematics, by our use of mathematics in physics, engineering, statistics, etc., and by our other interests. We are not compelled to accept the conclusion of a formal proof in the way that we are compelled to accept the result of a calculation.[20] But that doesn't mean that we decide to accept it. No, much that we have accepted and can go along with makes it acceptable to us, or unacceptable, as the case may be. I imagined earlier a people whose life and culture makes unacceptable a proof that we accept. I tried to show that a decision to accept its conclusion is not singly open to them—and not because of any stupidity or ignorance on their part.

Decision plays only a very small part in the formation of concepts, and that part is confined to very special circumstances —where exceptionally gifted people initiate conceptual innovations. In all his later writings Wittgenstein insisted that what concepts we develop is conditioned on the one hand by the life we live and certain facts about our natural history and, on the other hand, by certain very general facts about nature (see *Inv.* II, xii). This is no less true of concept-formation in mathematics: 'A mathematician is always inventing new forms of description [new concepts]. Some, stimulated by practical needs, others, from aesthetic needs,—and yet others in a variety of ways' (*Rem.*

[19] Michael Dummett, 'Wittgenstein's Philosophy of Mathematics', *Wittgenstein, The Philosophical Investigations*, ed. George Pitcher, p. 426.

[20] Compelled in the sense that if the calculation is correct and we accept its premises we would be *inconsistent* if we rejected its result.

I, §166). Here instead of 'reasons for making a decision' it would be more appropriate to speak of an historical account of developments in mathematics. Such an account will make us see why we have developed these techniques, concepts and operations, and how, given other features of our life, these have grown out of others. It will not, of course, provide a justification of these techniques.

IV

In the *Tractatus* Wittgenstein had characterized propositions which express necessary truths as 'senseless'—they do not say anything. So he referred to them as pseudo-propositions. We have seen that he wanted to contrast them with empirical propositions and that he did not mean to deny their significance. He even suggested that mathematical propositions or equations play a useful role outside mathematics—in transitions from propositions that do not belong to mathematics to others that likewise do not belong to mathematics (6.211). In other words they are instruments of language.

This should not be taken to mean that they are 'mere instruments' of language. For empirical propositions too are instruments of language—though Wittgenstein did not speak of them in this way in the *Tractatus*. Later he contrasted their use: 'A proposition which it is supposed to be impossible to imagine as other than true has a different *function* from one for which this does not hold' (*Rem.* III, §4). There is no longer a need to characterize such a proposition as 'senseless'—which may wrongly suggest that when we say we understand a mathematical proposition we must be under an illusion.

To understand a mathematical proposition, where it is obviously correct and there is no question as to whether it hides a contradiction, is to accept it, or know it to be true, and be able to use it. To understand it, of course, one must be familiar with that part or branch of mathematics to which it belongs—which means that one must be able to carry out the relevant operations and do so not merely as in an exercise but in connection with actual problems. Where there is room for doubting whether or not a mathematical proposition hides a contradiction, to understand it is to be able to prove it.

But what does one do in proving it? One derives it from or reduces it to mathematical propositions which one does not doubt and in this way demonstrates its internal consistency. Doubting its truth and doubting its consistency mean the same thing. When it is in doubt, its sense or internal consistency and its truth are established by one and the same procedure, which means that the truth of a mathematical proposition is not anything over and above its sense. One who understands it knows it to be true. Showing it to be self-consistent *is* to establish its truth. When I speak of knowing it to be self-consistent I mean recognizing it oneself and being able to demonstrate it. One who can do so obviously knows how to use it—for what is being able to use it in mathematics but being able to carry out such derivations?

It may be objected that we can understand self-contradictory propositions in mathematics and that it is a mistake, therefore, to equate the sense of a mathematical proposition with self-consistency. It may be argued that we can understand mathematical propositions without knowing whether or not they are true: 'We may well understand the expressions on the two sides of the equality sign and we may know what it means to equate such expressions. Hence we can understand an equation, or a proposition which states it, prior to knowing whether it is true. Take, for instance, the mathematical statement that the three roots of the equation $x^3 + x^2 + x + 1 = 0$ are -1, $+ \sqrt{1}$, $- \sqrt{1}$—or 'if $x^3 + x^2 + x + 1 = 0$ then $x_1 = - 1$, $x_2 = + \sqrt{1}$, $x_3 = - \sqrt{1}$'. (This is in fact incorrect and the roots are $- 1$, $+ \sqrt{-1}$, $- \sqrt{-1}$.) Surely we understand what it is for an equation to have a certain number of roots, and what it is for these roots to be any number one cares to think of. The above proposition speaks about a particular equation and wrongly states its roots to be $- 1$, $\pm \sqrt{1}$. What it says is wrong and can be shown to be so; but we do understand it.'

There is, I think, something right about this objection, but also something wrong. It is true that if we understand differential equations we shall understand what it is for *any* such equation to have this or that for its roots—that is we shall understand the expression 'a differential equation whose roots are a, b and c, where a, b and c are given specific values'. This makes it seem that we can and do understand the suggestion that the above equation $(x^3 + x^2 + x + 1 = 0)$ has these specific roots, namely -1, $\pm \sqrt{1}$, even when we do not know it to be true, or know it to be mistaken. If, however, we ask ourselves what it would be for these to be really the roots of the equation in question we cannot say. We think it out, i.e. calculate, and see the suggestion to be nonsense.[21]

To be sure we may know or understand what it means for an equation of this form to have roots and we may know how to solve it. So there is a sense in which we understand the proposition in question in contrast with someone who knows nothing about such equations. It is in a language we understand. In this sense if someone knows how to check it, he understands the proposition. So it seems that here too, as in the case of empirical propositions, we can understand such a proposition even though we do not know whether or not it is true. But this is a mistake. For when we check it and find it to be false we also see that the particular suggestion makes no sense. If the checking is carried out more or less automatically and we keep the particular equation, so to speak, at a certain distance, especially where the checking operation is lengthy and complicated, we may think to ourselves that the checking operation could have turned out otherwise. But the moment we see clearly that it could not, we have to admit that we do not understand what it would be for the proposition in question to be true.

We can, of course, *suppose* a self-contradictory mathematical proposition to be true. We do so in *reductio ad absurdum* proofs. But it does not follow that we understand what we suppose. It is true that when we make an empirical conjecture, when we say 'Suppose that we were able to overcome gravity and walk on air' we must understand what we are supposing—what we suppose must be something intelligible. But this condition does not hold in the case of mathematical conjectures; the word 'suppose' is used differently in the context of a *reductio ad absurdum* proof.

---

[21] There is a parallel to this outside mathematics. Someone says something rather involved which strikes us as perfectly intelligible. But when we try to think out what he could have meant we find that we had not understood or even that there was nothing to understand—that what was said (uttered) makes no sense.

Where such expressions as 'suppose that two parallel lines were to meet' or 'suppose that there were more than one perpendicular from a given point to a particular line or plane' are used in geometry, we are not being asked to imagine what it would be like for this to be the case. We are simply asked to explore what sense the suggestion makes, if any—perhaps with a view to recognizing that it is absurd or has absurd consequences. This is how 'suppose that . . .' is used in mathematics. The fact that there is a use of the word 'suppose' in mathematics where it is followed by a self-contradictory expression does not imply that we can understand such expressions in mathematics and that we should not, therefore, equate intelligibility with self-consistency.[22]

On the other hand if we do equate them we run the risk of forgetting how much the sense of the formulae we can construct within a calculus is bound up with their application—with the fact that the calculus has a use.[23] Thus it would be best to say that while the self-consistency of a mathematical proposition, its being a member of a system, allows it to have sense, it is not sufficient for it to have sense. What gives it sense is its role in the many things we do.[24] As for its truth, this is not anything over and above its sense. What establishes the possibility of its sense (i.e. its self-consistency, its membership of a mathematical system) also establishes its truth. There is no further question whether it corresponds to a reality, or whether the system itself does so. That is not what 'true' means here.

The conclusion of a deductive argument is true if the premises are true. If we know the premises to be true but are not sure about the validity of the argument then we are equally unsure about the truth of the conclusion. What establishes the validity

[22] For a fuller discussion of this point see Alice Ambrose, 'Self-contradictory Suppositions', *Essays in Analysis*.

[23] I am not forgetting what I argued earlier, namely that we cannot make sense of the idea of consistency in separation from a practice. But one has to distinguish between a practice and its connection with other things we do, its role in those activities. It is the latter that is relevant to the sense of mathematical propositions.

[24] There are, of course, mathematical concepts and theorems for which there is no known application. What gives them sense is their connection with other concepts and theorems which have an application and the possibility that they may be given an application in the future.

of the argument also establishes the truth of its conclusion. What we have to look at in order to make sure that the conclusion and the premises are so connected that the argument is valid is *language*. There is no further question whether language itself is true or corresponds to facts. It is the same with an argument in pure mathematics. If the argument is correct and the premises from which it starts are true then the conclusion is true. If we are in doubt about the premises we try to prove them; and if we are in doubt about whether the argument is correct we try to check it. What makes the premises true and the argument valid is *mathematics*. There is no need to go outside it to make sure that the conclusion is true. There is no further question whether the mathematics we use in proving the premises or checking the validity of the argument is itself correct or trustworthy.

Both what makes the premises true here and what makes the argument valid is mathematics. Here lies the difference between an argument in pure mathematics and a formal argument from contingent truths to other contingent truths. In the latter case the truth of the premises cannot in the end be established formally; and where a contingent truth is known by deductive inference it can be known without such an inference. That is why we can and must distinguish between propositions which serve as premises in our arguments and the principles in accordance with which we reason and argue. In pure mathematics, however, there is no such distinction since what may serve as a premise in one argument will be a principle of inference in another. And if we refer to it as a premise in a particular case then we must not forget that what makes it true is not different in kind from what makes the argument valid. The real distinction here is not between premises and principles of inference, but between those principles which admit of proof and those whose proof would be 'a curious exercise, a sort of game'[25]—that is between 'theorems' and 'axioms'.

My main point is that whether or not there is any sense in proving it the *truth* of a mathematical proposition is wholly determined by mathematics, and there is no further question whether mathematics itself is true. Wittgenstein asks whether

[25] See Malcolm, 'Knowledge and Belief', *Knowledge and Certainty*, pp. 63–4.

there is not some truth corresponding to the sequence of numbers we follow when we count. His answer is that 'it can't be said of the series of natural numbers—any more than of our language— that it is true; but: that it is usable, and, above all, *it is used*' (*Rem.* I, §4). Language itself cannot be true or false; only what is said in language can be. If we speak of the relation between language and reality we are thinking of the possibility of what is said being true, the possibility of distinguishing between truth and falsity. Similarly for counting—and adding, subtracting, multiplying, dividing, weighing, differentiating, and so on.

The result we obtain when we count a group of objects may be true or false. But whether true or false, it has been obtained by counting—and that means counting like this. Is that correct or trustworthy? Are we right in counting as we do? Is what we call 'counting correctly' counting correctly? Is there not a justification for counting objects in the way we do? We have already seen that the idea of truth and falsity, the idea of an independent reality which one can investigate, measure, and speak about, and with which one's results and statements can accord or conflict, presuppose norms that one can maintain, rules that one can observe, methods that one can follow. The norms, rules, and methods cannot themselves be true or false, correspond to reality or fail to do so—though this does not mean that they are arbitrary.

Wittgenstein warns against the danger of giving a justification of our procedure, or a justification of the criteria for a correct move. The move itself is justified if it accords with the appropriate norms. But as for whether we are justified in counting as correct those moves that accord with them—there can be no such question (*Rem.* V, §45). We do call those moves correct; that is what we call counting—adding, weighing, etc. (II, §74). 'This is simply what we *do*. This is use and custom among us, or a fact of our natural history' (I, §63). But it is connected with much else that we do—it is 'an important part of our life's activities, a technique that is employed daily in the most various operations of our lives' (I, §4). It is part of what enables us to understand things as we do; it makes possible the kind of understanding we seek and achieve in various fields of inquiry. Hence Wittgenstein says that 'the *truth* is that counting has proved to pay' (I, §4).

This does not make Wittgenstein into a pragmatist. For the criteria of what makes our ways of counting and calculating practical, useful, or advantageous to us are internal to the life and language of which our mathematics is a part and to which it contributes. It isn't as if we have certain practical aims independently of the language we speak and the mathematics we use, and that our particular ways of calculating and counting happen to fulfil them. It is abundantly clear that Wittgenstein never thought so when he asked us to consider language and mathematics as instruments and when he argued that the possibility of sense and truth belong to language by virtue of the work it does.

The peculiarity of mathematics, as we have seen, is that it is a network of *norms*, a motley of techniques for developing new norms and establishing new connections. What gives these norms and techniques their reality, so that calculating is not merely a pastime, is their application. They do not correspond to some reality. We speak of *truth* in connection with these norms partly because there is a procedure of proving (most of) them, and partly because we accept and use them, and they serve us well—given the kind of life we live, our interests, and certain very general facts of nature. (This is not the only connection in which 'truth' carries no implication of any kind of correspondence with facts. There are other kinds of norms of which we mark our acceptance by characterizing them as true.)

SUMMARY

In the second part of this book I have been concerned with deductive reasoning. I tried to understand the nature of the steps we take when we reason deductively and the relation between the principles that govern these steps and the language we speak. I tried to do so through a discussion of difficulties and misunderstandings. I took Wittgenstein's remarks in the *Tractatus* as my starting point in each chapter. I attempted to understand what lies at the core of these remarks and in what sense, as Wittgenstein himself came to see, what he says in them is defective or limited. I also tried to appreciate how much of what he says here foreshadows what he said later and how his later discussions deepen and develop what is to be found in the *Tractatus*. The problems on which I concentrate are not, of course, the only ones in the field, nor are they the only ones that Wittgenstein discusses. There are others, some equally important, which I left out.

The problems I discuss here all centre around the idea of a deductive step or connection, the principles with which such steps agree and the propositions in which such connections are stated or expressed: In what sense are these steps taken and justified *a priori*? How is their validity dependent on nothing but the language in which we take them? In what way is knowing the principles which govern them nothing more than being able to draw logical inferences and judge their validity, being able to calculate and check one's conclusions? How is logical practice inseparable from the practice of using words intelligibly? In what sense are the results of a formal operation determined in advance and how is it that nothing that happens, no accidents, can upset them? What does it mean to speak of principles of formal reasoning as true? In what sense is their truth necessary and their falsehood unthinkable?

Chapter 8 starts with an elucidation of Wittgenstein's account

in the *Tractatus* of the sense in which deductive relations are
'connections of meaning' or 'internal relations'. Chapter 9
considers why there is no need to go outside or beyond the propositions that enter a formal inference in order to justify it. It
examines both Wittgenstein's view that the principles to which
we may appeal in justifying such an inference are tautologies, his
later view that they are rules of our language-games, and the
connection between these views. This later view is further examined in chapter 11, section II, when considering the inexorability of such rules, the necessity of the propositions in which
they are stated.

Chapter 10 starts with a consideration of Wittgenstein's
opposition to the idea that a necessary connection is a 'material
connection', that there must be a causal nexus to justify a
formal inference. I examine some of the confusions responsible
for this idea. I try to show how easy it is to confuse the kind of
reasoning which an engineer may carry out on paper in designing a machine and the kind of reasoning that leads him to make
predictions about the machine he has constructed. The relation
between the engineer's drawing and what it is intended to represent is an internal one, whereas that between the drawing and
the actual machine is not. The failure to distinguish between
these plays a large part in the impression that we can make a
formal inference 'from the existence of one situation to the
existence of another, entirely different situation' (5.135). What
the engineer infers formally is not how the machine will actually
move, but how it *ought* to move *if* its parts are 'perfectly rigid'.
We have seen that this rigidity is something he stipulates when
he designs the machine. It is a rule we follow in reading the
drawing and in our kinematic derivations. Hence the way the
successive positions of the parts of the machine in the diagram
are determined is like the way the successive numbers in a formal
series are determined. It is different from the way the successive
movements of the actual machine are determined. The latter
may be called 'causal determination', whereas in the former case
our results are determined by the rules we observe in reading
the drawing or diagram—rules which make the lines on paper
into a diagram.

Chapter 11 again takes its start from a consideration of the

Tractatus where section I examines how a formal operation determines all the possible values of a system or series thus fixing its limits or boundaries. It is a continuation of the discussion in the previous chapter—the kind of determination we have in a kinematic derivation or other calculation. Here I examine the sense in which accidents are excluded in a calculation and how a calculation or other formal operation differs from an experiment.

If one could accept Wittgenstein's truth-functional account of language one would have to admit that he managed to avoid a conception of logic that makes logic into a kind of ultra-physics without falling into any form of conventionalism. The line that he takes in his later writings confronts one who wishes to avoid conventionalism with difficulties greater than those Wittgenstein faced in the *Tractatus*. The question whether logic or grammar (not the same thing) is arbitrary is one of the questions in which Wittgenstein faces these difficulties. The second section of chapter 11 is partly a discussion of this question. It takes the grammatical proposition that there is no colour between red and green as an example and asks what makes it a *necessary* truth. I argue that if we wish to understand what makes it so we have to understand both its role as a rule, norm or method of description, so that it is unfalsifiable, and its position in connection with a great many things we say and do, so that we find it unthinkable to deny or reject it.

Section III turns to the example of mathematical propositions and considers the source of their necessity in the fact that mathematics forms concepts. I argue that the necessary truths of mathematics are not analytic and that they contribute to our comprehension of things through the concepts they synthesize. Mathematical reasoning guides us in our apprehension of contingent truths by forming concepts. I discuss the relation between formal proofs (such as we have in mathematics) and concept-formation by means of four examples. The differences between these examples are as important as their similarities. Here as elsewhere I don't believe that Wittgenstein was putting forward a theory. His general remarks about mathematics in general, and proof and concept-formation in particular, should be taken in the spirit in which they were given. Sections II and III continue the discussion started in chapter 10. There I had concentrated on the sense in which a rule determines the steps that I take when I observe the rule, which I contrasted with causal determination. This is obviously important for understanding what is meant by logical necessity. But there I said very little about the point of the kind of rule we follow in the example of the kinematic derivations I considered. Here I emphasize the significance of the *application* of logic and mathematics for their very character—for the necessity that is characteristic of the steps we take in our deductive reasonings and calculations. Also the fact that the rules of grammar, logic and mathematics form networks. In this way I supplement what I said in chapter 10 about the idea of a formal connection.

The final section of this chapter may be entitled 'sense and truth in mathematics'. It is not a full treatment of this topic, but meant to tie together some ends that were left loose in the previous sections.

In one sentence the second part of the book may be said to be about what sense, truth, necessity and justification mean in connection with deductive reasoning.

CHAPTER 12

CONCLUSION: PHILOSOPHY
AND LOGIC

I

Wittgenstein's chief interest was always in logic and mathematics, and he considered the study of logic to be fundamental to philosophy. His discussions in *Philosophical Investigations*, for instance, always gravitate towards questions in the philosophy of logic. Unless one sees how much these are at the centre of his interest one will miss much of what he says on other issues.

The kind of study of logic to which Wittgenstein devoted himself is one that aims at understanding questions like the following: What makes it possible to construct a formal system such as Russell and Whitehead constructed in *Principia Mathematica*? (see *Tract.* 5.555). What kind of relation is there between the principles of logic and the propositions that occur in our arguments? How is it that nothing actual can contradict any proposition of logic? What gives logical propositions the kind of generality they have? How are we to understand the kind of sway they have on our thoughts? We have studied some of these questions in the second part of this book (chapters 8–11) and have tried to appreciate Wittgenstein's contribution to their study. An investigation into questions of this sort is what I mean by a philosophical study of logic.

But the difference between a philosophical and a non-philosophical study of logic is not one of method and, of course, Russell too in *Principia Mathematica* was concerned with the nature of logic, although his work looked very much like a treatise in logic and mathematics. For in that work Russell and Whitehead are trying to formalize and to unify the whole of mathematical thought, to derive it from a few non-mathematical axioms, to prove that every part of it does follow logically from these axioms, and to remove any contradictions that may arise in it.

In this respect they may be said to be doing logic and mathematics, to be engaged in a logico-mathematical investigation.

Yet the motive-power of this whole venture comes from philosophy. It was, I think, largely with philosophical questions in mind that Russell and Whitehead embarked on this venture. Their aim was not to extend mathematics, nor to improve it for practical purposes. If they said that they were concerned to remove certain defects in mathematics, then we should remember that these were not defects which interfered with those using mathematics to solve problems. If one wishes to say that they made mathematical discoveries, then one should remember how these differ from other mathematical discoveries.

Russell himself stated this difference lucidly. He said that the difference between mathematics and mathematical philosophy does not lie in their subject-matter, not in the propositions with which each is concerned. Nor does it lie in their techniques. Mathematical philosophy, as Russell practised it, uses purely mathematical and logical techniques, but differs from ordinary mathematics in the direction in which it proceeds and in the interest which inspires the kind of research Russell carried out. The direction in which mathematics proceeds is 'constructive, towards gradually increasing complexity; from integers to fractions, real numbers, complex numbers; from addition and multiplication to differentiation and integration, and on to higher mathematics'. Mathematical philosophy proceeds in the opposite direction, 'by analysing, to greater and greater abstractness and logical simplicity; instead of asking what can be defined and deduced from what is assumed to begin with, we ask instead what more general ideas and principles can be found, in terms of which what was our starting point can be defined or deduced' (*Intro. to Math. Phil.* pp. 1–2).

Characteristically Russell regarded this as part of his programme of making philosophy 'scientific', 'precise' and non-speculative. In the preface to his *Introduction to Mathematical Philosophy* he says: 'Much of what is set forth in the following chapters is not properly to be called "philosophy", though the matters concerned were included in philosophy so long as no satisfactory science of them existed. The nature of infinity and continuity, for example, belonged in former days to philosophy, but belongs now to mathematics.' He means that these questions can be treated in a purely formal way and are susceptible of final and definite answers. Wittgenstein's way of thinking about these same questions in both the *Investigations* and *Remarks* were so different from Russell's, indeed so 'unmathematical', that Russell did not recognize that Wittgenstein continued to be concerned with the questions they had discussed together when Wittgenstein was a young man.

In what sense were Russell's formal researches inspired by philosophical interest and directed to philosophical difficulties? Russell says that many mathematicians learn certain techniques, which they employ with great skill, 'without troubling to inquire into its meaning or justifications' (*Intro. to Math. Phil.* p.194). It is well known that such questions as 'What does it *mean* to say that one is in pain?', 'What kind of reality does a mental image have?', 'What is the ultimate *justification* of our moral judgments and religious beliefs?', 'What are our reasons in the end for believing in the existence of the chair we sit on or the desk on which we write?', 'What are we really saying when we say of someone that he feels angry?', 'What kind of claim are we making when we say that what someone did was a shabby thing to do?'—these are philosophical questions. Philosophers who asked questions like these have often wanted to look for *deductive connections* between one kind of statement and another —for instance, between statements about chairs and tables and reports about our sense impressions, propositions about feelings and desires and descriptions of human behaviour, moral judgments and statements of fact. It often seemed to them that unless such a connection could be established they would be forced to admit that we cannot have any binding reason for the kind of judgment we constantly make.

What drove Russell to base mathematics deductively on non-mathematical logical propositions is very similar to what so often drives philosophers to look for deductive connections between one kind of proposition and another, to look for a deductive justification for the principles that govern various forms of reasoning. There is an additional feature in the case of mathematics which equally threatens to give rise to sceptical doubts: mathematical propositions hang together in a very special way

o

and are not independent of each other. Hence it seemed to
Russell that unless one can provide a general guarantee that it is
impossible to derive contradictory propositions from any one
or more of the 'fundamental' propositions of mathematics one
cannot be certain that one is ever calculating in using mathematics. His concern to prove that mathematical propositions
form a consistent system and his concern to prove that mathematics is finally indistinguishable from logic, therefore, stem
directly from his concern to meet philosophical scepticism. For
it seemed to Russell that unless mathematics is finally indistinguishable from logic one would have to admit that it is
arbitrary. Similarly it seemed to him that unless one can guarantee
that the different parts of mathematics will, under no circumstances, come into conflict with each other there is no denying
that they may be just *arbitrary* techniques. Thus the attempt to
found mathematics on logic and the attempt to prove it consistent are part of the same concern.

II

Speaking of the indistinguishability of logic and mathematics
Russell says :

The proof of their identity is, of course, a matter of detail: starting with
premises which would be universally admitted to belong to logic, and
arriving by deduction at results which as obviously belong to mathematics, we find that there is no point at which a sharp line can be
drawn, with logic to the left and mathematics to the right. If there are
still those who do not admit the identity of logic and mathematics, we
may challenge them to indicate at what point, in the successive definitions and deductions of *Principia Mathematica*, they consider that
logic ends and mathematics begins. It will then be obvious that any
answer must be quite arbitrary (*Intro. to Math. Phil.* pp. 194–5).

This is a typical case where it is claimed that a philosophical
conclusion has been proved by demonstrative arguments. It is
impressive, it seems incontrovertible: it seems that here we have
a philosophical conclusion which has really been proved demonstratively. So much so that it seems almost as if the conclusion
proved was all along a mathematical one. But this is not so, and

one can contest the philosophical conclusion for which Russell argued without contesting the mathematical proofs he gave.

One may ask: Is the reasoning we employ in solving arithmetical problems, for instance, the same as formal, deductive reasoning which involves no mathematical ideas, if it is established that the principles that govern the one and those that govern the other are deductively connected? Does deductive connection give an adequate criterion of identity? This is a question which Russell does not raise and to which he assumes the answer would be obviously in the affirmative. But this unspoken assumption can and must be questioned, and it cannot be investigated by the kind of deductive procedure employed by Russell. In other words, there is an important question about what it is that Russell's and Whitehead's proofs establish: Granted that one formula is shown to follow from another, what does this actually prove? That these formulae follow from those ones is perhaps unquestionable. But is Russell's conclusion about the identity of mathematics and logic itself unquestionable? I do not think so.

Put it this way. Perhaps Russell does succeed in showing that all mathematical procedures are in accordance with the rules of logic. All this means is that 'mathematics is a logical method' (*Tract.* 6.2, 6.234). As Wittgenstein puts it in the *Remarks*: '*So much is true about saying that mathematics is logic: its movement is within the rules of our language*' (I, §164). Does this mean that mathematical and non-mathematical deductive reasoning are identical? The answer to this question is by no means obvious. As Rhees once put it: The questions (i) whether you can show that all mathematical procedures are in accordance with the rules of logic, and (ii) whether the mathematics that we learn and use, all of it, is something which could have been developed from the principles of logic—these are quite different questions.

We have already seen that a man does not have to be a logician to be able to argue and to evaluate arguments; and he can do so even if he cannot formulate any general principles. It is enough that he speaks a language. For he will have learned logic as he learned to speak. But this is by no means sufficient for him to be able to count, add, subtract and multiply. These are techniques which he has to be taught directly. It is, I think, possible for people to be able to carry out such operations in various situations in their lives even though they have never heard of pure mathematics. Still these are specific operations which they will have learned in particular. As for the techniques of pure mathematics, competence in them are quite specialized skills. Whether or not a people need and develop such skills, or have any use for them, depends on the rest of their lives. How mathematics develop, what mathematical ideas come up during this development, is not something that can be determined by logic. It depends on the culture and interests that flourish in the surroundings which produce these developments. They cannot be foreseen in the way that the conclusion of a deductive argument can be. Thus while Russell and Whitehead may well have shown that all mathematical procedures are in accordance with the rules of logic, they did not show that our mathematics is something that could have developed from the principles of logic. The ideas and principles which Russell and Whitehead arrived at by analysis and from which they derived our mathematical ideas and principles are not logically more primitive than the ideas and principles which Russell and Whitehead based on them. It is what people actually do in mathematics that give them content and not the other way around as Russell and Whitehead thought. Their attempt to justify mathematics by deriving it from logic is, therefore, yet another instance of what Wittgenstein calls 'putting the cart before the horse'.

We have already studied this point in connection with the principles of inference which may be used to justify particular inferences (chapter 9). These principles, which are 'superfluous', are abstracted from the practice of drawing inferences and evaluating arguments. The axioms of *Principia Mathematica*, however, can hardly be said to be abstracted from mathematical practices. For they specifically do not contain any mathematical ideas. Besides, while the principles of inference which one finds in logic textbooks are superfluous, they are convenient and useful. They can help us to see whether a complicated deductive argument is valid or not, they can help us to exhibit the validity of such an argument in a way that is easy to take in. The axioms and proofs of *Principia Mathematica*, on the other hand, do not have any such practical role. As Professor Malcolm puts it:

There *can* be a demonstration that $2 + 2 = 4$. But a demonstration would be for me (and for any average person) only a curious exercise, a sort of *game* (*Knowledge and Certainty*, p. 63).

Of course Russell's and Whitehead's proofs are not games, and there is much in them worthy of a mathematician's admiration. Still the fact remains that they were constructed for philosophical reasons. Russell's and Whitehead's interest was not in their *outcome* (*Knowledge and Certainty*, p. 63, fn. 3). For what they proved is not less certain than the assumptions or axioms from which their proofs started. It is the reverse that is the case.

As I said, whether Russell's proofs are valid is one question and whether, if valid, they establish the identity of mathematics and logic is another question. Were it possible to identify mathematical reasoning with the rules that govern it, there would still be the question of the identity of the rules. Merely formulating them does not settle this question. For we must not forget that we have a multiplicity of rules and that what gives them content is what mathematicians do in particular cases. It follows that the fact that these rules can be deductively connected with others in which no mathematical ideas appear does not establish any identity between the forms of reasoning which are governed by them or which they characterize. Wittgenstein would say that the identity of a form of reasoning cannot be decided in separation from the kind of context in which it is exercised and the kind of activities into which it enters: it cannot be decided on purely formal grounds.

In any case, why were Russell and Whitehead so concerned to establish that mathematics is founded on logic? Briefly, because they thought that without such foundations mathematical techniques would be arbitrary, that their employment in particular cases would lack the force of calculation. We have seen that Wittgenstein questions this assumption and shows that what gives the use of these techniques the kind of force they have, what makes mathematical propositions express necessary truths, is to be sought elsewhere.

III

Can there be a deductive guarantee that the methods developed by mathematicians will not be upset by the appearance of some case for which they have not provided? To Russell it seemed that unless such a guarantee can be provided, unless it can be proved that what was for him the foundations of mathematics can *under no circumstances* lead to a contradiction, one has no right to trust mathematics. In *My Philosophical Development* he writes of how in 1901 he discovered a contradiction in mathematics. He explains there that it was a consideration of Cantor's proof that there is no greatest cardinal number that led him to this discovery.

Some classes, Russell explains, are not members of themselves, while some others are. For instance, the class of the books in this room (the example is his) is not another book in this room, but the class of things that are not books is itself one of the things that is not a book. Now take, says Russell, the class of classes that are not members of themselves. Is this class a member of itself? (A) If it is, then like the rest of its members, like the class of books, for instance, it must be a class that is not a member of itself. (B) If, on the other hand, it is not a member of itself, then it must lack the defining property of the class, and so it must be a member of itself. There are only these two alternatives, and each leads to its opposite. In other words, the class of classes that are not members of themselves can neither be a member of itself, nor not be a member of itself, and yet it must be one or the other. In short, it cannot be what it must be. This is paradoxical. The concept of a class of classes that are not members of themselves hides a contradiction. Yet here is a concept which is at the centre of Russell's account of number and therefore, according to Russell, one which occurs at the ground-level propositions which support the whole superstructure of mathematics.

Russell writes: 'I wrote to Frege about it, who replied that arithmetic was tottering. He was so disturbed by this that he gave up the attempt to deduce arithmetic from logic, to which, until then, his life had been mainly devoted. For my part, I felt that the trouble lay in logic rather than in mathematics and that it was logic which would have to be reformed.' Thus the theory of logical types (writes Russell) 'recommended itself to us in the first instance by its ability to solve certain contradictions'.[1]

There is one point on which Russell and Frege are in agreement, namely that the contradiction must be removed. Frege said that arithmetic was tottering; Russell thought that the contradictions, if not removed, would vitiate the whole of human reason. He thought that either they can be removed or universal scepticism is inescapable. In his later work Wittgenstein questions not only the formulation of this particular paradox[2] and the connection between the notions of class and number,[3] but the whole conception of logic and reasoning behind this view. In the *Investigations* he writes:

> It is the business of philosophy, not to resolve a contradiction by means of a mathematical or logico-mathematical discovery, but to make it possible for us to get a clear view of the state of mathematics that troubles us: the state of affairs *before* the contradiction is resolved.
>
> The fundamental fact here is that we lay down rules, a technique, for a game, and that then when we follow the rules, things do not turn out as we had assumed. That we are therefore as it were entangled in our own rules.
>
> This entanglement in our rules is what we want to understand.
>
> It throws light on our concept of *meaning* something. For in those cases things turn out otherwise than we had meant, foreseen. That is just what we say when, for example, a contradiction appears: 'I didn't mean it like that.'
>
> The civil status of a contradiction, or its status in civil life: there is the philosophical problem (§125).

This is not only a remark about philosophy, but also one about logic.

The desire for a general guarantee that the rules or principles in accordance with which we proceed when we calculate will *in*

---

[1] Second. Introduction to *Principia Mathematica*, Cambridge Paperback, p. 37.

[2] *Remarks* V, §29.

[3] In the *Tractatus* he had already questioned Russell's conception of number (see especially *Introduction to Mathematical Philosophy*, pp. 132–3) which requires the existence of aggregates and the Axiom of Infinity.

no circumstances lead to a contradiction, the desire to cope with every conceivable situation in advance and not to have to cope with difficulties as they come up—this is part of what Wittgenstein called 'a craving for generality'. He thought that the attempt to systematize logic in abstraction from the practical situations in which it is employed, of looking at logic in separation from the way the language we speak enters our lives in different situations, is misconceived. This way of looking at logic, exemplified by the mathematical logician, contains or encourages a misconception about the very nature of logic (see *Remarks* IV, §48).

It is this misconception which is at the centre of Wittgenstein's attention when in the *Investigations* he discusses how a rule or formula determines the steps taken by someone who is observing the rule or using the formula. He argued there that rules and formulae, and also gestures and definitions, examples and illustrations, hints and pictures, can always be meant and so taken or understood in a variety of ways. Hence the statement of a rule, a definition, cannot *itself* give us a criterion of the right way to act, the correct way to use the word: 'Does the sign-post leave no doubt open about the way I have to go? Does it shew which direction I am to take when I have passed it? But where is it said which way I am to follow it? And if there were, not a single sign-post, but a chain of adjacent ones or of chalk marks on the ground—is there only *one* way of interpreting them?' (*Inv.* §85). What determines which is the correct way of understanding a gesture, rule, or definition, is *general practice*. It is there that how the rule or definition is meant and so how it is to be taken is to be found. A particular person will be able to take part in the practice if he can be trained in certain ways—and that means if he naturally reacts or is brought to react as a matter of course to certain instructions, gestures and examples in ways which participants in the practice regard as being in agreement with their own reactions in similar situations. The important point for the moment is that it is the practice, founded on a consensus of reactions, that enables us to say of a person that he is following a particular rule, say, in arithmetic, that what he does at one step or on one occasion is consistent with what he does on another. It is this that enables us to distinguish between a correct and an incorrect procedure; such words as 'correct' and 'consistent', such notions as accordance and conflict, mean nothing apart from an established way of doing things: 'A person goes by a sign-post only in so far as there exists a regular use of sign-posts, a custom' (§198). In short, what people confronted by a sign-post or formula *actually do in particular cases* determines what the sign-post says, what the formula means: 'Not only rules, but also examples are needed for establishing a practice. Our rules leave loop-holes open, and the practice has to speak for itself' (*On Certainty*, §139).

Derivations in accordance with a formula is an abstract and mechanical procedure. But what are and what are not correct derivations—this is determined *in the end* by what people do in particular situations. The lines followed mechanically by a purely formal, abstract procedure cannot overreach actual practice. A proof, an abstract procedure, can lay down 'new tracks' along which the practice may be extended. But there is no compulsion on the practice to develop just this way, in just this direction. To put it differently, if people did not actually, in their lives, actions and speech, follow the lines suggested by such an abstract procedure there would be no grounds for saying that they were not being true to their commitments. It could not be said that they were being inconsistent with any part or feature of their practices in refusing to follow the guide lines suggested by this purely formal procedure. For, as we noted, the notions of consistency, necessity and commitment have sense only within an established way of doing things. The meaning which the formal logician gives to words and symbols which are used in certain ways by people in certain situations in drawing inferences which take him beyond actual use is *not* the only possible meaning that could be seen in or given to these words and symbols and the rules which govern their use. The people who use them can always tell the formal logician that they 'didn't mean them like that'.

So if by a purely deductive procedure a contradiction were derived from the rules in accordance with which we reason this need not show that there is anything wrong with these rules. As Wittgenstein puts it: 'The sign-post is in order—if, under normal circumstances, it fulfils its purpose' (*Inv.* §87). The point is that you cannot talk of whether or not the sign-post is in order in separation from the circumstances in which it is used and what role it plays there. To elaborate an example of Wittgenstein (*Remarks* II, §79): If someone asks you the way to the hospital, you may point to the right or to the left according to which way the hospital lies. But if you were to point both to the right and to the left he would not know which way to go. We would say that the directions you had given him were contradictory. But if the street were circular then these would be alternative directions and they would not contradict each other. Whether or not they are contradictory, whether or not we should avoid pointing both to the right and to the left in answer to the question 'Which is the way to the hospital?', depends on the circumstances.

This is equally true of the rules of logic. The formal logician needs to be reminded that 'it is for practical, not for theoretical purposes, that the disorder is avoided' (*Remarks* II, §83). That is why Wittgenstein directs the philosopher's attention to 'the civil status of a contradiction'. Here we should not forget that the contradictions in question are not contradictions in an argument, but contradictions generated by the principles of logic. Such a contradiction can be 'sealed off' (II, §80), if we actually come upon it, by specifying that the principles or rules in question are not meant to be taken in that way.

We have already seen that the meaning of any rule lies in the practice in which it is observed. If we think that we can and must 'seal off' every possible disorder or contradiction, we have once more given way to that 'craving for generality' which Wittgenstein was combating. We should, therefore, ask ourselves what 'every possible disorder' could mean here. As Wittgenstein puts it very succinctly:

> If I had to fear that something somehow might at some time be interpreted as the construction of a contradiction, then no proof can take this indefinite fear from me.
> The fence that I put round contradiction is not a super-fence (*Remarks* II, §87). (Also see *On Certainty* §§26–7.)

In the *Investigations* Wittgenstein wrote: 'That is not to say that we are in doubt because it is possible for us to *imagine* a doubt' (§84). Similarly one could say: That is not to say that the mathematics we use or our logic is defective because it is possible to imagine a contradiction, i.e. to derive one from its rules in a purely abstract manner.[4] The possibility of such a contradiction is not anything we could remove or need to fear: 'It is not the eternal correctness of the calculus that is supposed to be assured, but only, so to speak, the temporal' (*Remarks* II, §84).

The problem, as Russell saw it, was *how to reform logic* so as to make it consistent, so as to remove the contradictions he came upon in the course of his work. This is a problem in mathematical logic.[5] What makes it of philosophical interest is that the impetus to reform logic comes from a certain conception of logic. It is *this* conception which Wittgenstein was concerned to change.[6] It is this conception which is behind Russell's philosophical problem—namely how scepticism is to be met. He thinks that it could be met by removing the contradiction. This, in turn, is a mathematical problem. Wittgenstein, on the other hand, suggests that if one took a different conception of logic, if one gave up the habit of 'looking at language without looking at the language-game', one would see that there is no need to worry as Russell did. In other words, the scepticism which Russell wanted to counter comes from a misconception of logic, from a 'misunderstanding of the logic of language'[7]—a misunderstanding concerning the relation between logic and language. So the scepticism in question will be met not by reforming logic, but by removing the misconception.

Removing such misconceptions means coming to a better understanding of the nature of logic. This is the sort of study of logic that is at the centre of Wittgenstein's interest. Such a study, as we have seen, cannot be pursued in a purely formal and abstract manner. Equally important, I submit, is the fact that the questions that such a study investigates are those which a deep investigation of almost *any* philosophical question is bound to bring us up against. It is in this sense, I believe, that a study of logic is fundamental in philosophy. Hence Wittgenstein's interest in logic and mathematics was not just an interest that he

---

[4] See *On Certainty* §392. [5] See *Remarks* V, §16.
[6] See *Remarks* II, §82. [7] *Investigations* §93.

happened to have. In it we have a measure of the depth of his interest in philosophy. In fact, Wittgenstein's interest in logic and mathematics and his interest in man and in human life and culture interpenetrate one another. When one sees the kind of interest he had in logic one will not find this surprising.

APPENDIX
RULES AND LANGUAGE

A mark that is written down or a sound that is uttered without any regularity or consistency is not a word and means nothing. The primitive idea that a word has meaning by its attachment to an object makes us think that it is the object which secures the consistency with which it is used. As Wittgenstein puts it in *Zettel*: One may ask, 'How do I manage always to use a word correctly—i.e. significantly?' and one may be tempted to answer, 'The fact that I mean something—the thing I mean, prevents me from talking nonsense' (§297). He argued that the truth is the reverse of what we are inclined to think. It is the consistency with which a word is uttered that enables it to attach to or signify anything at all. The particular way in which it is used determines what it means.

We tend to think of words as names and of names as labels that we attach to different things. We learn to attach words to objects classified in different ways—in accordance with their shape, use, colour, chemical analysis, etc. Thus we learn to use the word 'red' because we can tell that blood, pillar boxes and telephone booths are *the same* colour. We can see the similarity between them. But when, as children, we learn to speak, how do we know what similarities are in question when we are introduced to a new word? Perhaps our teacher points to a red object and utters the word 'red'. It is no use for him to say that he means the *colour* of the object. For that presupposes that we know the meaning of other colour words, only not this one. So the question arises what it means to point to the colours of things, to give names to their colours, to compare things with respect to their colour. If we think of a name as a label we may forget the enormous amount of stage-setting in the language that is pre-supposed when we successfully attach it to anything, when we are able to attach it to the same kind of thing on different occasions.

This is what Wittgenstein brings into prominence in his idea of a language-game: A word can only have meaning, a name can only signify what it does, in a language-game—and that means in connection with other words and expressions, in the course of certain activities where it has a role. It can only name the same thing on different occasions in the surroundings that are part of a language-game. A person cannot understand what it means until he is familiar with the language-game it enters. You may be able to teach him what it means by pointing to examples. But such teaching will achieve its purpose only when 'the overall role of the word in language is clear' (*Inv.* §29). The word, if it means anything, must have a place in our life, a position in certain activities in which we engage. This is what Wittgenstein means by its *grammar*. His concern with grammar is his concern with this common understanding—this understanding we share with people whose language we share and from whom we can learn. A word's use is one of the various activities that constitutes a language-game; these are as much part of the language-game as is the utterance of the word. They provide the post at which a word is stationed and thus both underlie the possibility of its having a meaning at all and delimit the kind of meaning it has—i.e. the kind of thing that we can intelligibly say with it. If we leave them out we cannot give a satisfactory account of what it means for a word to have the same meaning or to be meant in the same way on different occasions.

We can see this more clearly in the case of words whose meaning we think can be given in separation from the surroundings in which they are normally used. Take colour words, for instance. We are inclined to think that what we see when we look at red objects is sufficient to determine what we mean by 'red'. What do you mean by 'red'? This—pointing to a drop of blood. But what if the colour impression I have when I look at it is different—perhaps green? If I consistently see green where others see red, then presumably when I say 'red' I would mean green. And if we were each to get different colour impressions when we look at the same things and came to attach the same colour word to them, we would each attach a different meaning to the same word. Yet we would never know this. When someone said that blood is red, for instance, we would take it that he means what we mean when we say this. We would never be able to find out that each of us sees colours differently, because we agree both in the words we use and in our reactions. One driver would stop when he saw red, another when he saw green, and each would say that they stop when the traffic light is red. We cannot know that this is not so. For all we know it may be.

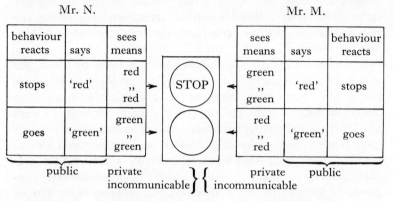

The idea is that in each case what is seen is private, what is meant incommunicable, and it is only contingently tied up with utterances and behaviour. So we say: 'When M looks at a red object he sees *the same* as N sees when he (N) looks at a green object. When M says "red" he means *the same* as N means when he (N) says "green". When they look at the same object (the stop light) and say "red", each sees a *different* colour and means a *different* colour.'

What we do not ask ourselves is whether these comparisons are even intelligible: If I can never carry out such comparisons, if I cannot know whether someone else sees red (and not another colour) when he looks at the stop light, if I cannot understand what he means when he calls it red, how can I understand what it would be for him to see the same colour as I see, or a different one? How can I understand what it would be for him to mean the same colour, or a different one? If it is impossible for me to make such comparisons how can I understand what it would be like to make them? How can I even have the idea of such comparisons? How can I attach any sense to 'same' and 'different'?

If we can and do in fact understand such comparisons, that is because the language of colours is a public language—what each of us means by colour words is not merely contingently connected with what other people say and do when we use particular colour words. There is an overwhelming agreement in what colour words we use on particular occasions and on how we react to colours. This is part of a common form of life in which our criteria of meaning and identity, and our norms of comparison are embedded. Because there is general agreement in what we say and do, we can disagree on a particular occasion and one of us may be mistaken.

'He took off his glasses and we saw the same colours.' 'He and I see a different colour when we look at this—he is colour blind.' 'We both said "magenta" and thought that we were talking about the same colour, but it turned out that we were not.' If these judgments have sense that is because we agree on a great many occasions, because there is such a thing as a normal reaction with which what we mean by 'red', 'green' and 'blue' is connected. Sever that connection and the comparisons and judgments of identity in terms of which our problem is set can no longer be given an intelligible content.

Neither can a person make comparisons which he alone can understand. For instance, he says to himself 'This is blue.' The claim is that the present colour impression is the same as the ones he had in the past when he called things blue. Unless this is so the word 'blue' means nothing. But what does its being the same mean here other than it seeming so to him? Unless it can mean something more whatever seems to him to be the same colour as what he called blue on a past occasion will be correctly describable as blue. This, however, only means that here we cannot talk of the *correct* application of the word (*Inv.* §258). And neither can he. He is not justified even before himself to call what he sees blue. For there is nothing outside his impressions, nothing independent of how things *seem* to him, to which he can appeal. Therefore his colour words cannot have a regular or consistent use, only at best one that seems so to him. The rules that govern them are no more than *impressions* of rules (§259).

Let me put it differently. If I mean anything by 'green' I must mean the same thing each time I say 'This is green.' But if each time I look at a leaf and say 'This is green' I could not know that it hadn't changed colour then neither can I know that I kept the meaning of the word 'green' constant. Of course I can know whether the leaves on the tree in my garden are the same colour as they were yesterday, or whether the curtains I hung up at the beginning of the summer have faded. I may remember them as being a darker blue than they are now. The possibility of my knowing this is inseparable from the possibility of its seeming so to me when in fact it isn't so. I mean that if I can know this then it must be possible for me to be mistaken. Thus I may remember them as being a darker blue than they are now; I may think that the curtains have faded when in fact they have not and it is my memory that is at fault. If this could be the case, as clearly it can, then I can have evidence independent of my memory. I can, for instance, ask my wife or the shop-keeper from whom I bought the material or compare the curtains with the rest of the roll that never left the shop. Even here I can be mistaken, which presupposes that others may have better eyes or can correct me by the use of instruments. But if none of these things bear on the question whether what I see now is the same colour as what I saw on another occasion, then surely my saying that it is means no more than that it *seems* so to me. In other words, there is nothing to guarantee that I am using the words 'blue' and 'green' consistently. In that case do I really mean anything by them?

Wittgenstein's discussion of whether one can understand something which cannot be said in a language that anyone else can understand, whether one can attach any sense to the words 'red' or 'pain' independently of the language we all speak and understand, is part of his discussion of the relation between words and behaviour, language and life.[1] This relation is an important part of what his idea of language-games was meant to bring into prominence. Naming, referring, meaning, using a word in the same sense on different occasions, presuppose an established practice with words in which people living together take part; a sentence is meaningful only in the traffic of human life.

[1] It is not, as many people have read it, a discussion of the problem of other minds.

P

If you want to understand what a word means consider its use. This means bringing into focus the circumstances in which it is used. Just as if you want to know what it means to mate one's opponent in chess you have to think of that last move in relation to the whole game (§316). Wittgenstein means to compare using a word or sentence with moves in a game. The move is a move in the game, and likewise a word or utterance has its identity in a language-game. What moves are possible in a game is determined by the rules of the game. The meanings of words too are fixed by rules. Grasping a definition, understanding what is said, using a word to say something, all involve the ability to follow rules.

Yet this does not mean that we should be able to give or formulate a rule for every word we understand and can use correctly. Nor, of course, do we learn new words by being given rules and definitions. As Wittgenstein puts it in connection with calculating—multiplying for instance: 'We did not learn this through a rule, but by learning to calculate . . . But then can't it be described how we satisfy ourselves of the reliability of a calculation? O yes! Yet no rule emerges when we do so.' He adds that 'the rule is not needed' (*Cert.* §§43–6). He says elsewhere that 'there may be such a language-game as "continuing a series of digits" in which no rule, no expression of a rule is ever given, but learning happens *only* through examples' (*Z.* §295). Even a game 'can be learned purely practically, without learning any explicit rules' (*Cert.* §95). But still he says: 'We do calculate according to a rule' (*Cert.* §46). His point is that it makes sense to say such a thing as 'What I did here is *the same* as what I did there' and that this is something I can teach other people.

Even where we are given rules, or are taught by rules and definitions, it is what people actually do in particular cases that gives content to these; and learning to follow a rule or keep a definition is learning in what circumstances and connections one can use the word in question to say something true. One normally learns this by means of examples. There is a point at which examples are indispensable. In teaching elementary techniques of arithmetic, for instance, the teacher can only show the pupil the right continuation of series (e.g. in counting) *in examples*.

He cannot yet use any expression of the law of the series. But in doing so he is 'forming a substratum for the meaning of algebraic rules or what is like them' (*Z.* §300). Later it may be possible for the pupil to learn to develop new series by means of rules. It is the same with words and definitions. Once one is off the ground so to speak, rules and definitions may come into the teaching, though there is *no need* for them to come in at all even then. One can imagine a people who learn to continue different series *only* through examples and to whom the idea of justifying individual steps by something like a rule or pattern is quite alien (*Z.* §295). But, in any case, whether or not rules come into the instructions we receive, they *cannot* take us off the ground: 'At *this* level the expression of the rule is explained by the value [i.e. what is the correct thing to write down or say *here* and *here* and *here*], not the value by the rule. For just where one says "But don't you *see* . . .?" the rule is no use, it is what is explained, not what does the explaining' (*Z.* §§301–2). This is where Wittgenstein speaks of *training*: we simply learn to do what we are told as in a drill—without question. We learn if in the end we can grasp what we are meant to do without reason or explanation, if the examples in which this is exhibited speak to us directly.

When Wittgenstein speaks of rules in connection with the use of words he is not thinking of the kind of rules we have in arithmetic. Certainly he did not think of language as a family of techniques. He says explicitly that learning to speak about people's character, feelings and motives, for instance, is not acquiring a technique. One is learning correct judgments. Still he does not deny that there are rules here: 'There are also rules, but they do not form a system, and only experienced people can apply them right. Unlike calculating-rules' (*Inv.* p. 227). This is given greater prominence in *On Certainty*: 'We do not learn the practice of making empirical judgments by learning rules: we are taught judgments and their connection with other judgments' (§139).

Speaking, of course, is not merely following rules—as in constructing sentences in an exercise. Even doing sums is more than this. Wittgenstein certainly never thought otherwise. Nor is learning to speak learning to behave as other people do, as in learning a skill—learning to drive in traffic for instance. A child who learns to speak learns to *say* things. His having something to say (for himself) is bound up with what he learns. He learns to ask questions, to investigate, evaluate, criticize and respond to criticism, learning to do so in ever newer connections. He learns whole ways of doing things and meeting eventualities that may arise in the course of these activities. He learns to relate himself to people who take part in them. But above all when he learns to speak he can bring something new to the conversations and discussions he has with people. In the questions he asks, for instance, or the comments or jokes he makes. This is part of learning to speak.[2] Without it we should be no more than parrots; we should not grow in the process of acquiring a language. Whereas our whole intellectual, emotional and moral development is made possible by our ability to take part in linguistic intercourse.

If Wittgenstein stressed the importance of acquiring skills and habits in the learning of language that is because he was thinking of the learning of what underlies the possibility of asking questions and understanding explanations. But he never thought that the learning of language could be confined to this. If there is something in language that we begin to learn by rote, almost like an animal, there is much in connection with speaking, thinking and expressing ourselves that goes beyond what can be learnt in this way. Consider the development of judgment, imagination and talent in the use of language in literature, for instance, or in scientific research, or in human relationships.

Wittgenstein emphasized the importance of rules in connection with the use of words because he wanted to bring into prominence the way in which the distinction between using words correctly and incorrectly underlies the possibility of using them to say something. Because he wanted to show that apart from a consistent use of words there can be no meaning. It was this that turned his attention to the relation between words and behaviour. For it is what people do and the agreement in what they do that gives meaning to rules. His attempt to oppose the tendency to think of meaning as something private—some-

---

[2] See Rhees on 'having something to say'—'Wittgenstein's Builders', *Discussions*, pp. 80–1.

thing that each person can determine regardless of whether others can understand it or not, something that can be confined to a particular occasion—is part of this discussion.

BIBLIOGRAPHY

AMBROSE-LAZEROWITZ, Alice, *Essays in Analysis*, Allen and Unwin 1966
CARROLL, Lewis, 'What the Tortoise said to Achilles', *Complete Works*, Nonesuch Press
EINSTEIN and INFELD, *The Evolution of Physics*, Cambridge 1947
HUME, David, *An Inquiry Concerning Human Understanding*, New York 1955—*Inq.*
MACH, Ernst, 'On the Principle of Comparison in Physics', *Popular Scientific Lectures*, trans. Thomas J. McCormack, Chicago, Open Court 1898
MALCOLM, Norman, 'Knowledge and Belief', *Knowledge and Certainty*, Prentice-Hall 1965
——*Ludwig Wittgenstein: A Memoir*, Oxford 1967
——'Wittgenstein on the Nature of Mind', *Studies in the Theory of Knowledge*, ed. Nicholas Rescher, Amer. Phil. Quart. Monograph Series No. 4, Blackwell 1970
MOORE, G. E., 'Certainty', *Philosophical Papers*, Allen and Unwin 1963
RHEES, Rush, *Discussions of Wittgenstein*, Routledge 1970
——*Without Answers*, Routledge 1970
RUSSELL, Bertrand, *Introduction to Mathematical Philosophy*, Allen and Unwin 1963
——*The Problems of Philosophy*, Oxford 1950
——*My Philosophical Development*, Allen and Unwin 1959
RUSSELL and WHITEHEAD, *Principia Mathematica to* $*56$, Cambridge 1964—*P.M.*
TOULMIN, Stephen, *The Philosophy of Science, An Introduction*, Hutchinsons 1955—*P.S.*
WISDOM, John, *Other Minds*, Blackwell 1952—*O.M.*
——*Philosophy and Psycho-Analysis*, Blackwell 1964—*P.P.A.*
——*Paradox and Discovery*, Blackwell 1965—*P.D.*
——'Proof and Explanation', Unpublished Lectures given in Virginia, Spring 1957—*V.L.*
WITTGENSTEIN, Ludwig, *Tractatus Logico-Philosophicus*, trans. Pears and McGuinness, Routledge 1961
——*Note-Books 1914-16*, Blackwell 1961
——*The Blue and Brown Books*, Blackwell 1958—*B.B.*

———*Zettel*, Blackwell 1967—*Z.*
———*Remarks on the Foundations of Mathematics*, Blackwell 1956—*Rem.*
———*Philosophical Investigations*, Blackwell 1963—*Inv.*
———*On Certainty*, Blackwell 1969—*Cert.*

Secondary Sources

BERKELEY, George, 'Principles of Human Knowledge', *A New Theory of Vision and Other Writings*, Everyman's Library 1950
BLACK, Max, *Problems of Analysis*, Routledge 1954
DESCARTES, René, *Meditations on First Philosophy*, The Liberal Arts Press, New York 1960
DUMMETT, Michael, 'Wittgenstein's Philosophy of Mathematics', *Wittgenstein, The Investigations*, ed. George Pitcher, Anchor, New York 1966
HUME, David, *An Abstract of a Treatise of Human Nature*
KANT, Immanuel, *Critique of Pure Reason*, trans. Norman Kemp Smith, Macmillan 1961
LOCKE, John, *An Essay Concerning Human Understanding*, Everyman's Library 1959
RUSSELL, Bertrand, *The Analysis of Mind*, Allen and Unwin 1921
STRAWSON, P. F., *Introduction to Logical Theory*, Methuen 1952
WEIL, Simone, 'Scientism: A Review', *On Science, Necessity and the Love of God*, trans. and ed. Richard Rees, Oxford 1968—*S.N.L.G.*
WINCH, Peter, *The Idea of a Social Science*, Routledge 1958

INDEX